ALSO BY THE MOTLEY FOOL

THE
MOTLEY FOOL
PERSONAL FINANCE
WORKBOOK

*A Foolproof Guide to Organizing Your Cash
and Building Wealth*

DAVID and TOM GARDNER
WITH ROBERT BROKAMP AND DAYANA YOCHIM

A FIRESIDE BOOK
PUBLISHED BY SIMON & SCHUSTER
New York   London   Toronto   Sydney

FIRESIDE
Rockefeller Center
1230 Avenue of the Americas
New York, NY 10020

For information about special discounts for bulk purchases,
please contact Simon & Schuster Special Sales:
1-800-456-6798 or business@simonandschuster.com

The Motley Fool and the jester logo are registered trademarks
of The Motley Fool, Inc.

Designed by Katy Riegel

Manufactured in the United States of America

3   5   7   9   10   8   6   4

Library of Congress Cataloging-in-Publication Data

Gardner, David.
The Motley Fool personal finance workbook : a foolproof guide to organizing your cash and building
wealth / David and Tom Gardner, with Robert Brokamp and Dayana Yochim.
p.   cm.
1. Finance, Personal. I. Title: The Motley Fool personal finance workbook : a foolproof guide to organizing
your cash and building wealth. II. Gardner, Tom. III. Motley Fool, Inc. IV. Title.

HG179.G317 2003

332.024'01—dc21   2002030675

ISBN 0-7432-2997-5

This publication contains the opinions and ideas of its authors. It is not a recommendation to purchase or sell the securities of any of the companies or investments herein discussed. It is sold with the understanding that the authors and publisher are not engaged in rendering legal, accounting, investment, or other professional services. Laws vary from state to state, and federal laws may apply to particular transaction, and if the reader requires expert financial or other assistance or legal advice, a competent professional should be consulted. Neither the authors nor the publisher can guarantee the accuracy of the information contained herein.

The authors and publisher specifically disclaim any responsibility for any liability, loss, or risk, professional or otherwise, which is incurred as a consequence, directly or indirectly, of the use and application of any of the contents of this book.

This book is dedicated to our community at Fool.com, who, through their ongoing discussion, have helped light a path to financial freedom that you may travel in these pages.

ACKNOWLEDGMENTS

The Motley Fool Personal Finance Workbook did not just happen. Its creation is unusually wonderful for us. No book of ours has so relied upon the help of our staff at The Motley Fool. You would not be holding this Foolish blueprint for financial security without the wit and wisdom of Dayana Yochim and Robert Brokamp. Their late-night research and tireless creative energy—even through the birth of a Brokamp child (way to go, Elizabeth!)—have made this book what it is. (By the way, please tell us what you think of the book by sending us a message at *Books@Fool.com.*)

Our team of supporters extends beyond Yochim and Brokamp to Trudy Bowen, David Braze, Ann Coleman, Paul Commins, Kristin Garrison, Shannon Zimmerman, Charlie Hennessy, Roy Lewis, Paul Maghielse, Selena Maranjian, Duffy Winters, David Wolpe, Poesy the Office Dog, Jocelyn the Office Baker, Reggie Santiago, and Bob Bobala. And then it all returns right back to Brokamp . . . Elizabeth Brokamp. Thanks, all.

We'd especially like to thank Alissa Territo for keeping all the files and pages and spreadsheets and punchlines in order. We'd like to thank our dedicated agent at William Morris, Suzanne Gluck. And we'd like to applaud our editor at Simon & Schuster, Doris Cooper.

We offer this book up to you, dear reader, in the hopes that from it you will win financial stability that leads to new opportunity that all ends in joy.

CONTENTS

INTRODUCTION

Welcome to *The Motley Fool Personal Finance Workbook*. It may not look very high tech, but what you have in your hands is a streamlined financial Global Positioning System. Snazzy. It'll tell you where you stand right now, and it'll help you find where you want to be. And it comes without the mess of instruction manuals you can't figure out.

In these pages, we'll explore as many ways that money touches your life as we can—from saving and spending to insurance, retirement, taxes, and big purchases. At every turn you'll get step-by-step directions to help you make the best decisions every day, week, month, and year. No matter who you are, what you earn, what you own, what you owe, or what you drive, a sound financial GPS—you know, Global Positioning System—can help you find the most direct path to your goals.

B-o-o-o-o-R-I-N-G.

We hear ya. The topic of money management is rife with dry how-to textbooks, mountainous budgeting spreadsheets, and countless unsolicited lectures, letters, and e-mails from lenders, bankers, brokers, newscasters, mothers, and dental hygienists. It's just no fun.

That's why we've hidden crisp five-dollar bills throughout the pages of this workbook to entice you to press on.

Go ahead, look.

Okay, welcome back.

As you can see, we haven't hidden *actual* currency in these pages. (So, yes, please put the other Fool Workbooks neatly back on the bookstore shelf and apologize to that toddler for shoving her stroller.) What you *will* find here is an easy and fun guide to managing your money. If you implement just a few of the suggestions you read here, you'll save hundreds of dollars over the course of a few months. That we guarantee. (And sorry about pulling that five-dollar-bill stunt. We hope that there's far more in this book for you.)

So there you have it—a guarantee that you'll save a bucket of money by using this book. But we still feel cheap, *real* cheap, relying on that gimmick to win you over. So try this on for size: What would it be like to know that you made the very best decision for every dollar you spent or saved? Can you imagine looking forward to balancing your budget at the beginning of next month? Wouldn't it be great to listen to a pro's advice and know whether or not it was right for your situation? What would it feel like to have in your hands a financial plan that would serve you for life?

Now we're talkin'!

So how can a bunch of *Fools* help you achieve all that?

Fools and their money, the long-running joke holds, are soon parted. Believe you and us, we're going to find out who started that vicious rumor and make them pay. Demons! Scoundrels! Nothing could be further from the truth. In Elizabethan times, the Fool was the only one who could tell the truth in the royal court without having his head severed. Look it up in Shakespeare. When the King's Wise men gave him bad, self-serving counsel, in stepped the clever Fool, the honest Fool, The Motley Fool. He (or she; there *were* female Fools) would set the record straight . . . while juggling flaming batons and generally making a ruckus.

We Fools are on hand to caution people not to overpay for insurance or stock trades. We're quick to point out which mutual fund is the best choice in a 401(k) plan. Some of us Fools even know what the "k" in 401(k) stands for! (It's the section of the tax code in which it resides, for the two of you who're curious.) We feel that the best person to manage your finances is, well, you! There are no conflicts of interest there. We do acknowledge the occasional need to call in an honest and good professional. Aha, but that in itself reflects *your* management decision. We believe we can help you sort through the charlatans who would sell you investment products and plans based on commissions.

Most of all, we love to share commonsense money management tidbits while, we hope, having a bit of fun along the way. So thank you for choosing to tackle your money matters with us and for politely laughing, even when Tom's jokes fall flat.

HOW TO DRIVE THIS WORKBOOK

With each page you turn, we'll toss another money-making/money-saving tool into your bag of tricks.

Rest assured, this isn't a typical workbook. We actively encourage cheating! In fact, we'll give you as many answers as we can.

Now, we know how hectic twenty-first-century life is. So we're doing our level best to meet you on *your* terms. Each topic in the book is broken out into bits so that you can take frequent breaks to check on the ball game, keep an eye on your kids, play a game of Ping Pong, or just check on your microwave popcorn (do you burn the stuff as often as we do?) without losing your place. You won't be graded on anything. And we promise not to humiliate you if you fill in a wrong answer.

Time is money, and we know that your time is priceless, or something near to it. Out of tens of thousands of years of human history, you'll get only a few decades around here. So we want to get you through this stuff efficiently. To help whisk you through, we kick off every chapter with a sixty-second overview. Use it to identify the main steps to mastering the given topic.

Then we go deep (well, deeper) by making lists, gathering some papers, crunching a few numbers (nothing harder than grade school math), and drawing turkeys (yep, you just might have to do that). Then at the end of each chapter we offer a ten-point refresher—your financial crib sheet.

As you progress, you'll be building a comprehensive savings and spending plan that, with minimal updating, you can use for years hence. We call it "The Global Master Asset Tracker T-4300 (Version XI.3)." Please fill it out in triplicate before you begin Chapter 1.

Kidding!

We *are* going to build a comprehensive savings and spending plan. But you'll complete it bit by bit. Since we couldn't come up with a better name, we're calling it the "Bit-by-Bit Budget Kit." Too bad we couldn't afford marketers at The Motley Fool. Regardless of the name, you'll be amazed at how much information you've amassed after just a few chapters without significant pain.

Go ahead and flip through a few pages to get a sense of what we're describing. We'll wait. And please know that we won't fault you for choosing to focus on particular sections now, leaving the rest for later. For instance, if you just want to save a few thousand bucks buying a car or want to be sure you're getting the right house, you can jump ahead to those chapters. The remainder of this book will always be there waiting for you.

WHAT'S AHEAD

Great, you're back!

Before we get started, let's get a bird's-eye view of the oncoming chapters.

• First we'll take a look at how you handle money and set some priorities to help guide your financial decisions.

• Next we'll get a clear picture of the state of your finances by taking a quick inventory. Based on that, you'll begin setting financial goals.

• We'll also attack the big bad "B" word—budget. Don't worry, we're going to make this as painless as possible. The "B" word is not a four-letter word. Budgeting isn't so bad when you realize that what you save now can make life in the future pretty sweet.

• The only thing less palatable than budgeting is facing debt. We'll tackle it head-on with a surefire system to help you pay it down and avoid it in the future.

• Then onto a sunnier topic: making your money grow by developing a basic long-term and short-term investing plan that lets you sleep well at night.

• Next, time to daydream. You'll map out your dream retirement and make sure that everything's in place for you to achieve it.

• And finally, because life happens, we've included a chapter about adjusting your Global Master Asset Tracker T-4300 (Version XI.3), er, we mean your Bit-by-Bit Budget, to account for major and minor life events.

Don't worry, we've also included chapters on hiring professional advisers, making big purchases, such as homes, cars, college, and RVs, getting insurance, and—the most riveting topic of all—taxes. We consider it a thrilling challenge, degree of difficulty 10.0, to make tax planning interesting. We also want to remind you once more that if you want to jump to the topics that matter most to you—perhaps skipping the tax section if your sister does all your returns for you (have her read it)—that sounds great to us.

One last thing: We can't take full credit for all of the great information you're going to get out of this workbook. As with all of our books, online seminars, and the thousands of articles we've published over the years, we continue to get great ideas—and jokes—from the community of Fools who join us every day at Fool.com. There are millions of them—seriously, we've counted—who gather at the forum we provide at Fool.com to share ideas and firsthand advice on money issues. Again, we would also like to thank our staff for their wonderful contributions.

This book is just another way for us to learn together—part motivation, part education, and part chocolaty goodness. We believe *The Motley Fool Personal Finance Workbook* will give you a customized financial plan that'll serve you well for life.

So let's get started.

THE

MOTLEY FOOL

PERSONAL FINANCE

WORKBOOK

CHAPTER 1

YOUR MONEY AND YOUR LIFE

SIXTY-SECOND GUIDE
TO YOUR MONEY *AND* YOUR LIFE

Let's kick things off with a one-minute preview of Chapter 1. We have to admit that this first chapter may seem frivolous. But play along with us for a few pages before we get down to business. We need you to figure out *who you are* before you can really excel at this workbook.

Remember, the next sixty seconds is just an overview of the different projects we'll work on together in the chapter. So here's where we're headed.

0:60 Take time out for self-reflection.

In general, would you call yourself a saver? A spender? A procrastinator? A realist? An avoider? An Abstract Expressionist? Reflect on the past and how you handled financial matters (and how they were handled—or mishandled—by the role models in your life).

0:51 Define in concrete terms how your spending matches up with your priorities.

When you make a big purchase, are you able to enjoy the item, or do you feel guilty? Do you spend money on smaller, less meaningful things because you feel you'll never be able to afford the ones you really want?

0:44 Go on a spending spree . . . in your imagination, that is.

Put that credit card down. Instead, commit to paper your list of goals—at least, those that will require capital. Don't dwell too much on the details; just write down a mega–master list of things you want to achieve (such as home ownership, a debt-free existence, a trip to China).

0:23 Pick the really important ones.

Scour your mega–master list of goals and pick out the top five that best match up with your priorities. Select only the ones that *really* count. That's what we'll be working toward in this book.

0:16 Make them real.

Put together a plan to figure what it'll take to achieve those five goals—what each will cost, when you want them to be completed, and so on. Break each one up into monthly or weekly savings goals and commit them all to paper.

0:03 Celebrate you!

Now bask in the glow of self-knowledge and self-actualization. You've completed the chapter, voilà.

. . .

There's the synopsis. Now let's get started.

KNOW THYSELF

Who are you? And what does that say about the way you use money? Think about it: Are you the sort who tirelessly searches out the four cents that won't let you balance your checkbook? Or do you believe, against all evidence, that there's money in your account just because there are still checks in your checkbook?

The Greek Oracle at Delphi read, "Know thyself." That's the first step in all good money management. We are all different. We all have unique talents and rare gifts. We all have flaws—terribly sad but true. The challenge, the great challenge, is to know ourselves and then to adjust our lives accordingly.

As this short lesson pertains to money, we'll be laser-focused in this chapter on how your strengths and weaknesses affect your financial circumstance. Money might not be the root of all evil for you. But it may be a hot button in your relationships (a bubbling cauldron, in some cases). It may be a source of worry. It may be a cause for celebration. Or it may hold the clue to your high blood pressure. (If so, eat more leafy greens, shorten your breathing, get eight hours of rest a night, and get a sound financial plan into place.)

At the very least, the topic of money has probably given you pause during some uncomfortable experiences. Now remember these moments, briefly.

Then proceed.

YOUR INNER FINANCIAL CHILD

Some of you *must* be rolling your eyes. *My inner child?* Hey, we don't want this to sound like daytime talk television. But before we get to crunching the numbers of your financial future, take a step back, just for a moment, and consider your financial history. The legendary Bob Marley put it right: "Don't know your past, don't know your future."

To get you started, we asked a couple from The Motley Fool Online to share some dark secrets from their past. In their own words, here are four financial discoveries they've made over the years. Consider this a starter list for your own journey:

Discovery 1: The past matters.

Shannon and I grew up very differently. Unfortunately, it took us a while to realize how much this matters in our relationship—especially when it comes to how we handle money as a couple. When you don't acknowledge the importance of where you come from, it comes back to haunt you in the form of agitation and misunderstanding.

Discovery 2: People react differently to their pasts.

My father worked at Walt Disney World his entire career, and my mom was a homemaker. I never worried that they couldn't pay the bills. Shannon's parents, on the other hand, divorced when he was seven, and his mom was the primary breadwinner. One result is that I'm much more of a short-term thinker in relation to money. I just have faith that everything will work out. Shannon is much more serious and interested in a long-term approach. Ah, how opposites attract.

Discovery 3: Your approach to money matters is as individual as you are.

One tangible result of our different backgrounds is the varying comfort levels we each have with debt and spending. We got married really young and moved to New York City. What does that spell?

Trouble—in the form of serious credit card debt. Because my parents didn't "believe" in debt, I totally freaked out about our credit card balances. I thought we were going to have to hit the streets. Shannon, on the other hand, seemed pretty comfortable with them. It took a while to develop a common language in this area.

Discovery 4: Knowing where you're coming from helps.

Shannon values having a secure retirement plan, whereas I value living our dream lives (the specifics of which change as we mature together). Again, developing a common language and really taking in what your partner needs is more than half the battle.

YOUR RUMINATIONS

Now it's time for your self-reflection. As a warm-up, we present ten questions about money management. Your answers will help set priorities later in this chapter. Be frank. It's *okay* if you're not the ideal chief financial officer yet.

1. Do you balance your checkbook? (Circle the appropriate answer.)   Yes   No

2. Are you a long-term planner?   Yes   No

3. When was the last time you *really* took a hard look at your finances (meaning more than glancing over your account statements)? _____

4. On a scale of 1 to 5 (5 being *very much*), how important are the following?

- Cutting coupons   1   2   3   4   5
- Going to the gas station with the cheapest gas   1   2   3   4   5
- Renting videos instead of going out to the movies   1   2   3   4   5
- Comparison shopping   1   2   3   4   5

5. How much is too much to spend on . . .

- Going out to dinner? $ _____
- A gift (for a friend, a significant other, children, a pet)? $ _____
- Vacation? $ _____
- A wireless sterling silver ab buster? $ _____

6. If you were to inherit $10,000, would it be most important to:

- Pay off debt
- Buy a new car
- Invest the money
- Take a vacation
- Throw an awesome party for your other relatives so that they, too, can see what an awesome and deserving daughter (granddaughter, nineteenth cousin twice removed) you are
- Other _____

7. What are a few comforts you wouldn't want yourself or your loved ones to do without?

_____

8. When do you expect to buy your next car? Will it be new or used?

_____

9. What are your top three long-term financial goals?

_____

_____

_____

10. Who shot J.R.?

_____

ALL ABOUT *YOU*

Now let's get really personal.

What's your ATM PIN?

Kidding.

Here's our legitimate question: From your past, what primarily has affected the way you approach money?

Think about how your family handled financial issues when you were growing up. Reflect on the last time you had to make a big purchase or found yourself even just a bit worried about your financial situation. What do these tell you about yourself?

Now list a few of your own financial self-discoveries. This may sound a bit sappy. But remember, our task right now is to help you understand yourself and how you approach money.

_____

_____

_____

_____

_____

_____

_____

_____

SETTING PRIORITIES

Excellent. You're learning about yourself. You're glowing. Doesn't it feel good to be so self-aware? You can really do this stuff. Stand up from your chair and beam for a minute, Fool. You really are amazing.

While most of that's true, let's face it, you haven't done much yet. Now let's get planning. We need to figure out your priorities. Provide answers to the following questions.

List five uses of your money that have made a significant positive difference in your life.

1. _____

2. _____

3. _____

4. _____

5. _____

List five uses of your money that have added little to your quality of life.

1. _____

2. _____

3. _____

4. _____

5. _____

List five uses of your money that will affect your life *positively* a decade or more from now.

1. _____

2. _____

3. _____

4. _____

5. _____

List five uses of your money that will affect your life *negatively* a decade or more from now.

1. _____

2. _____

3. _____

4. _____

5. _____

Kinda interesting, no? We don't often take the time to *really* think about the role money plays in our lives, beyond putting a roof over our heads and funding the purchase of a polka CD collection without rival (speak for yourself on that one).

As you look over what you jotted down, you'll begin to get a sense of where you'd like to redirect your money.

SETTING GOALS

Having set your priorities, you now need to form some goals. Making the above dreams a reality is the mission of this book.

BIG GOALS

Setting major goals and priorities means identifying the one or two things you really want to strive for—things that keep you excited and motivated. The best goals are the ones that you love *so* much that the steps required to achieve them become easier. It turns into a game. So when you delay buying a new car, instead of thinking, "My Yugo is the oldest one on the block!" you think, "By driving this old carriage for a few more years, we'll be able to afford a down payment on that cabin in the mountains."

BABY STEPS

Being able to achieve a lofty goal such as a new house or a wedding or a beveled-edge Corian countertop won't happen overnight. It requires smaller tactics that help you save money for your monster goal. The best tactics are:

1. **Specific:** Define exactly what you're going to do differently. For example: "I will increase my 401(k) participation from 5 percent to 10 percent of my salary per year to save for retirement faster." Or "I will limit shoe shopping to one pair every two months," rather than just "I will buy fewer shoes."

2. **Realistic:** You know yourself. You know what spending patterns are "must haves" versus "nice to haves." We won't ask you to deny yourself every new polka band release, if that's what makes you happy. Instead, we'll acknowledge the realities of temptation and have you allocate a certain amount of money to spend on your burgeoning CD collection.

3. **Well known:** Goal-setting theorists (yes, there are such people!) have long known that people are more likely to meet goals if they've made them public. Those with the best chances of quitting smoking, for example, have told all their friends and family about their dream. Tell your friends so they can help you meet yours. Put goal "check-ins" on your calendar. Use online "nag" services to remind you via e-mail (e.g., "Have you paid an extra $100 on your credit card bill this month?").

FOUR TACTICS FOR THE GOAL-AVERSE

What if you've tried this all before? You are awful with money. You spend like royalty but are paid the wages of a chimney sweep. Here are four tactics for people who hate goal setting.

1. Set up (many) automatic deductions from your paycheck—to your 401(k), a government savings bond program, a brokerage account.

2. Start tracking all of your expenses, even if only for one month. You'll probably end up curtailing them just to save yourself the bookkeeping.

3. Specifically budget "play money" and create an envelope with that play money in cash. Give yourself permission to freely spend that money—you'll feel rich! You'll likely spend less than if you had no budget. Remember, when the envelope is empty you need to stay home. Read a book. Or reread this workbook.

4. Leave your credit card and checkbook at home when you go out. Make cash your king. When you have to pull out actual dollar bills, you may find that you're more reluctant to part with them.

DAYDREAM BELIEVER

Now close your eyes and daydream. Where are you? What are you doing? Sitting on the beach, drenched in the proper SPF (30 or higher, please), drinking something with rum in it, and giggling? Maybe you're raising a family in a quiet setting, leaves rustling high in the trees around your patio, kids playing sweetly together (dream on!)? Or maybe you're raising a glass of bubbly with _____ (fill in the name of your heart-throb here)?

Here are some *other* common goals. Depending on where you are in your life, one of your big goals may be:

- Buying a home (or a vacation house)
- Getting out of debt
- Having/adopting a child
- Living on one salary
- Retiring early
- Sending a child to private school/summer camp/college
- Starting a business
- Getting a new car
- Giving money to those in need

- Getting a new chin
- Changing careers
- Taking a dream vacation (from the aforementioned children)
- Going to graduate school (to show off the aforementioned new chin)
- Remodeling the kitchen

GOAL-SETTING FREE-FOR-ALL

Now it's your turn. Jot down all the goals that you can think of, large and small:

_____

_____

_____

_____

_____

_____

_____

_____

_____

_____

_____

_____

_____

_____

_____

_____

_____

Nice job!

Most likely, not all of them are realistic. (Well, you *might* suddenly become U2's background vocalist. But let's play it safe for now and assume you won't be hanging with Bono anytime soon.) Achieving your goals will mean focusing on *one or two* now, then setting new ones. If you try for everything at once, you'll likely end up with nothing. (We don't want *that*.)

In a perfect world, your spending-to-saving ratio would directly align with what you list as your priority goals. Now, we want your mind to be focused on this stuff. So flip back and find your answer to the question "What are the comforts you wouldn't want yourself or your loved ones to do without?" And see what your list looked like after you pondered this one: "List five uses of your money that will affect your life *positively* a decade or more from now."

Those are some of your priorities. They'll vary greatly from person to person. But whether you're looking to buy a stone house in the Scottish highlands or pay off a credit card, the only way to get there is through some planning. Dreadful thought, we know, yet true. So, let's keep on at this. A few more questions for you to answer:

Q: Do you have debts to pay off? How important is it to pay off those debts as soon as possible?

For example, you probably want to pay off credit card debt as soon as possible, but you may choose not to put extra money toward your mortgage. As a general rule of thumb, debts with interest rates in the double digits should be paid off before you do anything else.

Q: Are the necessities taken care of?

These could include establishing a six-month cash emergency fund, fully funding an IRA or 401(k) account, getting life insurance policies, etc. The reason? Well, for instance, without an emergency fund your savings plan could be completely thrown off course by an act of God.

_____

_____

_____

Q: What major life events are you expecting in the next three to five years?

Is your income likely to change in any big ways—going back to school, changing careers, becoming a stay-at-home parent, retiring?

_____

_____

_____

REAL GOALS FOR REAL PEOPLE

We hope these questions have focused your attention on just a few goals. Now it's time to write 'em down. Think carefully before committing them to the blanks below, though. Why? Because we're going to spend much of the rest of this book trying to help you finance these dreams. Name your top five dreams that demand capital. Also, pick a date by which you want to meet that goal.

GOAL	DATE TO ACHIEVE IT BY

TEN TIPS ON PUTTING MONEY INTO PERSPECTIVE

1. Remember that every financial decision you make is emotionally informed by your past. Strange but true.

2. Regularly take time to think about how you handled past financial situations. Don't simply dwell on your distant past, but analyze decisions you made even just the previous week. What would you do differently if you had it to do all over again? Now call your therapist.

3. Keep your most important goals in the forefront of your mind.

4. If it helps, carry around a list of your goals so that with every dollar you spend your cash is directed towards the things that truly bring you joy.

5. Make sure you have both short- and long-term goals. It's hard to work toward achieving your dreams if the payoff for all of them is years away.

6. If you don't mind the cleaning lady psychoanalyzing your lifestyle, post your list of goals—including the dates you want to achieve them by—on the fridge or your bathroom mirror.

7. Do a reality check, especially if your financial situation changes. If your goals are unrealistic, you're setting yourself up for disappointment.

8. Regularly review your list. Life happens, and goals change. We won't think you're flaky.

9. Do some extra research. If you want to buy a château in Provence or a French mastiff puppy, chat with someone who already has done so. Get a sense of what it'll take to get there.

10. Call your best friend and brag about how in touch you are with your inner financial child.

ONE LAST THING: YOUR BIT-BY-BIT BUDGET ENTRY

In the Introduction (you didn't skip it, did you?) we promised to help you build a master saving and spending plan to serve you for life. We also promised not to overwhelm you with it all at once. So here's your first painless assignment. Turn to the Bit-by-Bit Budget on page 223 in Chapter 12. Now transfer your five main goals to the first column of the Bit-by-Bit Budget under "Expenses." Please use pencil, though. It's not that we think you're fickle; it's just that your goals may change as you work your way through this book. (Okay, that means we *do* think you're fickle.)

In the coming chapters, we're going to figure out how much money you have coming in and how much is going out to cover your necessary expenses. Then we'll divide up the leftovers (we're crossing our fingers right along with you here) to help you pay off any debts and start socking away dough to reach all of your goals.

CHAPTER 2

SPENDING AND SAVING

SIXTY-SECOND GUIDE TO SPENDING AND SAVING

The heart of your finances is your money—you take it in, you pump it out. But you can't expect to be fiscally fit if your money's gushing all over the place. Let's take a minute to review what's ahead.

0:60 Follow the money.

Do you know how much you spend on electricity each month? On groceries? At the racetrack? Time to don your sleuth suit. Watson, your first assignment is to follow the money trail.

0:40 Direct the flow of your dough.

Once you know how much you're recklessly spending on shoes, you can see how it matches up with your priorities. Remember those goals you set in Chapter 1? Now you can start strategically redirecting the flow of your money, socking it away for the things that count.

0:30 Build a b—b—b— (you can say it) budget.

We know—budgeting ranks right up there with de-gunking the microwave on the thrill scale. But keep this in mind: *You* are the captain of your cash flow. *You* decide what kind of budget you create, how you follow it, and what sacrifices you have to make—if any. *You* decide whether to put money toward a new house or your Barry Manilow collection. You are the CEO of your own personal finance business.

0:20 Snuff out fluff.

Find yourself coming up short? There's no shortage of ways to sock away more money and thus reach your goals sooner. Welcome to the world of Living Below Your Means (LBYM)—a whole village of Fools sharing tips on how to spend less and save more.

0:10 Seize control of your goals.

We're not necessarily promoting penny-pinching, but we are encouraging you to squeeze the most power out of each dollar. That's the primary way you'll make your financial dreams come true.

• • •

Now that you have a bird's-eye view of what we're going to do about spending and saving, let's take it from the ground up.

START BY FOLLOWING THE MONEY

So where's your money going? Start by making some guesses. How much do you think you spent last month on the following items? Fill out the "Your Guess" column. We're just looking for a ball-park figure, so don't sweat the small stuff (and it's all small stuff . . . sorry, had to toss that in).

Category	Your Guess	Actual Amount
Groceries		
Eating out		
Gasoline		
Electricity		
Retirement savings		
Gifts		
Beano		

Okay, let's see how accurate you were.

You'll be able to fill out the "Actual Amount" column right now only if you've used your checkbook, debit card, or credit card for most purchases. (If you primarily use cash, don't worry, we'll follow the *real* money trail later.)

Review your account statements and/or checkbook to see how much you actually spent on these items in the past month. You don't have to be exact; roughly adding them up in your head is good enough for now. Add your estimated actual amount to the chart above. If you're feeling frisky, check out the last two months to see if the amounts are similar.

Were you . . . uh . . . on the money? Were you surprised? Shocked?

The reality is, most folks don't know where their money goes. They pay their bills, spend as they see

fit along the way, and if there's money left over, great. If not . . . plastic. But that's no way to make life better for you and your family.

The good news is that you may not have to track each expenditure for the rest of your days. Working through this book and henceforth spending responsibly may be enough. But keep this in mind: You spend a huge chunk of your waking hours trying to make a buck. Don't you think you should be sure that your time is worth it? That's the point of examining your spending habits.

In fact, there are many benefits of tracking your money. Here are a few, followed by a statement. Rate yourself from 1 (strongly agree) to 5 (strongly disagree) according to how much you concur with the statement.

AWARENESS

As you perhaps saw in the earlier exercise, you may not know where your money's been going. In the course of a single day, money spills out of your checking and savings accounts every which way. The daily portion of your rent or mortgage, the electricity to run your fridge and light your house, the water for your showers, the cereal you eat for breakfast, the burger you buy for lunch, the gas that powers your car to work, the per diem share of your phone service . . . the list goes on and on. Why, you're practically exhaling money with each breath. How will you know if you're getting your money's worth if you don't know exactly how much is going where?

Rate Yourself

I know the flow of my dough (1–5): _____

CONTROL

Every person should be in charge of his finances, not the other way around. It's a question of allocating limited resources to seemingly unlimited choices. Some of those choices put you into the driver's seat (e.g., a sufficient emergency fund, a retirement nest egg, prudent investments). Others put you into the paddy wagon (e.g., excessive debt, unaffordable luxuries, speculative long shots). So which way is your money going?

Rate Yourself

I am in control of where my money goes (1–5): _____

GOAL ATTAINMENT

Remember the goals you set in Chapter 1? Unless your main financial mission in life is to collect Happy Meal prizes, your goals will probably cost more than a few hundred smackers. We'd also guess that you'd prefer to realize your goals sooner than later. Tracking your finances—and ensuring that more money is going to priorities than frivolities—will increase the chances that you'll reach your goals and shorten the time it takes to realize them.

Rate Yourself

I am directing as much money as possible to my goals (1–5): _____

SECURITY

When people are asked why money is important to them, one of the most common responses—besides "I'd like to dabble in world domination"—is "peace of mind." Money can't solve all of life's problems, but it's nice to have some when the furnace blows up, the chimney falls down, or termites gather. Knowing how much things cost, where you can cut back, whether you're adequately insured, and exactly how much you can afford to spend on an emergency goes a long way to providing economic equanimity.

Rate Yourself

The movement of my money allows me and my family to weather most storms (1–5): _____

BECAUSE WE TOLD YOU TO

Many of the exercises in this book will require that you know how much you spend on various items. You might as well find this information out now (and have it handy as you work through subsequent chapters). And, hey, you wouldn't buy a really useful appliance and not use it as directed, would you? So put this book to proper use!

Rate Yourself

I want to get my money's worth from this book, so I will do all the exercises to the best of my ability (1–5): _____

So how did you rate? Tally your score and consult the table on the following page.

ON THE MONEY TRAIL

So let's see where your money's gone over the past six months. Gather the statements of any account from which you pay bills. If you don't have the statements handy, you may be able to access them via the Internet. It may help to have your checkbook available, too, as long as you keep accurate records in the registry.

You can use the handy-dandy sheet we provide for categorizing and totaling your expenses. Or, if you have a computer and a spreadsheet program (such as Excel), you may want to use the program and let the computer do your math.

IF YOU JUST DON'T HAVE THE TIME

If following the trail of every one of your dollars is too daunting, boil your expenses down to broad

Score	Recommendation
5–9	Very impressive. It seems you're on top of your game. You may not need to go through your last six months' worth of expenses since you probably already have a grasp of where your money's going. However, it couldn't hurt. Consider at least reviewing your statements for confirmation of your assessment.
10–15	Not bad. A few modifications to your budget and procedures, and all your dollar ducks could be in a row. You could still stand to learn a lot from examining your spending and saving.
16–20	As they say, acknowledging your problems is half the battle. Now it's time to get to work. Taking a good long look at the inflow and outflow of your money will prepare you for the rest of your life.
21–25	It sounds as though your finances and your habits could use an overhaul. (Aren't you glad you bought this book?) Closely examine how you feel about money, and how you make financial decisions. Don't worry, we're here to help.
26–100	Take a math class. The highest possible score you could have earned is 25.

categories. Choose two or three of your biggest categories (such as food) to break down into more detail (e.g., groceries, eating out, lunch, sugary cake snacks). This will provide you with enough information to get started—and may provide some shocking revelations. ("I spend $50 a month on Ding Dongs?!") Once you have a grip on the bigger categories, you can gradually become more detailed as necessary.

THE CASH CONUNDRUM

Cash is wonderful.

It's accepted everywhere; it won't ruin your credit record; you don't get an account statement and concomitant mail to add to your paper pile; you don't have to suffer the grocery store cashier pretending to be a handwriting expert by comparing your signature with the one on your credit card; and you can laugh at the crazy hairdos presidents used to have (tame those flyaways, Andrew Jackson!).

Unfortunately, from a money-tracking perspective, cash is like youth. It seems to disappear overnight, you don't know where it went, and you can't get it back.

If greenbacks are your main mode of payment—or if you find far too many ATM withdrawals on your bank statement with nothing to show for them—you'll have to expend a little more effort to track your money. Here are some suggestions. Remember that if you've done none of this before, it'll just be great that you're thinking about it. Implement a few of these ideas, gradually. And remember that once you've mastered basic budgeting, you'll have to do less and less work each month. Here they are:

• Give up cash for a while. Use checks or debit or credit cards and let your bank keep your transaction records for you. (Of course, pay off your credit card balances in full at the end of the month. See Chapter 3 for details and scary tales.)

• Keep a small memo pad with you, and record any transactions you make. Or just fold a piece of paper in fourths and keep it in your pocket for jotting expenditures down.

• Every time you make a purchase, keep the receipt. If the items purchased aren't listed on the receipt, write them down. When you get home, put the receipts into a jar. At the end of the month, total up your expenditures.

• Use your PDA. We're talking about "personal digital assistant" here—such as a Palm or Handspring—not "public displays of affection," which earned you several detentions in high school. Record your purchases as you make them. You can categorize your expenditures then and there if you have a spreadsheet program.

Earlier, we suggested that you analyze your last six months' worth of expenses. However, if you'll have to develop a cash-tracking system to follow the money trail, we don't suggest that you wait until you get a half year's information before scrutinizing your spending habits. Glean what information you can from bank account statements, see where your cash goes for a month or two, then move on.

DIRECTIONS

1. Use the "Single-Month Money Tracker Worksheet" beginning on page 15 to record and add up your expenditures within each category.

2. Once you have a total for each category for the month, move each total to the "Six-Month Money Tracker Worksheet" on pages 17–18.

3. Move on to the next month, rinse, and repeat steps 1 and 2.

4. Once you have data on six months' worth of spending, calculate your average monthly expense for each category. Simply add up the total amount of money you spent on that line item over the half year, then divide that total by 6. Record the result in the far-right-hand column of the "Six-Month Money Tracker Worksheet."

MONEY AUTOPSY-TURVY

Whew! Did you know you spent so much at Bed, Bath & Boomerang?

You may have uttered a few *hmms, a-has,* and *uh-ohs* while filling out the Money Tracker Worksheet. Let's take some time to look at what you may have learned.

In the previous chapter, you made some guesses as to what uses of money are affecting the quality of your life. Take a look at what you wrote, then look at where your money actually has gone over the past six months. Any revelations? Confirmations? Consternations? Write down the top five lessons you learned from this exercise:

1. _____

_____

_____

2. _____

_____

_____

3. _____

_____

_____

4. _____

_____

_____

5. _____

_____

_____

Now let's see how much money you spent on your priorities—the goals you wrote down in Chapter 1. Just for perspective, include a few other categories.

GOAL	AMOUNT SPENT	PERCENTAGE OF TOTAL EXPENDITURES*
1._____	_____	_____
2._____	_____	_____
3._____	_____	_____
4._____	_____	_____
5._____	_____	_____
Clothes	_____	_____
Entertainment	_____	_____
Mortgage/rent	_____	_____
Paying down debts	_____	_____

* To calculate a percentage, use this formula: Total spent on item divided by total amount of money spent over the month, then multiply the result by 100.

SLASH YOUR SPENDING

Were you surprised at how much you spend on the necessities—and luxuries—of life? We know—living isn't cheap these days, and death isn't much fun. So how can you fund your dreams as well as cover your expenses? Welcome to the world of Living Below Your Means.

Back at the Fool.com ranch, there's a discussion board called "Living Below Your Means," affectionately known as LBYM. The board is consistently one of our most active, buzzing with tips on how to live life more cheaply. (We host many active conversations via our online community discussion boards. You can interact with and learn from others at Fool.com about a wide range of topics—finances, investing, and many other important facets of life. You can enjoy a thirty-day free trial in the Fool Community to see what it's all about.)

THE LBYM WAY

Money means different things to different people. One thing's for sure, however: money is more than a bunch of pieces of stiff paper. And Living Below Your Means is more than checking movies out from the library rather than paying Buckbuster Video. It's a way to think about money. It's a philosophy, a way of life, an attitude. It's telling marketing executives, "I'm tired of you trying to manipulate me. Game over." It's saying to yourself, "The time I spend working is worth more than the fleeting pleasure I'll get from buying this trinket."

Now that we're done with the lofty introduction (and self-promotion), we'll leave it up to you to get down to details. In the Appendix of this book (right behind the pancreas and liver) is a list of some of the best ideas from the Living Below Your Means community. Please check them out. They are worth the price of admission here. If you want even more, hop on the Internet and surf over to The Motley Fool. You can save a fortune by reading the top fifty posts ever on our Living Below Your Means folder at http://boards.Fool.com.

WAYS TO THINK ABOUT MONEY

As we said, money isn't just pieces of paper, nor is it just a number on your bank statement. When it comes down to the tough spending decisions, it'll help to have an accurate and clear idea of what money really means to you. Here are a few ways to think about money:

- Break your expenditures into how long it took you to earn that money. To do this, you have to estimate your hourly pay. For folks who work a forty-hour week, your hourly pay is roughly half

SINGLE-MONTH MONEY TRACKER WORKSHEET

EXPENSES Month:	WEEK 1	WEEK 2	WEEK 3	WEEK 4	Total
Room and board:					
Rent/mortgage					
Electricity					
Water					
Oil/gas					
Telephone					
Cell phone					
Trash removal					
House maintenance					
Real estate taxes					
Improvement/furnishings					
Groceries					
Dining out/take-home food					
Transportation:					
Car loan payment					
Gas					
Maintenance					
Other/commuting costs					
Internal and external care:					
Medical/dental expenses					
Clothing purchases					
Laundry and cleaning					
Personal care					

(continued)

SINGLE-MONTH MONEY TRACKER WORKSHEET, continued

EXPENSES Month:	WEEK 1	WEEK 2	WEEK 3	WEEK 4	Total
Recreation:					
Entertainment					
Cable/satellite TV					
Internet access					
Vacations					
Gifts					
Other:					
Business/professional expenses					
Child care expenses and allowances					
Tuition/educational expenses					
Child support and alimony					
Donations to church and charities					
Insurance:					
Vehicle					
Homeowner's/renter's					
Life/disability/other insurance					
Debt repayments:					
Loan payments					
Credit card payments					
Taxes:					
Income taxes (federal and state)					
Social Security and Medicare taxes					
Miscellaneous:					
Miscellaneous expenses					
Others (list):					
Total Expenses					

SIX-MONTH MONEY TRACKER WORKSHEET

EXPENSES	MONTH 1	MONTH 2	MONTH 3	MONTH 4	MONTH 5	MONTH 6	TOTAL	AVERAGE MONTHLY EXPENSE
Room and board:								
Rent/mortgage								
Electricity								
Water								
Oil/gas								
Telephone								
Cell phone								
Trash removal								
House maintenance								
Real estate taxes								
Improvement/furnishings								
Groceries								
Dining out/take-home food								
Transportation:								
Car loan payment								
Gas								
Maintenance								
Other/commuting costs								
Internal and external care:								
Medical/dental expenses								
Clothing purchases								
Laundry and cleaning								
Personal care								

(continued)

SIX-MONTH MONEY TRACKER WORKSHEET, continued

EXPENSES	MONTH 1	MONTH 2	MONTH 3	MONTH 4	MONTH 5	MONTH 6	TOTAL	AVERAGE MONTHLY EXPENSE
Recreation:								
Entertainment								
Cable/satellite TV								
Internet access								
Vacations								
Gifts								
Other:								
Business/professional expenses								
Child care expenses and allowances								
Tuition/educational expenses								
Child support and alimony								
Donations to church and charities								
Insurance:								
Vehicle								
Homeowner's/renter's								
Life/disability/other insurance								
Debt repayments:								
Loan payments								
Credit card payments								
Taxes:								
Income taxes (federal and state)								
Social Security and Medicare taxes								
Miscellaneous:								
Miscellaneous expenses								
Others (list):								
Total Expenses								

your annual salary, divided by 1,000. For example, if you earn $40,000 a year, you make about $20 an hour. So the next time you're tempted to spend $100 on a fleeting pleasure, ask yourself, "Is this worth five hours of my labor?"

- Consider how much the money would be worth if you invested it instead. For example, let's say you could shave $100 off your food budget each month. Instead of spending that money, you could deposit it in an investment that earns 8 percent annually. After five years, you would have more than $7,300.

- Every time you open your wallet, think of your goals. The more you spend, the less you save. So every time you spend money, you are prolonging—and perhaps undermining—your ability to buy a new car, fund your children's education, or build a tree house with a hot tub.

- When you think money, think chicken. According to Heifer International, an organization that offers families around the world a way to feed themselves and become self-reliant, a batch of chicks is worth $20. A goat or a pig costs $120, a buffalo fetches $250, and a heifer is worth $500. So the next time you want to buy a CD or two, ask yourself if they'll be worth that poultry sum.

- Speaking of charity, if altruism runs in your veins, think about how much could be done with your money. Finding a way to trim $100 from your monthly budget could do wonders for a worthwhile charity.

CONTROLLING CASH FLOW

Looking at what you've learned about yourself in this chapter, how do you feel? We'll assume that you're like us: you feel you could do a little better job of managing your finances. After all, that's what living in a compulsive society is all about (and why you bought this book). Which brings us to the "B" word.

"SON OF A BUDGET!"

When you think of budgeting, what comes to mind? Control? Self-denial? Domination? Prison? An uninvited dinner guest?

It's likely that you associate budgeting with boredom, unpleasantness, futility—or any other of a rogue's gallery of unsavory emotions.

Hey, wait! Don't skip ahead to the next chapter! We'll make this as easy as possible by creating the budget bit by bit as you work through the book. As you do so—and think, "I'd rather be watching an infomercial for skin care products"— keep this in mind: Devising and following a budget will lead to better decisions. You'll spend less on things that aren't important to you and more on your life's goals. You'll think twice about buying something that will provide merely fleeting satisfaction.

Here are a few helpful (and healthy) ways to approach the budgeting process:

1. **A budget doesn't control you—you control the budget.** You decide on the priorities—what deserves your hard-earned dollars. Unless you're a member of the Gates (Microsoft founder) or Walton (Wal-Mart founder) families, you'll probably need to curb your spending on some unnecessary items. But that's only to fund the really important things in life. You're not just giving up your fifteen magazine subscriptions, you're saving for that house with the wraparound porch, fireplace, and dormer windows.

2. **A budget is all about knowledge, not about self-denial and stinginess.** Once you've gathered all of your financial facts, you have the necessary information to make good decisions. The point is not to squeeze the enjoyment out of your life, one dollar at a time; it's about giving each saved dollar greater power.

3. **The best budget is the budget that works for you.** Don't abandon the idea of budgeting because you can't do it perfectly or you don't have enough

time to go over piles of receipts and input each one into your financial database. With a little creativity, you can come up with some quick, easy ways to stay on top of your inflow and outflow.

THE MOST IMPORTANT ITEMS TO ADD TO YOUR BUDGET

To meet your financial goals, you need to set aside money for them on a monthly basis—and consider this money as important as your mortgage, your food money, and your water bill. Hoping that there'll be money left over after you pay your bills, go out to eat, and buy another pair of shoes is *not* the way to turn your dreams into reality.

SIXTY-SIX TIPS ON SPENDING AND SAVING

For this chapter, we had more than ten tips, so we refer you to the "Living Below Your Means" Appendix, which has many tips on saving money.

THE BIT-BY-BIT BUDGET

You won't be finishing the budget in this chapter; rather, you'll be filling in the blanks as we go through the book. Plus, your priorities may change as you go from chapter to chapter, so make sure you use a pencil.

Right now, go to the Bit-by-Bit Budget in Chapter 12 (beginning on page 223) and complete the following tasks:

1. Fill in the "Income" line items. Candidates: Your pretax monthly paycheck, dividends, or interest from investments, alimony, or child support—in other words, any source of spending money.

2. Fill out the Chapter 2 items in the Bit-by-Bit Budget beginning on page 223 using the numbers in the "Average Monthly Expense" column of the Six-Month Money Tracker Worksheet. (Again, we have copied below the portion of the Bit-by-Bit Budget that you're going to fill out in Chapter 12, just so you know what to look for.)

3. Go eat some ice cream; you deserve it. (If you're counting your calories, then go have some fat-free, nondairy, additive-free, fruitless, non-anything-else yogurt—a.k.a. water.)

BIT-BY-BIT BUDGET

	Amount from Money Tracker Worksheet	Budgeted Amount	Month 1	Month 2	Month 3	Month 4	Month 5	Month 6
Room and Board:								
Rent/mortgage								
Electricity								
Water								
Oil/gas								
Telephone								
Cell phone								

	Amount from Money Tracker Worksheet	Budgeted Amount	Month 1	Month 2	Month 3	Month 4	Month 5	Month 6
Trash removal								
House maintenance								
Real estate taxes								
Improvement/furnishings								
Groceries								
Dining out/take-home food								
Transportation:								
Car loan payment								
Gas								
Maintenance								
Other/commuting costs								
Internal and External Care:								
Medical/dental expenses								
Clothing purchases								
Laundry and cleaning								
Personal care								
Recreation:								
Entertainment								
Cable/satellite TV								
Internet access								
Vacations								
Gifts								
Other:								
Business/professional expenses								
Child care expenses and allowances								
Tuition/educational expenses								
Child support and alimony								
Donations to church and charities								

CHAPTER 3

GETTING OUT OF DEBT

SIXTY-SECOND GUIDE TO GETTING OUT OF DEBT

Picture yourself debt-free (and having a really good hair day, if that kind of thing matters to you). Think about it: No more bouts of anxiety over mounting credit card balances. No more shuffling out of the checkout line in shame after your card's refused. No more Very Uncomfortable Phone Interactions with people to whom you owe money. Sound good? Then let's get you out of debt! The average American adult has $8,000 of credit card debt today. Ouch.

0:60 Resolve to spend less than you make.

Make it a habit as fundamental as stopping for red lights. If you can't pay for it today, you can't afford it.

0:55 Distinguish between Bad Debt and OK Debt.

Acceptable debt has an interest rate well under 10 percent—preferably with some tax advantages to boot (think mortgage). In the best case, the thing you bought with borrowed funds will appreciate in value. Bad Debt is everything else—from your tita-

nium credit card to the 35 percent loan from Larry's Kwik Cash. That's what you want to tackle first.

0:50 Pick a winner.

From your Bad Debt column, pick the one major credit card that features the lowest annual interest rate. Cut up your other cards, including all department store cards, into lots and lots of little pieces. (If you have plenty of ventilation, you can fashion a handsome mosaic side table with the shards and some hot glue.) Promise yourself that you'll use the one card left intact for emergencies only.

0:41 Gather the latest bills from all Bad Debt accounts.

Line these up on the kitchen table. Find the minimum monthly payment for each account and then add these up to get an overall monthly minimum. Pledge to pay this overall minimum *plus* a hefty additional chunk every month—enough to make a solid dent in the outstanding balance of at least one account. (Don't fret, we'll show you how in a moment.)

0:34 **Ask for a lower rate.**

Grab a bill from any account charging you more than 14 percent interest. Dial the toll-free number on the bill and ask to have your rate lowered to 11 percent. Tell them that you'd really like to stay with it out of customer loyalty (embellish according to your acting skills) but that you have received offers for much-lower-rate cards. Expect to be made very uncomfortable, but stand firm and remember that, to the credit card company, you are both a customer and a profit center. You also stand to save a bundle.

0:26 **Pick the highest-interest-rate account and attack! Lather, rinse, repeat.**

Order the latest bills according to annual interest rate charged. Apply the "hefty additional chunk" (beyond the minimum) to the highest rate account(s). Repeat monthly until the last Bad Debt account is paid in full.

0:18 **Be prudent.**

Be aggressive in paying down Bad Debt, but don't get so ambitious that you risk missing minimum payments on your mortgage, automobile, or any other secured credit account. (Secured means that if you miss enough payments, the bank can show up and take your stuff. Yes, even the ugly stuff.)

0:12 **Seek out support.**

If you're plugged in, spend time on our Consumer Credit/Credit Cards discussion board at Fool.com. You'll find plenty of emotional support and great ideas. Help others celebrate their victories over debt with the traditional "happy dance."

0:05 **Dance, Fool!**

When your Bad Debt is 100 percent exorcised (and you can make remaining OK Debt payments with ease), it's your turn to dance.

• • •

THE GREAT DEBT DIVIDE

We Fools are highly committed to turning debtors into savers, replacing the drudgery of monthly payments with the joy of expanding investments.

Indulge us for a moment: Somewhere in every mountain range there is a line that divides water flow. On one side of the line, water flows east. On the other, it flows west. Regardless of direction, these rivers and streams start out as a trickle but quickly pick up speed as they head down the mountain, finishing as raging torrents.

Money and wealth work exactly the same way. Over time, you'll end up on either the savings or the debt side of the personal finance divide. It doesn't take much to nudge you one way or the other. But once a direction is established, the momentum tends to build and it gets harder and harder to go back. "Paddle faster, honey! *Faster!*"

If you want to "nudge" yourself in the savings direction, just remember that *it all boils down to spending less money than you make, on a consistent, long-term basis.* (We're hoping you've noticed that this is an important point.)

So here you are in Chapter 3. You've set some financial goals (is one of them killing your debt?) and have started to build a workable budget. Worst-case scenario: an overwhelming debt burden is pushing you to the edge of financial disaster. If so, you should probably skip to the end of this chapter, where we help you perform some Debt Triage.

If debt is not currently a problem—you're just here to head off future problems—a hearty "Huzzah!" to you. Let's keep debt from nipping at your heels and get started with the basics of managing debt and the fundamentals upon which you will build your financial success.

BEATING DEBT IS SIMPLE, BUT NOT EASY

Getting out of debt and staying out is actually pretty simple, at least compared to most money management topics. (Just wait until you get to the taxes chapter!) It boils down to spending less money than you make, on a consistent, long-term basis. That's it. Nothing else will get the job done. Nothing.

And it's easy, too. Right? Wrong! While conquering debt won't send you scrambling for thick math textbooks, it's an ocean away from easy. One moment of weakness—or worse, one cruel act of fate—and you're scratching and clawing your way back out of the hole. It's *not* easy.

So how did something so simple get to be so hard? Because beating debt demands a lot of willpower over a long period of time. If you've been a human being for any length of time, you know that this is one tough combination to nail down. We're afraid there's no getting around it. Over the long term, regularly spending more than you make—even just a little more—will bring your financial house down, even if you are the most responsible of bill payers. Until you take this basic lesson to heart, even bankruptcy is just a temporary solution.

HOW CAREFUL DO YOU HAVE TO BE?

Consider two simple examples, starting with a positive one. Let's say that you begin setting aside $75 every month in savings earning 5 percent interest. If you can pull this off for five years, you'll end up with a comforting $5,100 in emergency savings.

Now let's turn this picture on its head, and assume that you come up *short* by the same $75 per month, on average, over the same five years. Further, assume that you routinely patch over this difference with a credit card. Note that we're talking about less than $20 per week here—hardly a symptom of reckless "retail therapy." Nonetheless, at the end of five years you'll be looking at more than $7,200 in debt, assuming an 18 percent credit card interest rate.

That's an extra $2,100 in debt, beyond the $5,100 earned by *saving* $75 per month. That's the difference between saving and paying down debt. Saving is hard enough, but paying down debt is $2,100 harder!

And the difference just gets bigger as time passes. While your bank savings work hard twenty-four hours a day to make you more money, any outstanding credit card debt is likely to be working three times harder, *charging* a much higher interest rate than your savings *pay*.

Moreover, as a saver you have the force of com-

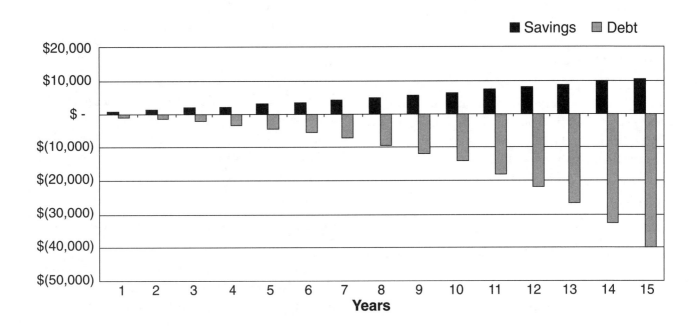

pound interest on your side, the idea that your balance starts to snowball as you earn interest not only on your deposits but also on the interest payments you leave in the account. As a debtor, this same powerful compounding force works against you, and the higher the interest rate, the faster the snowball builds. Our aim here is to keep that snowball to a handful of unpackable powder.

GOOD DEBT VERSUS BAD DEBT

We've been talking tough about consumer debt, but we do realize that some debts are an inescapable part of life for most of us. Still, even when we carry debt, there are some basic debt management rules that will keep the lid on problems:

• Be especially wary of double-digit debt—credit cards and loans that charge 10 percent or more in annual interest. At this level, balances snowball quickly, and it's tough to get a return on the borrowed money that beats this cost.

• Good debts, like some mortgages and student loans, combine two things: (1) a relatively low, tax-adjusted interest rate and (2) the potential to invest in something that, over the long run, will grow in value.

• Ignore bankers' rules for "acceptable" levels of debt. These are designed by banks to maximize *their* income. Their calculations cleverly keep you far enough under water that you continue to pay them interest, but not so deep that you go broke. Don't be a prisoner of your own debtor's jail. Set tighter rules of your own.

WHERE DO YOU STAND?

In order to get where you want to go, you need to know where you're starting. Let's start by listing all

your "bad" debt. Let's also take a look at how much interest you'll pay this year. This'll involve a little math, but only a little. Don't worry. It's not too complicated if you do it the right way: with a calculator! Just follow our example (see page 26).

DO YOU HAVE TOO MUCH BAD DEBT?

Look at your total bad debt—not your interest payments, but the debts themselves—and compare this number to your annual after-tax income.

Now pick up the adding machine you just dropped and apologize to your cat for yelling at him.

Since you'll want to pay off this bad debt as soon as possible, you don't want it to take up too large a chunk of your income. If you've been reading other financial advice, you may think we've made a mistake. A common suggestion is to divide your after-tax income by your annual debt payments (the money you have to come up with just to pay the mortgage, other loan payments, and credit card minimums). Because we're aiming to get you out of debt—not to just leave you afloat so that you remain enslaved to the banks—we're doing two things differently:

1. **We're leaving good debt out of the equation.** It's tougher to give a rule of thumb for the whole ball of wax. Suffice it to say that if you're having trouble just paying all the minimums—you're not regularly saving or paying down debt—you probably have too much debt, period, good or bad.

2. **We're dividing your after-tax income by total bad debt.** That's because we want to focus on eliminating all of the bad debt as quickly as possible, not just keeping up with the payments.

Here's an example, using numbers we stole from our coworker Will Robinson by rummaging around in his personal stuff. (We changed his name from Willy Robison to Will Robinson to protect his identity.)

WORKSHEET: BAD DEBTS

(CREDIT CARDS, STORE CHARGE CARDS, CAR LOANS)

NAME OF CARD/LOAN	AMOUNT OWED	INTEREST RATE	ESTIMATED ANNUAL INTEREST PAYMENT
Example: First Bank of Firstness Visa	$4,379.27	17.65%	$4,379.27 × 0.1765 = $772.94*
Total			

*This is just a rough estimate—all we need for this exercise. It's the amount you would pay in interest if your balance (amount owed) remained unchanged for one year. Ideally you'll pay down your balance over the next year, reducing your total interest payments from this estimate. On the other hand, if you miss payments or charge more on this account, your total interest could be higher.

Total bad debt: $6,437
Total after-tax annual income: $30,000
Bad debt–to-income ratio:
   $6,437/$30,000 = 21.4%

Danger, Will Robinson! A 21.4 percent bad debt–to-income ratio is awfully high, especially if it's all—or mostly—credit cards and charge cards. If it includes a car loan at below 10 percent annual interest, that's a little better, but a debt load of this magnitude (relative to income) is still going to take a serious effort to bring down.

The ideal number here is zero, but at the very least you want to keep bad debt—including car loans—to 15 percent or less of your after-tax income. Otherwise, your debt payments will eat up too big a chunk of your paycheck. Sure, some banks will advise you to go well beyond 15 percent, but remember who profits if you stay on the debtor side of the divide—they do!

Your key take-away here is that your bad debt–to-income ratio needs to head toward zero—and get there.

HOW MUCH ARE YOUR TOTAL INTEREST PAYMENTS?

Now take a quick look at your total estimated annual interest payments for bad debt. Surprise you? This is how much you're spending annually—roughly—for the honor of being in debt. Too bad more college students don't encounter this point earlier in life. Unlike a mortgage or student loan, these interest payments are just money down the drain. More important, this is the money you could be saving annually if you were to pay off your bad debts. Imagine what you could do with all that dough!

HOW'S YOUR CASH FLOW?

There's one more aspect of debt to consider: You can have a retirement stock portfolio to beat the band and the biggest house on the block, but you still have to meet your minimum monthly debt payments. The bankers don't care how much you're worth. They want cash. Debt goes from a destructive, anti-wealth-building habit to a serious financial crisis all too easily. When the required monthly payments get so big, relative to your income, that you can no longer make minimum payments on a consistent basis, you're in trouble. For now, we'll just reinforce the point that this should be a serious red flag.

SO YOU'RE IN DEBT. LET'S GET BUSY!

Now that you have a sense of "good debt" and "bad debt," you might be worrying about one thing: that you have *way* too much of the bad stuff! (Or maybe not. If you're keeping the bad debt to a minimum, give yourself a pat on the back, go hug your ferret, and call your mother. She misses you.)

If you're like many people, you're staring at a big pile of credit card debt that is costing you plenty in monthly payments. Not to worry, though, because we're going to talk about how you can pay that debt down and keep your credit card use under control in the future.

THE SEVEN STEPS TO PAYING DOWN YOUR CREDIT CARD DEBT

Millions of Americans have paid off heavy credit card debt, and now it's your turn to join them. It won't be enough, however, just to make minimum monthly payments. Here are the six steps to getting your debt under control:

1. **Stop using your cards.** The last thing you want to do with heavy credit card debt is add to it. Take all your credit cards out of your wallet or purse and leave them at home. (Though you may want to keep one for emergencies. And, no, a really great sandal sale or a cool new garage gadget does not qualify as an emergency.)

Cut up the cards, if that's what it takes to stop using them. Some people keep their cards out of reach by freezing them in glasses of water. Heck, just go ahead and throw them behind a major appliance. You'll think twice about spending if you risk getting a hernia every time you're tempted.

2. **Stop the flood of credit card offers.** You can force credit bureaus to stop selling your name and address. Dial 1 (888) 5-OPTOUT to get the forms. If you're searching for a low-interest card, don't wait for it to come to you. Visit a site such as www.cardweb.com or www.bankrate.com to do your own research.

3. **Always pay more than the minimum.** The credit card companies are not just being nice when they require only a small minimum payment on

your total balance. They calculate this minimum to extend your payments for as long as possible, to boost their profits. Scrimp if you need to, and pay as much as you can above the minimum every month.

4. **Plan your attack.** Don't just throw yourself at a mountain of debt without preparation. How many cards do you have? What interest rates do they charge? Which have the highest balances? What a coincidence, you already recorded all that information a few pages ago!

Generally, you'll want to start by paying off the card with the highest rate first, then the next highest, and so on. After all, the higher the interest rate, the less of your monthly payment goes to paying down your balance. If you want a quick boost, go ahead and pay off a card with a low balance, just to have one paid-off card under your belt. In a moment we'll commit your attack plan to paper and line up those debt decoys in your sight line.

5. **Reduce the interest rate.** Most credit cards charge interest of anywhere from 16 percent to 20 percent. Heck, we've seen cards that charge as much as 41 percent. But you can negotiate with your credit card company for a lower rate, particularly if you've had any of your cards for a while. Call it up to demand a lower rate. Shoot for 11 percent or 12 percent. You'd be surprised at how easy it is.

While it may not work every time, you should definitely give it a try. Let's look at an example. We'll compare the total interest paid on $5,000 in credit card debt at two different interest rates—a typical rate of 18 percent versus a reduced rate of 12 percent. Assume that no further charges are made and that the cardholder makes a regular payment of $200 per month until the entire balance is paid off.

CREDIT CARD DEBT	INTEREST RATE	TOTAL INTEREST PAYMENTS
$5,000	18%	$1,358
$5,000	12%	$810

There you go—a saving of $548 with just one phone call! That's worth a few minutes of discomfort, eh? So what are you waiting for? Use our Rate Negotiation Dialogue—from the "Dialing for Dollars," box on page 29—to reduce the amount of interest you're paying to The Man.

6. **Consolidate your debts.** OK, so you know what the interest rates and outstanding balances are for each of your cards, and you've reduced the rate on at least some of them. Next, consider combining your debts onto one or two of your lowest-rate cards, if you have some credit room on them. (If you're maxed out on those cards, forget it.) Simply call your lender and ask how to transfer funds.

7. **Pour any windfall into paying off your debt.** Don't be tempted to double your money by gambling or even investing it in the stock market. Ask your kid, your niece, or the tike behind you in line at the grocery store, "Which sounds better, losing 18 percent of your cash each year or making 12 percent on every buck you sock away?" Go ahead, we'll wait.

In fact, while we're waiting, we'll do the math. Take an investor who comes into a $3,000 windfall. Although she has $3,000 in debt, she has heard about the great returns she can get in the stock market. Even if she scores an above-average year on the stock market, pushing her holdings up by 12 percent, can she beat the 18 percent growth rate on her debt? Nope.

STOCKS VERSUS CREDIT CARDS

	STOCKS AT 12% PER YEAR	CREDIT CARD AT 18% PER YEAR
At launch	$3,000	$3,000
Year 1	$3,360	$3,540
Year 5	$5,287	$6,863
Year 10	$9,317	$15,701

A decade later, her debt has grown to more than $15,000 and her investments have grown to more than $9,000. Though she started with enough money to eliminate the debt, she's now in the hole more than $6,000. Until she sells the stocks. Then she'll have to pay 10 to 20 percent of the profit back to the government in capital gains taxes. So she's actually out more than $9,000.

So you see, Fools, that money in your savings account earning 1.5 percent, that can of change atop your dresser, even that portfolio that is bringing in above-average returns will not beat the interest accruing on your credit card. So roll up the dimes and pennies, dip into that savings account, even hold off on investing, and pay down that debt.

DEBTS TO DEFEAT: THE ATTACK PLAN

On the worksheet on page 30, write down your balance on each card and their interest rates in order of highest to lowest. Then pick a time frame during which you'd like to have each debt paid off and break it down into months. In the last column you'll determine roughly what your monthly debt payment will be. (It's a rough number because we're not including the interest you're accruing on your remaining balance.) Leave the columns marked "Secured or Unsecured" and "Flexible or Inflexible" blank for the moment. You'll come back and fill those out in a minute.

For the most accurate calculation of what it's going to take to pay off your debt, head to the Web. There are a lot of calculators you can use to see:

- How an interest rate change will affect your balance.
- What it will take to pay off your balance.
- Whether a lower-rate card is worth the annual fee.

Come play with the calculators at www.Fool.com/credit.

DIALING FOR DOLLARS

Now that we've seen the difference a lower interest rate can make, it's time to make that call. Rarely do you get anything in this world without asking, after all. Start with a card that you've had for a while and on which you haven't made any late payments. Then consider this sample script—our exclusive Rate Negotiation Dialogue—for ideas on what to say.

You: "I just got this incredibly great offer in the mail for a new credit card that has an introductory interest rate of only 5.9 percent! I don't really want to switch cards, since your service has been great. But even though I've had your card for three years, I'm still paying a 17 percent rate on my balance. I'm going to have to transfer my balance unless you can lower the interest rate."

Customer service rep: (The sound of a flurry of keyboard rat-a-tat-taps and your credit and payment history being scrutinized.) "Hmmm . . . well, that is the going rate . . . let's see. . . ."

You: "Sure, but I can pay a lot less in interest if I transfer my balance. I really need you to reduce the rate to 11 percent or so."

Customer service rep: "Let me check with my supervisor . . . . OK, how about 11.8 percent?"

You: "No problem." (Now go treat yourself to a snack—a cheap one!—for saving some bucks!)

This may not work as well if you're frequently late with payments and deeply in debt. But it can't hurt to at least try on all your cards. If you have a solid payment record, don't litter, are generally polite, or can affect a halfway decent French accent during the call, you should be able to get a rate reduction, even if you haven't really gotten a recent offer for a card with a lower rate. (You may not want to take such an offer anyway, since those rates are usually only temporary.)

WORKSHEET: DEBT ATTACK PLAN

Name of Card or Loan	Amount Owed	Interest Rate	Negotiated Interest Rate (If Any)	Secured or Unsecured	Flexible or Inflexible Payment Schedule	Number of Months Until Paid Off	Monthly Payment Due (= Total Amount Owed ÷ Months Until Paid Off)

KNOW THY DEBT

You're on the final lap here! You've organized your debts from highest to lowest interest rate. And maybe by this point you've called a few of your lenders to discuss lowering your interest rate. You rock!

There are just a few niggling details about those debts you have rounded up that you should find out. Go back to each item on your list (c'mon, you can face 'em!) and ask yourself the following two questions:

1. Is this secured or unsecured debt?

First, the easy part: Credit cards are *unsecured* debt. If you get way behind on payments, you can be sure you'll be reminded relentlessly by the bank and its bill collectors. But that's really all they can do to you when the debt is unsecured. The most common types of *secured* debt are home mortgages and car loans. These are a fundamentally different can of worms. If you violate the terms of these loans, the bank can come and take your house or car away. When you signed for the loan, you agreed that the bank could take possession of your stuff and sell it to recoup its losses should you default on the deal. In general, any loan in which you put up some kind of "collateral" is a secured loan.

To do: Go through your list of debts on your Attack Plan worksheet and mark each with an "S" for secured or a "U" for unsecured.

2. How flexible is the repayment plan?

The ultimate in flexibility is the credit card. You have to pay only a tiny "minimum" each month (though we hope you have gathered that we caution against paying this way). Sometimes student loans have flexible repayment options, too, such as the ability to suspend payments for a few years if you go back to school. Installment loans, such as home or car loans, are on the other side of the flexibility

spectrum. Unless you refinance the loan—by signing a whole new contract—you more or less have to make the required payments on time, without excuses.

To do: Go through your list of debts again. This time, mark the flexible ones with an "F" and the inflexible ones with an "I" in the column labeled "Payment Schedule."

HOW MANY CARDS ARE ENOUGH?

Personal finance is confusing enough without a stack of credit cards to track. Your goal should be to carry only one or two credit cards and pay the balances in full every month. If you've gotten carried away and have five, six, or more cards, consider the benefits of closing out most of them:

- **Simplicity.** Fewer cards will be easier to track. In addition, you'll have a much better sense of your overall debt level when it's on one or two cards, rather than spread across a bunch of them.

- **Better credit record.** You'll want to have at least one credit card to help build your credit history. If you're married, your spouse should have at least one card in his or her name only, for the same reason. Too many cards can hurt your credit rating, particularly if they all have large unpaid balances. And a spouse's credit sins can put your plans for a home purchase, for instance, in jeopardy.

- **Less temptation.** The more cards you have, the easier it is to rationalize excessive spending. "After all, *this* card has only $500 on it!" (Never mind that you have two more that are carrying $5,000 each.) Remember that your card's credit limits are not like poker bets: You don't have to match (much less raise) them.

Fewer cards, lower balances: That's your goal.

THE BIG PAYOFF

Now you have a handle on the amount of your debts and are probably getting a good sense of what it's going to take to get you out of the credit hole you're in. Developing a budget, saving money, and sending out debt payments make for a pretty dull life. You have to let a little sun shine in, or you're bound to collapse under the strain and give up.

One good way to add some zest to the game—while providing a motivational edge at the same time—is to come up with a fun one-year (or however long it's going to take) savings goal.

So sit down and think about it. If there are a spouse and children involved—who will surely be wondering why money is suddenly so tight—get them in on the reward planning too. Together, come up with something fun that will keep you all focused and help you stand firm in moments of potential weakness. Make it attractive, write in the total amount you'll need to pay for the reward, and divide that number by the number of months you have to achieve your goal. Remember, no cheating! If you haven't achieved your get-out-of-debt goal, postpone the reward. (Sorry, but those are the rules. We didn't make them up.)

There's no substitute for putting your agreed-upon award in writing for all to see (even if it's just you looking!). Seeing it in black and white makes it real. Record your goal in the space below. Then cut it out and hang it on the fridge.

> *Through regular monthly savings of*
> *$_____, we will accumulate savings*
> *of $_____ over _____ months.*
> *This money will be spent on a really awesome*
> *[tasty, shiny, sunny, or other adjective] reward.*
> *We've decided that this reward will be:*
>
> *_____.*

As you work toward your goal, you'll probably need a few pick-me-ups to keep up the momen-

tum. Set some short-term goals—we find that weekly is a good measure—so you can watch your progress toward your debt-free life. Your weekly goals could be:

- Saving a certain dollar amount to put toward your debt
- Avoiding putting any new purchases on the card
- Negotiating a lower interest rate
- Transferring your balance to a lower-interest-rate card
- Brown-bagging your lunch and adding the lunch money to your debt payment pile
- Baking cookies (or making some other home-made treat) instead of buying a gift for some occasion

Record your minigoals here:

_____

_____

_____

_____

_____

_____

_____

_____

What will be the reward for achieving these minigoals? Make it something inexpensive but enjoyable. Maybe it'll be a sundae from your favorite restaurant or a frou-frou coffee drink one day before work. Perhaps it'll be a magazine, a free hour to read it, or a day off from chores. Record your minirewards here:

_____

_____

_____

_____

_____

_____

_____

_____

Now get out a calendar and pick a minigoal and a minireward for each week of the month. Write it down and put a gold star sticker next to it. If you get ambitious, insert your minigoals for the next few months. As you pick off each one, mark it with a big black *X* and dive into your reward! If it takes more than a week to complete the minigoal, just carry it over into the next week until you're done. Remember, hold off on the reward until the goal is achieved. Yes, we're watching you.

OTHER KINDS OF DEBT

So far, when we've discussed the details of debt, we've focused mainly on credit cards. But what should you do with those other loans once you pay off your high-interest debt?

In the worksheet on page 34, make a list of the other kinds of debt you're carrying, including stu-dent loans, car loans, your mortgage, that $200 you owe your brother-in-law (really, you shouldn't bet that kind of money on the Red Sox), and the two grand you borrowed to get your "deviated septum" fixed. (Your new nose looks *really* natural, by the way.)

Let's consider some common questions regarding these forms of debt.

Q: My credit card debt is under control. Should I aggressively pay down car loans? Student loans? My mortgage?

Ideally, we'd all be 100 percent debt free. But for many of us, this just isn't a practical option, at least not in the near term. And if we do have to carry a little debt, we at least want to control the terms. The risk in paying down debt too aggressively is that we can lose control of the terms. This is where saving for an emergency enters the picture.

For example, let's say that—in an effort to pay off their mortgage early—a couple is making double mortgage payments every month. They're cutting their financial margin so thin, however, that they fail to save any cash for emergencies. (You, however, will be learning how to stash some short-term cash in Chapter 5.) Then, all of a sudden, one of them is laid off. Now, instead of making double payments, they're having a lot of trouble making the required single payment each month. In the worst-case scenario, they're forced back into high-interest credit card debt to make ends meet.

So we're all for aggressive debt repayment, but don't spread yourself so thin that it's hard to sleep at night. And don't neglect your emergency savings. After you have that established, start investing moolah for your future. Moreover, the after-tax interest cost of mortgage loans can get down into the 6 percent range, a level at which investing any extra cash might be more profitable, over the long run, than paying down the debt. So be sure to start with the higher-interest, non-tax-deductible loans, such as car loans. For most homeowners, the mortgage should be the last loan you attack.

WORKSHEET: OTHER DEBTS

Type of Loan	Amount Owed	Interest Rate	Time Remaining Until paid in Full (in Months)	Monthly Payment Due (= Total Amount Owed/Months Until Paid Off)

Q: Besides emergencies, what other things can upset loan repayment plans?

When we talk about saving for emergencies, we're talking about *real* emergencies, such as losing a job or suffering from an extended disability. We're *not* talking about the car insurance payment that slipped your mind or even replacing a broken-down refrigerator. Try to budget beyond the monthly must-pay bills to cover things such as future appliance needs, vacations, and next year's tuition payments. Failure to do so can lead to a demoraliz-ing step backward—to credit card debt—just when you were starting to make real progress.

Q: Should I consolidate multiple debts under one loan?

Maybe, but there are some important pros and cons to think through first. The most obvious benefits of loan consolidation are:

• **Lower interest rate.** It may be possible to borrow at an attractive rate and then use this money to pay off higher-interest rate loans, effectively "moving" a chunk of your debt to a lower-cost loan.

- **Simplification.** It's easier to be disciplined if you're organized, and it's easier to be organized with fewer outstanding loans to track.

But consolidation is not without risks. Just as we saw above, planning for emergencies comes into play.

TRADING UNSECURED DEBT FOR SECURED DEBT

Lower-rate loans are commonly "secured," meaning that the debt is backed by your home, car, or some other tangible possession. Putting your valuable stuff "on the line," so to speak, is what gets you the lower interest rate. From the lender's perspective, it removes a lot of the credit risk from the deal. The downside to secured loans is that if you hit an extended rough spot and default on the loan, you can literally lose your stuff. Think about it: You could lose your home. Even bankruptcy laws may not protect your home if, for example, your mortgage turns out to be the secured loan that you can't pay.

For this reason, many personal finance experts lay down a firm line. They'll tell you *never* to trade unsecured debt, such as credit card balances, for secured debt. For example, the standard advice is *not* to roll credit card debt into your mortgage or a home equity loan.

On the other hand, this advice is too conservative for some. Borrowing against the value of personal possessions is sometimes the only way out of lousy high-interest-rate loans. If you do decide to put your stuff at risk, be sure to consider whether you have adequate life and disability insurance, a secure and stable job, and some emergency cash set aside before you take the plunge.

Q. Does paying off my mortgage early make sense? I've heard it isn't a good idea, but I've also heard you can save a fortune in interest.

Paying off a mortgage early *might* make sense, but not from a strictly financial point of view. You *do* save a fortune in interest. The question is, what will it *cost* you?

You've probably heard all the arguments about the value of the mortgage interest deduction and how mortgage interest rates are lower than probable investing returns, yada, yada, yada. Obviously that hasn't convinced you. It hasn't convinced a lot of folks. So let's run a real-world scenario that doesn't even consider the tax deduction for mortgage interest, assumes a moderately high interest rate (which would motivate one to pay the mortgage off faster), and assumes a mediocre return on invested dollars. In other words, we're stacking the deck in favor of paying the mortgage off early. Let's see what happens.

We'll compare two neighbors with identical mortgages of $100,000 at 8 percent for thirty years. The scheduled payments are $733 per month. Fred, at 601 Motley Drive, runs some numbers and finds that by paying an additional $300 a month on his mortgage he can save more than $103,000 in interest and pay the house off in thirteen years. That sounds almost too good to be true. He jumps all over that plan.

Philip, at 603 Motley Drive, never ran the numbers; he just made his mortgage payments as scheduled. He also put $300 per month into a tax-efficient S&P 500 index fund that he read about on some Web site. He earns an average return on his index investment of 10 percent per year. At the end of thirteen years, when Fred holds his mortgage-burning party, Phil's index fund account is worth $95,000—several thousand more than what Fred saved in interest and enough to pay off his mortgage in cash with some left over—if he chooses.

But now Fred can start putting *$1,033 a month* into savings, right? Putting $1,033 a month into an index fund for the next seventeen years and earning an average of 10 percent per year will give Fred an account worth $550,000 by the time Phil makes his last mortgage payment. Nice.

But . . . wait a minute. Phil kept socking away his

paltry $300 a month. By the time his house is paid off, his investment account has grown to over $680,000. Both guys own their houses free and clear, both have paid out exactly the same amount every month for thirty years, but Phil comes out way ahead.

If Phil had invested just the difference between his mortgage interest deduction and Fred's, his account would have been tens of thousands of dollars bigger. That would pay for one heck of a mortgage-burning party.

ON THE OTHER HAND . . .

So why might you want to consider paying off a mortgage early?

• **Guaranteed return.** When you pay off a mortgage early, your return is guaranteed. The market comes with no guarantees. If you have extra money that you're not willing to risk in the market, paying off your mortgage is better than adding more cash to your coffee can.

• **Emotional satisfaction.** There's nothing like owning the family farm and knowing that no one can ever take it away from you. Just don't confuse emotional reasons with financial ones.

In our example, by the time Fred, our early payer, held his mortgage-burning party, Phil, his investing neighbor, could have cashed out his investments, paid his capital gains taxes, and had enough left to pay off his mortgage. But had disaster struck either family a few years *before* Fred paid off the mortgage, Phil could have sold stock to keep making his mortgage payments, while Fred might have been forced to refinance or even faced foreclosure. *Cash* can be very emotionally satisfying, too.

• **Forced savings.** If you fear that you won't send $300 a month to an index fund but are sure you will make every mortgage payment, consider a shorter-term mortgage instead of a boat and big-

screen TV. Even better, tell your brokerage just to grab the cash from your checking account every month. It will be *happy* to oblige.

Three good reasons to pay off a mortgage, three good reasons to think twice about each. It's your call.

A FINAL REVIEW OF ALL OF YOUR DEBTS

Everything's down on paper now. And you should be proud. It takes a big person to face up to all of his debts, staring at you from the page in stark black and white. As you review your list, think of these debts as ducklings lined up in a row (no, not fluffy, vulnerable *actual* ducklings—we're talking about the mechanical bedraggled circus kind). The prize for popping them off one at a time far surpasses that foam pink elephant you'd get at the county fair. The prize is peace of mind.

It should be crystal clear by now why you should pay down credit card debt first. Not only do credit cards generally charge the highest rate of interest, they're also very flexible. We want you to live a blessed and calamity-free life. But if the worst does come knocking on your door, you can always fall back to running up the card balances again. Of course we hate to see this happen to anybody, but we have to admit that it beats losing a home.

The opposite of unsecured, flexible credit card debt is secured, inflexible home and automobile debt. At a minimum, then, you should have a big enough monthly income cushion to easily pay these in full every month. If this isn't the case, you'll have to make a drastic move to increase your income or lower your expenses or sell the kids. (Or, more practically, you may want to consider a smaller apartment, car, or house.) It's harsh, we know, but it's also an inescapable fact. And it just may end up improving your quality of life in the long run.

Before you start aggressively paying down "good" loans, such as mortgages and student loans, we ask you to consider the following four emergency planning steps designed to prevent you from falling back into debt, or having to climb out of a deeper hole than you're in right now. We're not trying to scare you. Really. We're just trying to steer you permanently clear of the growing "bankruptcy through bad luck" crowd.

PLAN FOR THE WORST

When most people think of debt, they think of careless spending. In truth, though, even prudent spenders find themselves in debt through no fault of their own—other than failing to plan for the worst. People lose jobs every day, often when they least expect it. And it gets worse. According to the Social Security Administration, "a 20-year-old worker has a 3-in-10 chance of becoming disabled before reaching retirement age." *Three people in every ten.* Divorce and medical emergencies can also cause sudden debt problems.

Sorry about the laundry list of doom. We don't mean to get you down, but these things do happen all the time, to people just like us. Being prepared for them is a big part of avoiding crippling debt—every bit as important as controlling your spending.

Beginning on page 38 is a list of debt prevention safeguards you should consider. We'll get into the specifics on all of them in later chapters. We encourage you to take this checklist seriously. It's your suit of armor when the debt monster rears his ugly head. Take our word for it, you'll sleep a lot better with these safeguards in place.

FICO, FICO, IT'S OFF TO BORROW WE GO

In search of: Soul mate to share sunsets by the lake and maybe more. Must be gentle and kind. Prefer FICO score above 720.

Don't laugh. Personal ads such as the one above could start popping among singles searching for a significant other with a clean record—credit record, that is. FICO scores—based on a formula developed by Fair, Isaac & Co—are the lending industry standard for quick, objective assessment of consumer credit risk.

So what's your score? You can get it for a fee at the FICO Web site, www.myfico.com. The number is included on most credit reports and plays a large role in determining if you are a good or bad credit risk, if you can get instant approval, and even what interest rate you'll be offered on a loan. The higher the score, the better chance your request will be approved. According to Fair, Isaac, the FICO score is used in 75 percent of residential mortgage applications.

CREDIT REPORTS VERSUS CREDIT SCORES

To be precise, a credit report is different from a credit score. Specifically, a *credit report* is a summary of various accounts, past and present, opened in your name, including credit cards, bank credit lines, mortgages, department store charge cards, and other bills, though usually not rent payments or utilities. A report also includes any collection actions taken against you and any public-record information that may exist, such as liens or bankruptcy proceedings.

This information is available directly from the three major credit-reporting agencies, for a fee. (See contact information on the next page.) If you have been turned down for credit within the past year, you can request a free report.

When you apply for a loan through a mortgage bank or other lender, it requests your credit report from one of the three major credit-reporting agencies, which then determine your *credit score* by calculating your FICO score based on Fair, Isaac's model. Since your credit report might differ among the different agencies, your FICO scores might differ as well. If you're not happy with one score, it may be worth getting a second opinion.

WHEN SHOULD YOU CHECK YOUR SCORE?

Certainly, it's not imperative that you know what your credit report looks like this very minute. However, if you're planning to buy a home or a car or make any other major purchase soon, or even if you're just curious, checking your credit history is worth the few minutes (and the few bucks) it takes. Even if a major purchase is a year or two away, checking your credit report well ahead of time will give you the opportunity to correct any errors that may exist or take steps to improve your record. You can also add comments to your report to explain your side of any disputes or other problems that resulted in negative factors on your credit report.

Mistakes are not rare: reports show that as many as 30 percent of credit reports contain inaccuracies.

WHERE TO GET YOUR CREDIT REPORT

The three major national credit bureaus have huge computer databases that keep track of all your loan and credit transactions. For a fee, they'll send you a copy of your current file (available free under certain circumstances). To get the full picture, you'll have to order from all three bureaus, though, since there will be differences in your file from bureau to bureau.

Experian

P.O. Box 2002
Allen, TX 75013
Telephone: (888) 397-3742

Online: www.experian.com

Equifax Credit Information Services, Inc.

P.O. Box 74024
Atlanta, GA 30374
Telephone: (800) 685-1111

Online: www.equifax.com

TransUnion LLC

Consumer Disclosure Center
P. O. Box 1000
Chester, PA 19022
Telephone: (800) 888-4213

Online: www.transunion.com

DEBT PREVENTION SAFEGUARDS

1. **Disability insurance:** According to government statistics, the average American twenty-year-old has just a 17 percent chance of dying before age sixty-five. These odds are much lower than the 30 percent odds of becoming disabled before retirement that we trotted out earlier. That's right, disability stamps out a lot more regular paychecks than death, yet more people have life insurance than disability insurance. Don't be one of them. Most disability insurance is sold through employers, so talk to your human resources contact at work about your disability coverage options. We'll provide you with some worksheets on this—and the next two items—in Chapter 4.

2. **Life insurance:** What will happen to your financial dependents if you should die? Please don't fail to address this possibility head-on, or you may drive your family down a one-way highway to overwhelming debt. It's hard enough to get out of the hole even when you and your paycheck are there, right?

3. **Health insurance:** Should you endure a period of unemployment in the future, the government provides a backup option—known as the COBRA plan—for your employer-sponsored health insurance coverage. In the midst of scrambling to find a new job, health insurance is likely to be one of the last things on your mind. Sign up for COBRA, and note when the plan will expire. Failure to bridge the gap could end up putting you into a debt hole from which you'll be hard pressed ever to get out.

4. **Emergency fund:** This just might be the most important element of sound financial planning.

Most experts recommend a goal of three to six months' worth of basic monthly expenses in an account with predictable interest payments, such as short-term CDs or a brokerage money market fund. It's a tall order for most people. Don't be afraid to start small on the path to achieving this goal. Moreover, the discipline required to amass this cash cushion is a major wake-up call for most people. It teaches firsthand (1) how tough it is to save this much dough; (2) how paying off an equivalent debt will be even more challenging, since compound interest will be working against you; and (3) how pleasant it is to be on the receiving end of significant interest payments for a change.

In Chapter 5, we'll help you establish an emergency fund that gets the best interest rates.

MAXIMIZING YOUR CREDIT SCORE

Keep a clean record—or work on improving it—by following these guidelines:

- Pay your bills on time, especially mortgage payments. Apart from extreme circumstances such as bankruptcy or tax liens, nothing has the impact of late payments. Anything more than thirty days late will hurt you. Never let a payment of any kind—even phone or utility bills—get ninety days past due.

- While nobody can tell you exactly how many credit cards to own, it's clear that not having any is likely to reduce your credit score. Having clean, active charge accounts established many years ago will boost your score. If you are averse to credit on principle, consider setting up automatic monthly payments for, say, utilities and phone on a credit card account and locking the card away where it's not a temptation. The sooner you get started, the better if you are currently renting but plan to buy a house someday.

- Beyond one or two credit cards, it starts to get complicated. It's not always a good idea to cancel extra cards, although it is always a good idea to keep the ratio of total owed to total credit available as low as possible (i.e., don't carry large balances from month to month).

- Be careful not to apply for too much credit in a short amount of time. Multiple requests for your credit history (not including requests by you to check your file) will reduce your score. If you are hunting around for good loan rates, assume that every time you give your Social Security number to a lender or credit card company, it will order a credit history.

- If you are using a loan search service on the Internet, ask how many credit file inquiries will be generated by the search and try another method if it can't keep this number low. Fair, Isaac claims to have improved its methods for clustering rapid strings of inquiries, so that they are treated as one, but it's safer not to even take the risk, if possible.

- Check your credit history for errors, especially if you will soon be requesting a time-dependent loan, such as a mortgage.

DEBT TRIAGE (FOR THOSE IN A DIRE SITUATION)

If debt troubles have pushed you to the edge of sanity, STOP . . . and take a deep breath. It may seem like the end of the world, but we can assure you that it's not. It's in everyone's best interest—both yours and that of the people to whom you owe money—to get you out of crisis mode and into a repayment plan that you can handle. Nobody wins if you spiral down to bankruptcy. The laws are actually on your side, although you'll have to get organized to take advantage of them.

If you're in the midst of a crisis, it can be next to impossible to think clearly and employ these steps. This section, then, is targeted for those in crisis mode. We want to steer you toward a more stable life, free of overwhelming and immediate stress. From there, you will be able to build and execute your measured plan for a long-term solution.

Unfortunately, there's not much we can do—directly—if you've fallen deep into the debt hole. We can, however, offer a list of valuable resources, and plenty of 'em. Take advantage of the law and credit counseling to get back on firm ground. These actions won't erase your debts. Chances are you'll owe just as much money. But at least you'll be in a position where you can think clearly and start laying the foundation for putting debt behind you forever.

No matter how bad it looks today, believe us when we say that you're not alone. You're likely one phone call away from somebody who's seen it all before—and worse. So pick up the phone or fire up your Web browser and get started.

GENERAL CONSUMER PROTECTION RESOURCES

• **The Federal Trade Commission (FTC)** is the national source of information about debt and credit laws that protect you, the consumer. It cannot address your individual situation—go to bat for you, specifically—but it can provide information either online or through the mail and track consumer complaints nationwide, looking for patterns that signal common problems.

- www.ftc.gov
- Telephone: (877) FTC-HELP

• **State attorneys general** cover some of the same consumer protection turf on the state level that the FTC covers on the national level.

- Your state's attorney general: www.naag.org
- Telephone: Check your state government listings.

• **Your local Better Business Bureau (BBB)** is a good source for complaints about specific compa-

nies and organizations in your area. It might be able to help you check out a particular debt-counseling service to see if it's a reputable organization or tell you if a particular creditor (somebody you owe) has a history of taking advantage of consumers.

- Find your local BBB: www.bbb.org/look up
- Check the complaint record of a local company: www.bbb.org/reports/bizreports.asp
- Telephone: Look under "Better Business Bureau" in your local phone book or dial (703) 276-0100 for the National Council of BBBs.

• **Consumers Union** is the nonprofit publisher of *Consumer Reports* magazine. Its Web site is a good source for information regarding the latest in credit and bankruptcy laws.

- Online: www.consumersunion.org
- Telephone (National Headquarters): (914) 378-2000

• **The Motley Fool** is serious about helping people get out of debt.

- Our "Getting Out of Debt" Education Center can be found at www.Fool.com/credit.
- Our Consumer Credit discussion board offers informal discussion support from a community of helpful people. A good source of both (1) tips and tricks and (2) emotional support, as many of the regular participants are themselves onetime heavy debtors who were helped by the board community. You can find it by searching Consumer Credit at: http://boards.Fool.com.

DEALING WITH BILL COLLECTORS

Are you being hounded by debt collectors or intimidated by lenders? If so, we have some good news and some bad news. The good news is that you are well protected by federal laws; the bad news is that it will take a disciplined effort on your part to take advantage of those laws.

Before we get into specifics, here are three general strategies that will help anyone battling a debt problem.

1. Start a record of every conversation you have, from here on out, with lenders, credit bureaus, bill collectors, and so on, by phone or in person. We provide some space on the next page for you to do this. Be aggressive on the phone. Get names and write them down, along with dates and key discussion topics, including any agreements reached or promises made.

2. Save all related mail, including postmarked envelopes. When it's your turn to send something important, go to the post office, ask to mail the letter by registered or certified mail, and request a receipt that proves it was received.

3. Be courteous and diplomatic, but make it clear to everyone involved that you know your rights, are keeping careful records, and won't be intimidated.

Yippee! Sounds like fun, eh? OK, we know these tasks are a drag. But if you can force yourself to do them, you'll be armed with the facts for each new round of battle against your creditors, and you'll gain a comforting sense of control over the whole process. Now for some specifics.

START AT THE SOURCE

Always start by contacting the businesses to which you owe money. Yes, we realize that this is about as much fun as giving a speech in your underwear, but it's generally to your advantage. When push comes to shove, most businesses would rather not bring in a costly bill collector. Faced with this option, most would rather work out a repayment plan that you can handle.

KNOW YOUR RIGHTS

- By law, debt collectors cannot contact you before 8 A.M. or after 9 P.M. and cannot otherwise ha-

rass you, your family, or your friends, or tell lies about you.

- If a debt collector threatens you with jail time, it's guaranteed to be a lie. Debtors are *never* jailed in this country, and nobody can even garnish your wages without a legal proceeding.

- You can prevent workplace calls or visits from a debt collector by requesting that you not be bothered there. Put the request in writing!

- Since debt collectors can be sued for failing to follow these (and other) rules, you can sometimes turn the intimidation tables on them by mentioning that you are familiar with the law.

Fair debt collection rules and regulations are enforced by the FTC. In general, contact either the FTC or your state's attorney general to report violations of the fair debt collection laws.

- Online www.ftc.gov/bcp/conline/pubs/credit/fdc.htm
- Telephone: (877) FTC-HELP and ask for information on the Fair Debt Collection Practices Act

FINDING A GOOD CREDIT COUNSELOR

A good credit-counseling organization can make all the difference. These offer everything from expert advice and a sympathetic ear to hands-on budgeting help. Many will even step in between you and those you owe to negotiate repayment plans that you can handle.

Many of these counseling services are nonprofit organizations that offer their services free of charge or for just a small fee to those who can afford it. A good place to start is the National Foundation for Credit Counseling (NFCC), a national network of Neighborhood Financial Care Centers (NFCC). Call it at (800) 388-2227 to find out if there is a center in your area. It offers a national, nonprofit network of in-person financial coun-

WORKSHEET: UNCOMFORTABLE INTERACTIONS WITH PEOPLE WHO WANT MY MONEY

Lender, Credit Bureau, Bill Collector, etc.	Contact Information: Phone Address	Person Contacted	Date	Key Discussion Topics	Any Agreements Reached

selors, an emergency phone number, and even on-line counseling. Along with your local Better Business Bureau, the National Foundation for Credit Counseling staff may also help you investigate other counselors (outside its network) in your area.

PROCEED WITH CAUTION

A good credit-counseling service can turn your life around, but please choose carefully. For some reason debt problems draw a lot of scam artists.

Unfortunately, for every such worthy organization, there are dozens of rip-off artists preying on vulnerable debtors. Anyone who promises to "quickly wipe your record clean" for a small fee, or similar magic tricks, is probably a thief. Be especially wary of high-pressure sales tactics. Most reputable counselors will wait for you to come to them.

WORKSHEET: QUESTIONS TO ASK A CREDIT-COUNSELING AGENCY
(FROM "FTC FACTS FOR CONSUMERS, CHOOSING A CREDIT COUNSELOR")

Use the following worksheet to interview a potential credit-counseling organization.

Name of organization _____

Date contacted _____

Contact information _____

Name of person interviewed _____

Action to be taken (e.g., call back to set up appointment, cross off the list):_____

_____

_____

What services do you offer? _____

_____

_____

Do you have educational materials? If so, will you send them to me? Are they free? Can I access them on the Internet? _____

_____

_____

In addition to helping me solve my immediate problem, will you help me develop a plan for avoiding problems in the future? _____

_____

_____

(continued)

WORKSHEET: QUESTIONS TO ASK A CREDIT-COUNSELING AGENCY
(FROM "FTC FACTS FOR CONSUMERS, CHOOSING A CREDIT COUNSELOR"), continued

What are your fees? Do I have to pay anything before you can help me? Are there monthly fees? What's the basis for the fees? _____

_____

_____

_____

_____

What is the source of your funding? _____

_____

_____

Will I have a formal written agreement or contract with you? _____

_____

How soon can you take my case? _____

Who regulates, oversees, and/or licenses your agency? Is your agency audited? _____

_____

What are the qualifications of your counselors? Are they accredited or certified? If not, how are they trained? _____

_____

How does your debt repayment plan work? How will I know my creditors have received payments? Is client money put in a separate account from operating funds? _____

_____

Can you get my creditors to lower or eliminate interest and finance charges or waive late fees? _____

_____

_____

What assurance do I have that information about me (including my address and phone number) will be kept confidential? _____

_____

TEN TIPS ON AVOIDING CARD TRICKS

Surprise! Some lenders don't have your best interests at heart. Even the most reputable ones bombard customers with "perks" that are designed to pad fees and interest payments. Customers can ignore those carrots—and we suggest that all Fools do.

In the pursuit of profit, some credit card companies resort to some rather underhanded practices. Here are a host of offenses to watch out for:

1. **Pursuing the un-credit-worthy.** Creditors often prey on those who are least credit-worthy by scanning credit records for telltale signs. If you are a student with no income or have recently emerged from bankruptcy, credit card solicitors would like to talk to you. They know that the recently bankrupt can't declare bankruptcy for another six years and that Junior probably doesn't know the first thing about budgeting.

2. **The magically appearing annual fee.** You signed up for a card with no annual fee. Then, blammo! Out of the blue you find one. Some lenders have started charging an annual fee to customers who pay off their bill every month. Your best recourse is to cancel the card.

3. **A sliding credit line.** One really abhorrent practice is to entice customers to use a cash advance check or a skip-a-month payment offer and then lower their credit limit. The maxed-out customer is then charged an additional fee for being above the limit. A variation on this theme is simply to lower the customer's credit limit once it is reached.

4. **Mysterious fees.** You may not have to pay a finance charge to get a cash advance. But most banks charge hefty transaction fees, which can be around 2 percent of the total amount and no less than $10. Also watch out for transaction fees for calling the toll-free number to check your balance and penalty fees for account inactivity. (Don't forget about that credit card buried in your sock drawer.)

5. **The disappearing grace period.** Watch out for lenders who pull the grace period out from under you, especially if you are a "freeloader," someone who pays his or her balance in full every month. Remember, if your grace period is eliminated, you'll accrue interest from the day you make a purchase. The only way to avoid a finance charge would be to pay your bill before you received it.

6. **The disappearing low interest rate.** Take a look at this one: "The Introductory rate from this offer will be maintained as long as you make at least the required minimum payments on your Account when due. Otherwise the regular Preferred Pricing rate will take effect from your last Statement Closing Date." That's a quote from a credit card solicitation one of our community members got in the mail. The translation: "You'll get the Very Special Introductory Interest Rate, as long as you don't pay any bill late." Further digging into the fine print revealed that the Very Special Rate was limited to six months, after which it would automatically go to the bank's Preferred Pricing rate, which, as you probably guessed, is much higher.

7. **Knee-jerk rate hikes.** Once you've figured out your APR, your lender will probably change it. What raises its ire? Missing a few payments certainly can. You could be subjected to a penalty rate of more than 30 percent. Lenders also scrutinize your spending habits. Even if you pay all your bills on time, you may get flagged. Your creditor may look at your credit records every quarter to evaluate the amount of debt relative to the amount of your current income. One recent notice received by a Fool staffer stated that customers could not increase "significantly" the amount

they spent on another unsecured card. It defined "significantly" as $2,000 or more. Keep your eye on your rates if you plan to make any big purchases.

8. **Teaser rates that don't treat all balances equally.** Like a cotton candy buzz, teaser rates don't last. But they are tempting. Creditors are now making it more difficult to continuously transfer balances from one low-interest-rate card to another. If you toss cards aside like Wet Naps after a rack of barbecued ribs, be prepared to pay a penalty. Before you sign up for a card with a low, low interest rate, find out what that rate applies to: new purchases? cash advances? balance transfers? Watch out for cards that force you to pay a retroactively higher rate or charge you a penalty fee if you cancel the card.

9. **Pricey "perks."** You're the picture-perfect plastic user. You pay your bill in full each month. You deserve a reward—go ahead, skip next month's payment. In fact, take this $1,000 "convenience" check to the mall and buy something pretty. Heck, we'll even extend your credit so that you can get the stereo you really want. That's what your card issuer would like you to do. In fact, most of the "perks" offered by lenders encourage impulse purchases and spending beyond your means. Fools know that they'll pay a king's ransom in interest if they skip a month's payment. And they recognize that those "convenience" checks usually come with a conveniently sizable fee, no grace period, and a higher interest rate.

10. **"Reward" cards that encourage bad money management behavior.** Don't get us wrong. There are indeed reward cards that offer genuine perks such as airline miles and football-shaped clock radios. With most, the rewards are based on the amount you charge, not your outstanding balance. But some require cardholders to carry a balance to cash in on the perks. Before signing up for a charge card offering a reward, look at the annual fee (most carry one) and interest rate. (Unlike unrewarding cards, these issuers usually can't be talked out of waiving the fee or lowering the interest rate.) Factor these into the reward you are trying to earn. It ain't much of a perk if you pay for it, then never use it.

ONE BIG LOOMING QUESTION LEFT HANGING IN THE AIR . . .

We hope you share our vision of two credit cards, maximum, with balance paid in full each month. At this point, however, you may be thinking, "Hey, this is all great advice, but you're forgetting one tiny, little detail, like, um . . . *Where am I going to get the money to pay off all these debts?"*

Of course this is a great question. And to answer it for yourself, we're afraid you're going to have to wait until you've completed a bit more of your Bit-by-Bit Budget. In the meantime, we provide lots of money-saving tips in the Appendix. You'll be amazed at how many money leaks you can fix with just a little bit of effort. And fewer holes mean more money to throw at your debts!

YOUR BIT-BY-BIT BUDGET ENTRY

All of this work boils down to a few line items on your Bit-by-Bit Budget. We know it's not very satisfying right now. But we promise that all the work you've done to organize your debts will pay off.

Directions: Go to the Debt Attack Plan Worksheet beginning on page 30. Take the list of your bad debts and the average monthly payments, and add them to the first and second columns of your Bit-by-Bit Budget (a copy of which appears on the next page). Then take the list of loans from your Other Debts Worksheet on page 34 and plug them and the monthly payments due into the lines marked "Loan."

BIT-BY-BIT BUDGET

	Amount from Debt Attack Plan Worksheet	Budgeted Amount	Month 1	Month 2	Month 3	Month 4	Month 5	Month 6
Debt Repayment:								
Credit card 1								
Credit card 2								
Credit card 3								
Credit card 4								
Loan 1								
Loan 2								
Loan 3								

Note: This is one part of your budget that we strongly encourage you to fill in continuously. Every month you'll be hacking away at those debts, watching the budgeted amount slowly (or swiftly!) dwindle to zero. We strongly encourage you to go above and beyond the budgeted amount to pay it all off. In the months when you have more money to put toward paying off your debts, by all means, pay your Visa! This is one area where we encourage going for extra credit. (The classroom kind, not the plastic kind that got you here in the first place.)

CHAPTER 4

INSURANCE

SIXTY-SECOND GUIDE TO INSURANCE

Welcome to the world of legalized gambling—except that in this case you hope you *don't* get to cash in your chips. Why pay for a service you pray you'll never need? Because it could save you and your family in the unfortunate case that you *do* need it.

0:60 Earn money while you're on your back!

Of course we're talking about disability insurance. Over the course of your career, there's a pretty good chance that you won't be able to do your job. Better make sure you have some money coming in when you're laid up.

0:50 Your money or your life.

No one likes to think about death—unless you believe in an afterlife loaded with chocolate. But you have to consider what will happen to your loved ones if you join that great sugar parlor in the sky. If folks are depending on your income, make sure it'll still be there when you aren't.

0:40 Determine what kind and how much.

When it comes to life insurance, you have a few choices. For most people, a convertible term life insurance policy is the best way to provide for your family when you're too far underground to do the job.

0:30 Crash, boom, bam.

Not only is it unwise to drive without insurance, it's also unlawful. But how much do you really need? Take some time to evaluate what's protecting your wheels.

0:20 Cover your assets.

What about your house? Your boat? Your gopher-hair couch? Just like cans of soup, insurance can be cheaper when you buy in bulk. See if you can get a discount for purchasing various types of insurance from the same carrier.

0:10 Get some armor against a suit.

Baseball, apple pie, and lawsuits are part of the American way. Protect the duchy from instant and utter destruction via a lawyer-led assault.

• • •

Insurance. That's all it takes to protect your empire from the forces of evil, or just life's random hiccups. So let's break it down into specifics, all without the accompaniment of an insurance salesperson.

Before we get started with the specifics, though, we should make our general bias clear. Simply stated, Fools always aim for self-insurance through savings and investment.

Note that we said "aim" because in many cases this just isn't a practical goal. Nonetheless, it does define our approach. We prefer to funnel money into our personal savings accounts instead of the insurance company's, whenever it makes sense, and take our chances with small claims rather than insuring against every unexpected event.

Broadly speaking, insurance protects either your paycheck or your stuff. Let's start by talking about the former group, which can be further broken down into disability insurance and life insurance.

DISABILITY INSURANCE

What's so magical about disability insurance? If you get injured or become ill and cannot work, disability insurance will replace a percentage of your income. It's money for nothin', and your checks for free . . . sorta.

Unfortunately, disability insurance seems to get lost in the shuffle. The Census Bureau says that while 62 percent of small companies include some life insurance as an employee benefit, only 22 percent provide long-term disability coverage. Listen up, this is important. There is a one-in-three chance—repeat: *one-in-three chance*—that a twenty-year-old worker will become disabled before retirement age. In fact, you're more likely to become disabled than to die before age 65. You need disability insurance.

IF YOU ALREADY HAVE
DISABILITY INSURANCE

Let us shake your well-protected hand. Check your policy against the following list of disability insurance "must-haves." If it falls short on any of these criteria, find out how much it'll cost to add those fea-

tures. If your policy is through your employer, get a copy of the policy from your benefits specialist. Also, find out if the plan offers extra coverage. A common option is a bump-up from a base of 60 percent of income replaced to 80 percent, usually at a competitive rate. If there is room in your budget for this extra payment, it's usually a good deal.

IF YOU DON'T HAVE DISABILITY INSURANCE

Here's the good news: If you pay for the policy yourself, with after-tax income, your disability checks will be tax-free income (should you ever need them).

Here's the not-so-good news: Disability is among the toughest insurance products to buy on the Web or via a quick phone call to a direct insurance provider. We're afraid it'll take a bit more effort.

Now down to business. Check your current policy, or a policy you're shopping for, for the following features:

Must Have

- The percentage of income replaced should be between 60 and 80 percent.

- Long-term disability should be covered to sixty-five years of age (not just five or ten years).

- The definition of disability should be liberal, including mental illness, stress disorders, back pain, and severe migraines, just to name a few common maladies that keep people out of the workforce.

Could Be Important

- Does the plan define commissions, bonuses, and overtime as income to be replaced? If a significant portion of your income comes from these sources, you should be sure they are covered.

- What's the maximum monthly payment? (High-wage employees may be cut off at a certain level.)

Complete the Protect Your Income Worksheet that follows. We've laid out the top things you need to ask (and know) about your policy. Policy comparisons based on these questions and premium costs should get you most of the way home.

WORKSHEET: PROTECT YOUR INCOME

Use this sheet to record your current disability insurance provider or to grade potential providers of the services they offer.

Name of disability insurance provider: _____

Date acquired: _____

LONG-TERM DISABILITY QUESTIONS

INCOME

1. **What does it cost, in premiums, to replace 60 percent of my income? 80 percent?**

$ _____

2. **Are overtime, commissions, and bonuses considered income?** If any of these account for a big chunk of your regular income, make sure the policy considers them as income when calculating your disability check.

Yes _____   No _____

3. **Is there a monthly maximum disability check?** Some policies cap replacement income. For example, let's say that a policy pays 60 percent of income capped at $60,000 annually. If you make anything more than $100,000 annually—i.e., 60 percent of your income is above the cap—you'll still receive just $60,000 in disability checks each year.

Yes _____   No _____

POLICY TERMS

4. **Will disability payments continue up to age sixty-five?** (Don't settle for five or ten years' worth of payments.)

Yes _____   No _____

5. **Is the coverage "any occupation" or "own occupation"? Is "own occupation" available, and how much more does it cost?** If you are a highly paid specialty professional—a brain surgeon or NBA power forward, for example—you may want to pay more for own-occupation coverage, since any-occupation coverage will require you to take any available job in your field and will not make up the difference between what it pays and what your higher-wage skills paid.

Any occupation _____   Own occupation _____ $ _____

6. **What is the elimination period?** This is the amount of time from the day you are disabled to the day you begin receiving benefits. The longer the elimination period, the cheaper the policy. An elimination period of six months is your best bet. Use your emergency fund for expenses until you begin receiving disability checks.

Elimination period: _____

7. **Is the policy noncancelable to age sixty-five?** This guarantees that premiums can't be increased as long as you pay them on time. Don't settle for "guaranteed renewable" or "return of premium" policies.

Yes _____   No _____

8. **Can I increase coverage as my career and income progress without a medical checkup?**

Yes _____   No _____

DEFINITION OF DISABILITY

9. **How is disability defined? What steps are required to prove I am unable to work?**

_____

_____

10. **Are these covered?**

Preexisting conditions? _____   Carpal tunnel syndrome? _____

Chronic fatigue syndrome? _____   Back pain? _____

Stress disorders? _____   Dangerous hobbies? _____

Mental illness? _____   Severe migraine headaches? _____

11. **Is it an "accident-only" policy?** If so, ask for something else. These policies cut out illness—more than half the reason for getting a disability policy in the first place.

Yes _____   No _____

WORTHWHILE

12. **Can I get a "residual benefits" rider or a "loss of income" policy?** These nifty options add an extra payment to cover the difference between the best job you can get, after becoming disabled, and the job you held before. This effectively locks in your current income and also avoids the awkward situation where you're forced to sit at home because getting a lesser job might reduce or eliminate your disability income.

Yes _____   No _____

13. **How much is a "cost-of-living" rider?** This will add important inflation protection to your disability payments. If it's affordable, get it.

$ _____

We're guessing you have exactly four more questions about disability insurance. What a coincidence! We have answers to four of the most frequently asked questions about disability insurance right here.

Q: What's the difference between short-term and long-term disability insurance?

Short-term covers absences of less than six months and picks up where paid leave, workmen's compensation, and so on leave off.

Don't bother paying for short-term disability insurance. Instead, rely on a good-sized emergency fund. Save money on premiums and get a policy that doesn't pay benefits until you've been disabled for six months.

Q: I have no dependents, so I don't need disability insurance. Right?

Wrong. You're forgetting about one person who depends on your income: you. Are you really prepared to go a few decades without a paycheck?

Q. Doesn't my health insurance cover illness?

Health insurance covers the cost of medical care—doctor and hospital bills. Disability insurance replaces your income so that you can pay the rent, buy food, and so on. Although it's too broad to address here, it almost goes without saying that health insurance is an essential financial protection. Medical bills for some ailments will make a year of lost income feel like a pebble in your shoe.

Q. Does absolutely every working person really need disability insurance?

If you've acquired enough wealth that you could retire tomorrow, you don't need disability insurance. (As a side note, are you single? Are you free Friday night?) Likewise, if you're willing to risk a lifelong dependence on family and relatives—with a small Social Security check perhaps providing some spending money—you can skip this insurance. Otherwise . . .

LIFE INSURANCE

So you're covered if you become disabled, but what if you should die before your time and the paychecks *really* stop rolling in? Can we have some of your stuff?

Sorry. That was tasteless. If other people—such as kids, a spouse, or an elderly parent—are counting on your future paychecks to make ends meet, get life insurance. Should you die, a life insurance policy would deliver a big check to these dependents that could generate monthly interest income to replace a big chunk of your lost paycheck. It's a good idea. Period.

If no one besides yourself relies on your paycheck, you can skip the life insurance section for now, but come back to it if you pick up some dependents. For those with dependents, read on.

THE MAJOR PLAYERS

Life insurance can be broken up into two major types:

• **Term life insurance:** Term insurance is pure insurance, like typical health, auto, and homeowner's policies. Pay the premium; get covered for the policy term; renew as needed.

• **Cash value insurance:** Cash value insurance combines life insurance payments with contributions to a long-term, tax-sheltered savings plan. Be aware, though, that cash value policies are usually a lifetime commitment. It can be tough to spend your cash value savings if you want to use them for something other than insurance payments. Once you're in, it's tough to get out without a little financial pain. The most common examples are whole life, universal life, and variable life.

Our Suggestion: Term Life Insurance

We Fools think most people are better off with straightforward term life insurance. It's simpler, more flexible, and more easily compared by price. (And there are better places to invest your long-term savings than in cash value insurance.)

But That's Not All . . .

There are two kinds of term insurance:

- **Renewable annually:** You have to renew the policy every year, and—unless you can figure out how to stop getting older—the price will go up each year.

- **Level premium:** The price is fixed (level) for the extended policy term, as opposed to increasing each year with age. Typical terms are five, ten, and twenty years.

Our Suggestion:
Look for the Least Expensive Option
That Meets Your Needs

Level premium term will usually be cheaper than annually renewable term over the long run, but your initial premiums may be higher. Look for a policy that is guaranteed renewable without a medical exam. This locks in future premium increases based on only your age (at renewal) and not on potentially costly health problems that may arise.

Convertible Term

There is just one more option to consider to be sure your policy provides the maximum flexibility: con-vertibility. This gives you the option of converting to a cash value policy, usually without a medical exam. This is a potentially useful option with negligible extra cost.

There you have it: We recommend that you consider a convertible term policy for your life insurance needs.

HOW MUCH DO I NEED?

The rule of thumb about life insurance is that you should get a policy that is six to eight times the size of your annual salary. Again, we're assuming that if you're shopping for life insurance, there is someone sharing your life and your current paycheck. Also, for the time being we're not taking into account any kiddies or high-maintenance pets. In a moment we'll walk you through five easy steps to figure out a more precise number. Follow along on your Protect Your Dependents Worksheet.

Note that this is a "one-person" exercise and does not include the income of your spouse, who must be insured separately. You'll have to do all this twice if you have two people bringin' home the bacon. Also, don't overlook stay-at-home moms and dads either; it will cost you plenty to replace their child care and/or other indispensable contributions. For these folks without an actual paycheck, estimate their annual income by what it would cost to replace their "services."

Also, there are many insurance needs calculators on the Internet, including one at Fool.com. If you have access to the Whirled Wild Web, visit the Fool's insurance area (http://insurance.Fool.com) or just enter the words "insurance calculator" into any Internet search engine.

WORKSHEET: PROTECT YOUR DEPENDENTS

HOW TO DECIDE HOW MUCH LIFE INSURANCE YOU REALLY NEED

1. DETERMINE HOW MUCH INCOME YOUR DEPENDENTS WILL NEED.

A common rule of thumb is that life insurance should replace 80 percent of your pretax income.

80% of your annual pretax income $ _____
(0.80 × your annual pretax income)

But as with most things in personal finance, there are plenty of exceptions.

Need More or Less?

Think about some of the exceptions. Do you have debt? How much does your family rely on your income and benefits? Do you have a large amount of savings that might free up some other money?

_____ I might need more than 80 percent.
_____ I might need less than 80 percent.

When you've arrived at a target annual replacement income, write it down below.

My annual replacement income need is $ _____

2. FACTOR IN SOCIAL SECURITY.

Upon your demise, your widow(er) and your dependents may receive Social Security benefits. To arrive at this number you'll need to pull your most recent Social Security benefits statement (now sent out annually). It will tell you how much your heir(s) would receive. If the statement's not handy, fire up the Social Security Calculator (www.ssa.gov/planners/calculators.htm) or call (800) 772-1213. Eligible dependents are:

- A spouse who takes care of your children, until the youngest child reaches age 16
- Unmarried children until age 18
- Dependent parents age 62 or older

Note: If your spouse will work after your death, his/her benefit will be reduced by $1 for every $2 made above the annual limit, which for comparison's sake was $10,680 for 2001. This will affect only your spouse's benefit, not those received by other family members.

My estimated **monthly** Social Security death benefit is $ _____

× 12

My estimated **annual** Social Security death benefit is $ _____

Subtract the **annual** Social Security number from the replacement income you settled on in Step 1. This gives you the annual income that insurance will need to replace.

_____ − _____ = _____

Annual replacement   *Annual Social Security*   Revised annual replacement income
income (found in Step 1)   *death benefit (found in Step 2)*

3. DETERMINE A TOTAL CAPITAL AMOUNT.

Using the table below, determine the size of the lump-sum benefit you want your heirs to receive upon your demise.

ANNUAL REPLACEMENT INCOME	Years Until You Retire						
	10	**15**	**20**	**25**	**30**	**40**	**60**
$10,000	$92,000	$132,000	$168,000	$201,000	$231,000	$283,000	$361,000
$20,000	$184,000	$263,000	$336,000	$402,000	$461,000	$565,000	$722,000
$30,000	$276,000	$395,000	$504,000	$602,000	$692,000	$848,000	$1,083,000
$40,000	$368,000	$527,000	$672,000	$803,000	$923,000	$1,130,000	$1,444,000
$50,000	$460,000	$659,000	$840,000	$1,004,000	$1,154,000	$1,413,000	$1,805,000
$60,000	$552,000	$790,000	$1,007,000	$1,205,000	$1,384,000	$1,696,000	$2,166,000
$70,000	$643,000	$922,000	$1,175,000	$1,406,000	$1,615,000	$1,978,000	$2,527,000
$80,000	$735,000	$1,054,000	$1,343,000	$1,606,000	$1,846,000	$2,261,000	$2,888,000
$90,000	$827,000	$1,185,000	$1,511,000	$1,807,000	$2,076,000	$2,544,000	$3,249,000
$100,000	$919,000	$1,317,000	$1,679,000	$2,008,000	$2,307,000	$2,826,000	$3,610,000
$110,000	$1,011,000	$1,449,000	$1,847,000	$2,209,000	$2,538,000	$3,109,000	$3,971,000
$120,000	$1,103,000	$1,581,000	$2,015,000	$2,410,000	$2,768,000	$3,391,000	$4,332,000
$130,000	$1,195,000	$1,712,000	$2,183,000	$2,610,000	$2,999,000	$3,674,000	$4,693,000
$140,000	$1,287,000	$1,844,000	$2,351,000	$2,811,000	$3,230,000	$3,957,000	$5,054,000
$150,000	$1,379,000	$1,976,000	$2,519,000	$3,012,000	$3,461,000	$4,239,000	$5,415,000

First column: Annual income to be replaced.
Top row: Years of replacement income required.
Table body: Lump-sum life insurance required.
Assumptions: Annual inflation rate 4%; annual investment return 6%.

(continued)

WORKSHEET: PROTECT YOUR DEPENDENTS, continued

My total capital needed to produce income amount is $ _____

(This is the lump sum you want to go to your dependents upon your death.)

4. ADJUST THE TOTAL CAPITAL AMOUNT.

Before you head off to buy this much insurance, there are a few more adjustments to consider. These are simple additions to the lump sum you calculated in Step 3.

If you have little or no emergency cash savings, add $10,000 to $25,000, depending on how fancy a funeral your family will throw; how complicated your estate will be; how good your health insurance is; and how much ready cash your family is likely to have. This little nudge won't add much to the premium.

Emergency cash addition to lump-sum insurance payout $ _____

If your death will leave your family with a heavy debt burden beyond what you can *comfortably* pay on your current salary, you should add money to pay off some of these debts. Don't be in a hurry to pay down your mortgage, unless the monthly payments are already busting your budget. Your dependents will make more by investing the lump-sum insurance payment than they will save by paying down a tax-advantaged mortgage.

Debt burden addition to lump-sum insurance payout $ _____

If you don't have retirement savings, you may want to leave some extra cash to give your dependents a boost toward these goals. Remember, though, that the chances are good that you won't die before retirement, so it usually makes sense to save on insurance premiums and invest money on your own, where you're more likely to get something back.

Retirement and other key savings plans bump $ _____

5. THE FINAL NUMBER

Take the lump sum from step 3 and make the additions from step 4.

_____ + (_____ + _____) = _____
Lump sum from Step 3   *Bump-ups from Step 4*   Your final number!

WANT A QUICKIE?

If you're not inclined to complete the Protect Your Dependents Worksheet, or you want to compare your number to another method, try this chart. It's real easy: (1) Decide how many years your dependents will need life insurance (usually until your kids are grown and your spouse is retired); (2) lower your after-tax income (since life insurance benefits aren't taxable) by any annual Social Security benefits your dependents will receive; (3) multiply that amount by the income factor in the chart below; (4) add more to the sum, if you wish, to account for debt relief, college or retirement funds, and so on.

YEARS	INCOME FACTOR
5	4.5
10	9.0
15	13.0
20	16.5
25	20.0
30	22.5
35	25.0
40	27.5
45	30.0
50	31.5

If you already have life insurance, compare your current coverage (the death benefit) to what you just figured. Consider buying additional term insurance to fill any gaps. If your current life insurance is a cash value policy, don't automatically dump it. Since these policies charge heavy up-front fees, after a certain point it becomes cheaper to stick with them. Also, some cash value policies can be converted into regular old annuities. These aren't the best investment vehicles in the world, but an annuity may be preferable to a lousy insurance policy. Call your insurance company for more details.

ON TO THE NEXT TOPIC

As we said earlier, disability and life insurance protect your paycheck. Now we'll shift our focus and look at the types of insurance that protect your stuff: car insurance, homeowner's/renter's insurance, and liability insurance.

But we haven't grouped these types of insurance together just because they protect your stuff. We have another reason: if you purchase these coverages from the same provider, you can usually see some sweet savings. After we go through each type of insurance, we'll help you analyze the coverage you have (if you have it) and encourage you to shop around for a better deal.

A final point these types of coverage have in common: you can save lots of money by choosing policies with big deductibles. Insurance exists to protect you from catastrophic losses, not small claims. Use your emergency fund—which at least earns a little interest—for the small stuff, and save big time on your insurance premiums.

AUTOMOBILE INSURANCE

Car insurance provides a wide array of protections. We'll break the topic down into the three main types of coverage.

THIRD-PARTY COVERAGE

An insurance policy is a contract between you (the first party) and an insurance company (the second party). The wild card is always the other guy: the third party.

When you're piloting a ton of plastic and metal down the road at sixty miles per hour, there's a decent chance that your life will become intertwined with that of a third party, regardless of how carefully you drive. There's also a good chance that this third party will blame you for any damage done to his car and passengers. So you should be ever prepared to honor such a claim, and (this is America, after all) your protection should anticipate the possibility that Mr. Third Party will attempt to sue the trousers off you.

There are two types of third-party liability coverage: *bodily injury liability* and *property damage liability*. The first covers people costs: medical expenses, lost wages, and pain and suffering. The second covers the cost of stuff, such as somebody else's car, a telephone pole, or, heaven forbid, somebody's living room window. Both include legal protection up to the limits of your policy if the claimant files suit against you.

When it comes to these two third-party coverages, it's not hard to figure out whether you need them. Do you own a car? If so, you need them. In fact, the law requires that you carry these coverages in all but a few states.

Even if you live in a "no-fault" state, these liability coverages are important. No-fault laws were enacted to clear out jammed courts, and they eliminate garden-variety, low-dollar injury lawsuits as well as most claims for "pain and suffering." But no-fault laws will *not* save you from serious, megadollar injury claims that could lead to bankruptcy. Even pain and suffering claims are allowed under certain conditions. Remember, the potential for these low-probability, high-impact events is exactly why you buy insurance in the first place.

Each state has minimum required levels for these two third-party liability coverages. If you have assets or income to protect, however, these minimums won't be enough for you.

The bottom line: Most people should have a 300/100/100 policy. This means that you are covered for bodily injuries totaling $300,000 (limit of $100,000 per person) and property damages up to $100,000. The only exceptions are people who are low on the income scale and are not homeowners; they might be able to get away with the state minimums.

FIRST-PARTY *INJURY* COVERAGE

Now we get into the first party: you and your passengers. Here we're talking about *expenses* as opposed to *liability*. In other words, these are things you'll want covered, even if the law doesn't insist that you pay for them.

When it comes to injury-related expenses, if the other party is at fault, your first line of defense will be the other guy's third-party liability coverage. Take our advice, though: don't bank on it.

Your odds of a successful claim will depend on many things, including the opinion of others—including, potentially, a court of law—and whether the other guy has any insurance or assets for which you can file a claim. Even though liability insurance is required by law, many people—including 28 percent of all California drivers, according to a 1995 survey—still drive without it. Moreover, those who drive without insurance are the most likely to have few assets and little income.

Your health insurance (outside of your automobile policy) will cover some of your family's medical costs, and a good disability policy will cover a long-term loss in wages. However, these policies might leave holes. Disability insurance covers only family wage earners, and health insurance covers only your spouse and immediate dependents (not your other passengers).

Take a look at your overall insurance situation and see where your potential coverage holes may be. If you find some shortcomings, consider these additional auto policy coverages as the next line of defense:

• **Medical payments (MedPay):** Covers medical costs for the driver and passengers in your car, regardless of which driver is at fault. Most commonly offered in states that do *not* have no-fault laws. If a medical payments rider isn't required in your state, it may be unnecessary as long as you and your passengers have comprehensive medical insurance.

• **Personal injury protection (PIP):** In states with no-fault insurance laws, this coverage is often required. These states place the burden of injury coverage on *your* insurance policy regardless of who's at fault, so it's tough to sue the other guy. Basically, PIP just extends medical payments coverage to include lost wages. Some states allow you to waive PIP coverage for your family (assuming you already have adequate health and disability insurance) but force you to carry some PIP to cover other passengers in your car.

- **Uninsured and underinsured motorist coverage:** As the name suggests, this insurance covers you and your passengers when the at-fault driver is not properly insured or can't be located (as in a hit-and-run accident). Essentially, it takes the place of the phantom driver's third-party liability coverage, allowing you to make a claim against your own insurance company for *injury* costs and lost wages. If you have a good health insurance plan and disability insurance, you probably don't need this coverage. However, keep in mind that it does cover your passengers and does compensate for pain and suffering. Finally, if you live in a no-fault state, this coverage may be unnecessary since you're covered by your standard policy. If you do decide to get this coverage, purchase limits equal to your bodily injury coverage.

FIRST-PARTY *PROPERTY* COVERAGE

This is the most straightforward of the three main coverage areas. First-party property is just your stuff. In the world of auto insurance, this usually means your vehicle.

Collision insurance covers damage to your vehicle resulting from an automobile accident, regardless of who is at fault or even whether there was another car involved (sorry, you can't insure your pride). In the event that someone else is at fault, your insurance company may go after the other guy's company for the money, but this won't matter to you. Your collision insurance covers you either way.

The inaccurately named *comprehensive insurance* covers damage to your vehicle that is not caused by an automobile accident. Common examples include hail damage and theft. Check your

policy to see which acts of nature and fate are covered.

With collision and comprehensive coverage, you don't have to choose any limits. It's a yes/no question. If you still have a loan out on your automobile or if you are leasing, you won't even have to make this decision. The bank or lessor will require you to purchase both.

If you own your vehicle free and clear, your decision will depend on its book value. You probably won't get any more than this from the insurance company, regardless of how well you've taken care of your four-wheeled baby.

Check your declarations page for a premium breakdown. Collision and comprehensive are usually the two most expensive coverages. If continuing to pay for these premiums will quickly rack up a total bill that closes in on the book value of your vehicle (and you own the vehicle), you should probably drop these coverages. The rule of thumb: If your premiums for collision and comprehensive are more than 10 percent of the value of your car, or if your car is worth less than $5,000, you probably don't need these coverages.

If you purchase collision and comprehensive coverage, your last decision will be the size of your deductibles—the per accident, out-of-pocket expenses you pay before collision and comprehensive payments kick in. If you have a comfortable, liquid emergency fund, jack up these deductibles as high as you can stomach. You'll save money on both premiums and premium increases that might result from the small claims that come with a lower deductible. This is one place where self-insurance can save you big money.

Finally, some companies will try to sell you *un/underinsured motorist* coverage that covers your property (before, we were talking about UM coverage for bodily injury). If you already have collision and comprehensive coverage, this additional first-party property insurance is probably superfluous. Collision and comprehensive will cover you regardless of fault. Unless there is a decent chance that an uninsured driver will plow into your house or other possessions, don't bother with this coverage.

WHAT FACTORS AFFECT MY AUTO INSURANCE PREMIUM?

There are many factors that affect the premium you'll pay for auto insurance, including driver's gender, miles driven per year, purpose for using the vehicle (commuting to work, using for work, leisure only), and so on. Below, we've elaborated on some of the major risk factors that affect the price of insurance.

Age

Statistically, drivers under the age of twenty-five have a greater risk of being in an accident than those over age twenty-five. Drivers between the ages of fifty and sixty-five tend to have some of the safest records. These are not absolutes, just assessments based on historical data. But age is just one of the many factors used to calculate your premium.

If you're a parent, having your sixteen-year-old on your policy will be an added cost. If you have more drivers than cars, you can make Junior a part-time, rather than a full-time, driver, and that may lower his premiums. Check with your insurer to see if this is an option.

Driving Record

Being liable for an accident or having moving violations on your record (speeding tickets, DWI, reckless driving, etc.) put you at higher risk of accidents and will likely mean a higher premium. Depending on the state in which you live and insure your car, insurance companies can penalize you for your record for as many as five years from when the incident occurred. The good news is that as your record improves, many companies will lower your premium.

Where You Live

Where you live really can make a difference. People living in areas with little or no traffic are likely to spend less on insurance than those living in congested cities or suburbs. Why? Oddly enough, areas with a lot of traffic have been found to have more accidents. Some areas also have a higher rate of vehicle thefts, which can result in a higher premium.

Type of Vehicle

As we've said, many factors contribute to the cost of your premium, including the make and model of the car you drive. If you have a relatively new, pricey car, it will cost more to repair it. Unless it's been paid off, your lien holder will require you to carry collision coverage on it. More expensive repairs translate into a higher collision coverage premium. As your car ages, however, your premium may decrease. But the book value isn't the only contributor to your premium. Certain cars, regardless of age or initial cost, seem to be exceptionally attractive to thieves, and that can result in a higher premium.

Discounts

Car insurers offer many discounts that can result in some nice savings. Be sure to ask about them when you're getting a rate quote. Here is just a sampling of things that may qualify you for a discount:

- Having homeowner's or renter's insurance with the same company
- Having a young driver with an impressive grade point average on your policy
- Taking a defensive driving course
- Using an approved (by your insurer) antitheft device in your vehicle
- Some companies give discounts based on the number of years you've been with them with a good record
- Housing your car in a garage versus on the street
- Membership in some professional associations that provide bulk business to the insurer

HOMEOWNER'S/RENTER'S INSURANCE

This is perhaps the simplest type of insurance. Though your house is your biggest asset, it's not too difficult to erect an insurance dome around your domicile.

RENTER'S

First, let's address you landlord-lubbers, since your situation is less complicated. Since you don't own the place you call home, you just need to insure your bike, stereo, TV, couch, and so on, against theft and damage. Get enough coverage to replace all your personal property, or at least the personal property that would be financially catastrophic to replace.

HOMEOWNER'S

A homeowner's policy insures against the loss of your house and the loss of its contents (even if the contents aren't in your home at the time, in some cases). If you're still paying on your mortgage, chances are you're required to have this insurance. However, even if you completely own your home, you should have homeowner's insurance. Here's what to look for:

• Get a "guaranteed replacement cost" provision. This guarantees that the insurance company will pay for the costs of replacing your home, even if it's more than the coverage provided by your policy.

• Homeowner's insurance doesn't protect against any old disaster. Often, you have to purchase additional riders for specific disasters, the most common of which are floods and earthquakes. If you live in an area that is at risk for these types of events (and, believe or not, most of us do), look into adding these to your policy.

• Find out if your policy includes "off-premises" coverage, which comes in handy when you lose your luggage on vacation or someone slips on the banana peel you dropped in Miami.

Besides insuring against the damage or loss of your material goods, homeowner's and renter's insurance also protects you against another form of financial disaster: lawsuits. Thus, we enter the world of . . .

LIABILITY INSURANCE

Big-money lawsuits are a mainstay of American life these days, and nobody is immune. Although it's true that most lawsuits are directed at businesses, not individuals, there is always the chance that you could someday be held liable for costly injuries or property damage suffered by others. Doesn't leave you with a warm, fuzzy feeling, does it?

To protect yourself from being wiped out by such events, buy liability insurance.

The key here is to see:

1. What liability insurance coverage you already have
2. Whether it's enough

In all likelihood, you already have some liability insurance in the form of homeowner's or renter's insurance and automobile insurance.

IF YOU DON'T HAVE HOMEOWNER'S OR RENTER'S INSURANCE

Think very seriously about getting some. Maybe you're just starting out with a futon and a knapsack to lose. Or perhaps you're on the other end of the spectrum with a mortgage paid off in full and no bank calling the shots. Either way, a quick fluke (perhaps a flaming dessert dish gone awry) followed by a multimillion-dollar lawsuit could wipe out your financial future.

For the money, the liability insurance that

WORKSHEET: PROTECT YOUR STASH

Use this sheet to record the features of your current policies. Then do some shopping to see if you're getting the best deal for your insurance dollar.

	CURRENT PROVIDER PHONE:	POSSIBLE PROVIDER 1 PHONE:	POSSIBLE PROVIDER 2 PHONE:	POSSIBLE PROVIDER 3 PHONE:
Automobile insurance:				
Insurance for: _____				
Blue Book value: _____				
Bodily injury limit				
Property damage limit				
First-party injury limit				
Medical payment (MedPay)				
Personal injury protection (PIP)				
Uninsured motorist (UM)				
Collision				
Comprehensive				
Riders:				
Annual premium				
Renter's insurance:				
Riders:				
Annual premium				

	Current Provider Phone:	Possible Provider 1 Phone:	Possible Provider 2 Phone:	Possible Provider 3 Phone:
Homeowner's insurance:				
Percentage of replacement cost				
Guaranteed replacement cost				
Off-premises coverage				
Riders:				
Annual premium				
Liability insurance:				
Limits				
Riders:				
Annual premium				
Other:				
Discount for buying all types of insurance from same provider				
Total annual premium for all coverages				

comes with these policies is a powerful defense that not only protects you around your home but, in general, also covers you and your dependents outside the home.

PROTECT YOUR STASH

This is one of the few areas of insurance that doesn't have a handy rule of thumb to hang your hat on. Ultimately it's a pretty subjective decision, but we'll try at least to set the stage for you.

An "Umbrella Policy" and the Odds of Being Sued

A common insurance industry recommendation is to maximize both your auto and homeowner's/renter's policies' liability limits (usually $300,000 is the ceiling for each) and then tack on what's called an umbrella or excess coverage policy up to $1 million. It's usually cheapest to do the whole deal (auto, homeowner's/renter's, and umbrella) through one insurance company.

Whether this boilerplate advice makes sense for you will depend mostly upon your odds of being sued. There are some characteristics that greatly increase your odds of being sued. How many of these statements apply to you?

- I own a business.
- I'm a risk taker.
- I'm a bad driver. (Be honest.)
- I'm a thrill seeker.
- I have a nanny and/or other household help.
- I frequently host visitors and parties.
- My kids are risk takers.
- My kids are thrill seekers.
- My kids are bad drivers.
- I have a pool.
- I'm wealthy.

For every "yes," there is a greater need to get liability insurance.

How Willing Are You to Risk a Million-Dollar Legal Decision Against You?

Beyond a $1 million umbrella policy, the question becomes even more subjective. Although judgments in the tens of millions of dollars are remotely possible, covering all such possibilities is prohibitively expensive for most of us. Basically, you have to do the cost-versus-small-risk calculation in your gut and pick an upper limit that makes sense to you.

WHERE TO LOOK

For a good start on term life price quotes, check out our online partners in The Motley Fool Insurance Center (http://insurance.Fool.com). You can also give these places a try:

- ReliaQuote: www.reliaquote.com or (888) 847-8683
- SelectQuote: www.selectquote.com or (800) 963-8688
- InsuranceQuote: www.iquote.com or (800) 972-1104

Another Web site worth a look—especially for information about disability insurance—is www.insure.com. Note: Insure.com is sponsored by the insurance industry, which you should keep in mind as you use it (for example, it promotes cash value policies more than we're comfortable with) but overall it has some excellent consumer resources.

TEN TIPS ON INSURANCE

1. Buy from the same carriers.

2. Videotape or photograph all your property. Keep receipts of major purchases. Keep these in your desk at work, or at your mother's house.

3. Paying your insurance on a monthly basis—instead of annually—sounds like a good idea.

However, you're probably paying for that privilege—perhaps as much as 20 percent of the annual premium. Even if you are charged just $5 a month ($60 a year) to be able to pay on a monthly basis, that's a considerable chunk of change. If you can't shell out the whole premium at once, monthly installments are a good idea. Otherwise, you're paying a lot for that convenience.

4. Make sure to update all insurance beneficiary information after major life changes such as marriage, divorce, the birth of an heir, or discovering that your precious niece Janey is more deserving of your priceless *Garfield* etchings than her no-good brother Joey.

5. Do not buy life insurance for your children. Unless they support your family with the proceeds from their Broadway career, it's a waste of money.

6. Update your policies when you move, celebrate your twenty-sixth birthday (if you're a male driver), acquire Great-Aunt Anne's Fiestaware set, or sell your antique Vespa scooter collection.

7. If you have a beloved pet, look into pet insurance. It could save you thousands of dollars should little Poesy require costly treatment during her life. Some employers even help cover the cost of pet insurance.

8. Get items of major value appraised by a trusted independent appraiser. An independent appraiser will give you an honest assessment of value. The retailer who sold you the goods is under pressure to illustrate what a deal you got at her shop. A questionable appraisal could raise eyebrows in an insurance claims department.

9. If Junior's heading off to college (aren't you proud!), check if he's still covered under your health insurance policy. Also, see if the university provides health insurance. Many include it in tuition so that students can freely use the university health center.

10. The most meaningful items can never fully be replaced by an insurance payout. Get a fireproof safe for your cherished home movies, old photos, and that lock of hair from your first haircut that you keep in a Ziploc bag in the second dresser drawer under your good socks.

YOUR BIT-BY-BIT BUDGET ENTRY

Once you've shopped around and settled on an insurance provider, it's time to plug the info into your Bit-by-Bit Budget in Chapter 12. Here's a copy of the section you're ready to fill out. If you haven't had time to shop around, simply plug in what you currently pay for insurance in each of these categories. You may find that when you're done adding up your expenses, you'll want to return to this part of your budget and spend some time shaving costs.

BIT-BY-BIT BUDGET

	Amount from Money Tracker Worksheet	Budgeted Amount	Month 1	Month 2	Month 3	Month 4	Month 5	Month 6
Insurance:								
Vehicle 1								
Vehicle 2								
Vehicle 3								
Vehicle 4 (you gotta be kidding!)								
Disability insurance								
Renter's or homeowner's insurance								
Liability insurance								
Other insurance (boat, pet, flood, etc.)								

CHAPTER 5

SHORT- AND LONG-TERM INVESTING

SIXTY-SECOND GUIDE TO SHORT- AND LONG-TERM INVESTING

You have got big plans for your future. If only the Publisher's Clearinghouse Prize Patrol could find a parking space on your block. Forget the Prize Patrol. Forget the lottery. Forget those hopes that a long-lost, insanely rich and generous relative will bequeath her fortune to you. You don't need any of it to build a comfy nest egg. It's time to start investing—for real!

0:60 Line up those ducks!

Before you begin your illustrious investment career, you need to take care of a few things. First, pay off that high-interest debt. Next make sure you have an emergency stash of cash at the ready.

0:52 Set your expectations.

There are a lot of places to stash your cash. Obviously, you want to earn the greatest return on your dough. Luckily, the stock market rewards those with time, patience, and persistence—three virtues most of us have within our reach.

0:44 Set aside your short-term cash.

Got some money you'll need in the next five years or so? Do you have an emergency cushion to cover those inevitable bumps in the road? Put money you need in the near term into a suitably safe investment.

0:39 Get the most out of your long-term investments.

Maybe you're thinking about retiring sometime down the line. (We hear that's popular with the older crowd.) First use accounts that will help you keep more dough for yourself—and not in Uncle Sam's clutches. Then pick investments that will give you the biggest bang for your long-term buck.

0:20 Track your results.

Investing is not a contest. Well, it is, kind of. But it's a contest in which you should be happy taking the bronze. In this case, you want to make sure your long-term investments are keeping up with the stock market as a whole. No better and no worse. Doing so will put you ahead of most Wall Street pros!

0:07 Keep investing, and don't freak out!

No need to follow the TV ticker 24/7. Simply put a quarter (or however much you can afford) into a cup every day and invest it on a regular basis. Then stay calm and cool and watch your savings blossom over the long term.

• • •

A FOOL'S GUIDE TO INVESTING

We feel that the main purpose of the stock market is to help enrich those who methodically save and invest, employing a buy-and-hold philosophy. What's more, at The Motley Fool we make a big distinction between a "fool" and a "Fool." Be a Fool! Buy 'n' hold! The others, the fools, may well be made idiotic by trying to predict the daily swings of the market.

WHY INVEST?

Chances are that some future event will require you to pony up a not-insubstantial amount of cash. Is it an exotic animal menagerie? Or perhaps a vacation villa in the sun-baked hills of Tuscany?

Say you take $2,000 of your savings and put it into the stock market. If your money returned 11 percent a year (the S&P 500's historical average, which we'll explain in a moment), two grand would be worth $53,416.19 after thirty years. With that kind of money, you could buy that Tuscan villa (or at least come up with the down payment).

Maybe you don't have $2,000 burning a hole in your bank account, but perhaps you can afford to invest your lunch money. Brown-bag your lunch and sock away just $4 a day, 250 days a year. It's not a lot, but if you're in your early twenties, you have the investor's best ally on your side—time. If you invest $1,000 once a year in an investment that averages an 11 percent annual return—the average annual stock market return since 1926—it'll grow to more than $1 million after forty-six years, which is right around the time you'll be ready to retire.

Of course, as you get older and more financially stable, you should be able to invest more. Upping the ante to just $166 a month (lunch money plus about what you pay for basic cable TV and a movie channel) would put you at the million-dollar mark in just thirty-nine years.

Simply put, you want to invest in order to create wealth. It's relatively painless, and the rewards are plentiful. By investing in the stock market, you'll have a lot more money for things such as retirement, education, and recreation—or you could pass on your riches to the next generation so that you become your family's Most Cherished Ancestor. Whether you're starting from scratch or have a few thousand dollars saved, this chapter can help get you going on the road to financial (and Foolish!) well-being.

WHY SHOULD I INVEST?

Here are some reasons that some folks invest—perhaps one or more will strike a chord with you. Check any reasons that apply to you.

_____ To accumulate money for retirement because I have no retirement pension where I work

_____ To supplement retirement income from a pension fund

_____ To save enough money for a large expense I can foresee, such as sending children to college, buying a house, or starting an exotic animal petting zoo business

_____ To have resources for an unforeseen future emergency

_____ To make one heck of a lot of money and become Master of the Universe

_____ To learn more about the company at which I work

_____ To have something to talk to my dad about

If you checked at least one box, you're going to get your money's worth out of this chapter.

ARE YOU RICH AND STOCK MARKET–SAVVY?

Who cares? We Fools certainly don't. And neither should you. In fact, let's debunk these and other common misconceptions about investing.

1. You need *to be rich to invest.*

No, you don't. There are investment strategies appropriate to all income levels.

2. You need *to put a lot of time into investing.*

No, you don't. You can put in as much or as little time as you want. Anywhere from thirty minutes a month to as much of your day as you're willing to commit will work. Some people make a hobby of investing and regularly read about companies, financial news, and the latest in electronic doodads. Others make a hobby of mountain biking or newts and *still* invest by using strategies that require little effort and only periodic checks of their investment performance.

3. You need *to know a lot about stocks.*

Nope, you don't need this either. You just need to know about what you are investing in, or the strategy you are using. Some strategies, such as index investing, require no knowledge at all. Others, such as investing in small-cap growth stocks, require more time to learn the nuances of market mechanics and valuation.

4. Investing is deadly *boring.*

Again, no, it doesn't have to be—unless you're an MBA student assigned to follow the utility industry by a mammoth investment firm. Otherwise, it's good, clean, educational fun. We still can't believe the subject isn't taught to our children more. (If you have a teenager or know one, may we recommend our *Investment Guide for Teens,* to help them get started investing?)

Now go play with your pet newts.

THE INVESTMENT PROCESS

What is investing? Any time you invest, you are putting something of yours into something else in order to achieve something greater. You can invest your weekends in a good cause, you can invest your intelligence in your job, or you can invest your time in a relationship. Just as you do each of these with the expectation that something good will come of it (wink, wink), when you invest your savings in a stock, bond, or mutual fund, you do so because you think its value will appreciate over time.

Investing money is putting that money into some form of "security"—a fancy word for anything that is "secured" by some assets. Stocks, bonds, mutual funds, certificates of deposit—all these are types of securities. As with anything else, there are many different approaches to investing. Some of these you've probably seen on late-night TV. A well-dressed, wildly positive (and unnaturally tan) young man sits lazily waving palm fronds and shakes his head over how incredibly easy it is to amass vast wealth—in no time at all! Well, hey! That sounds fine! However, discerning minds will wonder: If it were so easy, wouldn't everyone who saw the same pitch be rich? Then, too, you always have to send in some money to learn the secrets. So we suggest you take the $25 you'd spend on the hardcover *EZ Secrets to Untold Billions* book and the $500 you would shell out for the EZ Seminar, and invest it yourself—after you've learned the basics here.

TIME IS MONEY

Why not take that $525 you saved by reading the previous paragraph and stick it under your mattress? You don't want to do that because the money will deteriorate. No, not the actual bills (unless you live in a particularly humid clime). But a dollar will not always be worth a dollar.

Sometimes a dollar is only worth 80 cents, and sometimes it is worth $1.20. (Say! You give us your dollar worth $1.20, and we'll give you ours worth 80 cents, in an even trade! Do we have a deal?)

But let's think about this. How can it be? Here's how: the value of a dollar changes dramatically depending on when you can take control of the dollar and invest it. The critical variable in the exact value of a dollar is *time*.

If someone owes you a dollar, do you want him to pay you today or next year? (Yes! Another trick question! The answer is "Today.") With inflation consistently destroying the purchasing power of a dollar, a year from now a dollar will be worth slightly less than it is today. "Inflation" is an economic term used to describe the gradual tendency of prices to rise over time. If inflation is 2 percent per year, that means that prices, on average, will rise 2 percent over the next year. That in turn means that your dollar will purchase 2 cents *less* in a year than it can today. That's right, all you mathematicians out there—with 2 percent inflation, a dollar today will be worth only 98 cents in a year.

However, if you got the dollar back today, you could invest it. If you invested it (along with a few of its cousins, we hope) in the stock market and your investment returned 10 percent over the course of the year (which is somewhat less than the market average has historically returned), then you'd have $1.10 at the end of the year. So your money would be growing instead of shrinking, and you'd be staving off the negative effects of inflation.

THE MIRACLE OF COMPOUNDING

In fact, if you leave this dollar invested, its value will mushroom over time through the miracle of compounding. The theory of compounding is pretty simple: as you earn investment returns, your returns begin to gain returns as well, allowing you to turn a measly dollar into thousands of dollars if you leave it invested long enough.

The more money you save and invest today, the more you'll have in the future. Real wealth, the stuff of dreams, is in fact created almost magically

through the most mundane, commonplace principles: patience, time, and the power of compounding. *BO-ORING,* we know. But thankfully those three virtues are within reach for most of us.

The table below shows you how a single investment of $100 will grow at various rates of return. Five percent is what you might get from a certificate of deposit (CD) or a bond, 8 percent is what you might get from a mix of bonds and stocks, and 10 percent is a little less than the historical average return of the stock market since 1926. (We'll talk about all of these options in greater detail a little later in this chapter.)

Why is the difference between a few percentage points of return so massive after long periods of time? You are witnessing the miracle of com-

Year	5%	8%	10%
1	$100	$100	$100
5	$128	$147	$161
10	$163	$216	$259
15	$208	$317	$418
25	$339	$685	$1,083
30	$432	$1,006	$1,745
40	$704	$2,172	$4,526
50	$1,147	$4,690	$11,739
60	$1,868	$10,126	$30,448

pounding. When your investment gains (returns) begin to earn money, too, those returns start to earn small amounts of money that can mushroom very quickly. Extend the time period or raise the rate of return, and your results will increase exponentially. For instance, if you start young, say at fifteen years of age, note how a single $100 investment grows to over $1,000 by the time you are forty. Ahhh . . . youth.

Looking at it another way, let's compare two teenagers and their lifetime savings habits. Bianca baby-sits a lot and spends most of her spare time reading. She saves $1,000 a year starting when she's fifteen and invests it in the stock market for ten years, earning 12 percent per year on average. After ten years, she comes out of her shell, stops adding money to her nest egg, and spends every penny she earns club hopping and on trips to Cancún. But she keeps her nest egg in the market.

Compare her account to that of her friend Patrice, who squandered her early paychecks on youthful indiscretions. At age forty, Patrice gets a wake-up call when her parents retire on nothing but Social Security. She starts vigorously socking away $10,000 every year for the next twenty-five years. Guess who has more at age sixty-five? That's right, Bianca. (You figured it was a setup, didn't you?) Her ten years of saving $1,000 per year (just $10,000 total—the same amount Patrice put away in just *one year*) netted her $1.6 million by age sixty-five. Patrice, on the other hand, scrimped for twenty-five years to invest a quarter-million dollars out of her own pocket and ended up with just under a million. Neither will be going to the poorhouse, but you see our point: Bianca's baby-sitting money grew for fifty years, twice as long as Patrice's, and Bianca barely missed it.

For now, suffice it to say that the power of compounding is the single most important reason for you to start investing right now. Every day you are invested is a day that your money is working for you, helping to ensure a financially secure and stable (and flush!) future.

How fast your cash will pile up depends on three factors: time, growth rate, and savings:

- **Time:** You have very little control over this. About all you can do is adjust your plans to give your investments more time to grow. So don't put off learning about and starting investing. It's never too early and rarely too late to begin!

- **Growth rate:** We'll tackle this in an upcoming section. When you finish this chapter, you will know how to match the growth rate of the market (which will beat most mutual funds and professional money managers).

- **Savings:** This is the one factor you can control most easily. We've offered you a million ways (okay, make that hundreds) to wring more money out of your (yeah, yeah, we know) already impossibly tight budget in Chapter 2. If you need motivation, just take another look at the glorious compounding chart. Ain't it a beaut?

GETTING READY TO INVEST

After seeing all those impressive numbers, you're probably itching to take the next step. You want to drop everything and start investing right now. But ho-o-o-ld on, cowboy! Would you start running a marathon without first stretching? Would you pour syrup on the plate before the pancakes are done? Would you take a sledgehammer to that light-obstructing wall in your dingy kitchen without first checking to see if it's a load-bearing wall? (Okay, that last one is a little obtuse.)

Having dazzled you with the power of compounded returns, we want to make sure it's not working against you. This means that you've got to get rid of your high-interest debt.

Why? Because, by the very same principle discussed above, a dollar of debt can quickly compound into a few *hundred* dollars of debt. Does it make sense to try to save money at the same time your debts are multiplying like bunnies? The first thing you should do to prepare for investing is to pay down all of your high-interest debt, such as credit card debt. Get thee back to Chapter 3 to develop your plan of attack. The first rule of thumb about investing is simple: Be free of high-interest debt when you begin.

PAY YOURSELF FIRST

Oh, hey there. You're back! Outstanding. Let's move on. How can you become a successful investor? By making investing a part of your daily life. It's not such a stretch—money is already part of your daily routine. Think about each decision that affects your finances, whether it's ordering a $4 glass of wine with dinner or getting a home equity loan to pay down your credit card debt.

We're not suggesting that you obsess over every penny you throw into a wishing well. (Please don't embarrass your spouse by diving in after it.) If you pay yourself first, you won't have to. What do we mean? When you pay your bills—the credit cards, the gas, water, electric, cable, and phone bills, the kid who mows your lawn, and the one who throws the newspaper onto your neighbor's porch instead of yours every other morning—add one more item to that list. In fact, we think it should be the first item. Put yourself at the top of that list: *Pay yourself first*. Then you don't have to think about it again until next month.

HOW MUCH SHOULD YOU SOCK AWAY?

The Motley Fool recommends that you put away as much as possible, with the goal being to save 10 percent of your annual income (your gross income—i.e., before taxes are taken out—not your take-home pay). Depending on your obligations, you may be able to save more or less. The more you save, the more wealth you create—but anything is better than nothing. Remember, even a few dollars saved now will be worth more than lots of dollars saved later. So take advantage of services that automatically withdraw money from your checking account and transfer it to some savings or investing vehicle. You'll be surprised how easy it is to live on

fewer dollars each month. You probably won't even notice the difference.

HOW MUCH *CAN* YOU SOCK AWAY?

Here's a quick exercise to get you started. How much can you afford to put toward your long-term savings each month? Go on, take a stab at it. Record your guesstimate here:

$ _____

Now let's see how far away your estimate is from that 10 percent savings rule of thumb we mentioned before:

Yearly Savings Goal	= Annual Gross Income	× 10% savings goal
	$_____	× .10
= $_____		
Monthly Savings Goal	= Yearly Savings Goal	Divided by months in year
	$_____	÷ 12
= $_____		

How far off were you? You can be flexible about this. If you find yourself eating beans and rice every night for a month (and you don't like beans and rice), maybe you're paying yourself too much, or perhaps you're not in a position to start paying yourself at all. But as soon as it's feasible, jump in. Remember Bianca and Patrice!

We hope that you check the first entry and the last, and leave the remaining ones blank in the following worksheet. We're just kidding about the others, which we consider to be wholly unnecessary (if not harmful). It's unfortunate that so many people don't consider investing in stocks and mutual funds because they figure they'll need a lot of money, a lot of expensive information, and a lot of graduate-level training. Nothing could be further from the truth.

Your success will mostly rely on the degree to which you understand *your own* circumstances. If you've come this far in the workbook, you should

WORKSHEET: ARE YOU READY TO INVEST?

Check the appropriate items below:

Have you:

_____ Eliminated your high-interest credit card debt?

_____ Finished your MBA?

_____ Stashed away at least $350,000 in your trading account?

_____ Quit your job so you can trade stocks full-time?

_____ Selected a full-service broker who will tell you what to buy and sell?

_____ Told your full-service broker just not to lose your money out there?

_____ Learned about options, futures contracts, and day trading?

_____ Learned about candlestick charting, the McClellan Oscillator, and trend lines?

_____ Paid $1,200 for expensive software and stock-quoting devices?

_____ Smiled and had a good laugh just now?

have a pretty good idea of what your financial goals might be. To get to this page, you should have taken care of all high-interest debt. Have you eliminated your credit card debt? Nice job, bravo! And have you set up at least a loose budgeting system that will allow you to sock away some savings each month? Encore, encore! Outstanding! So you've got some cash to invest, you have a regular stream of new money coming in, you haven't a lick of pre-payable short-term debt, and you're fired up for your money to start earning you money. Onward to the castle, then, Fool!

MAKING YOUR MONEY GROW, GROW, GROW

The goal of investing, as we said before, is to create wealth. To help put this into context, let's look at how various types of investments have performed historically. Bonds and stocks are the two major asset classes that have been used by investors over the past century. Knowing the total returns on each of these and their volatility is crucial to deciding where you should put your money.

- Putting money into cash reserves U.S.—*Treasury bills* or, more recently, *money market funds*—has yielded an average of roughly 3.8 percent per year over the last century.
- Long-term government *bonds* have returned an average of around 5 percent per year since 1900.
- *Stocks* have also been very good to investors. Overall, stocks have returned an average of 11 percent per year since 1900.

Consider this: According to research company Ibbotson Associates, if you had invested a dollar in long-term government bonds back in 1926, growing at 5.3 percent a year, it would be worth about

$48 today. How much would that dollar be worth if in 1926 you had invested it in large-company stocks, which grew an average 11.1 percent a year (a little more than twice that of long-term government bonds)? You might think that your dollar invested in stocks back in 1926 would be worth about twice the $48.10 your bond investment would have given you.

But no! That dollar invested in stocks would actually have grown to $2,682.59 in the same time period. Wow! That's almost fifty-six times more than the bond investment! Behold the power of compounding.

In fact, let's look at the power of compounding at different rates of return using the compounding chart from earlier in the chapter. We like it so much, here it is again!

Year	5%	8%	10%
1	$100	$100	$100
5	$128	$147	$161
10	$163	$216	$259
15	$208	$317	$418
25	$339	$685	$1,083
30	$432	$1,006	$1,745
40	$704	$2,172	$4,526
50	$1,147	$4,690	$11,739
60	$1,868	$10,126	$30,448

INVESTMENTS AND TIME FRAMES

You shouldn't treat all savings alike. Not by a long shot. You need to treat short-term and long-term savings very differently if you expect the money to be there when you need it. Here's one way to define the appropriate investment types for your personal schedule.

Time Frame	Investments to Consider
Short-term (up to 3 years)	Low-risk investments (money markets, CD)
Midterm (3–10 years)	Mix of low-risk investments and stocks
Long-term (more than 10 years)	Stocks

Short-term expenses are major expenses planned for the next three years—a down payment on a house, a family reunion cruise, college tuition. Short-term money should also include an "emergency fund," in case you ever find yourself *sans* paycheck. A single person with generous parents will need less in emergency cash than a single parent of three small children, but a cautious benchmark would be three to six months' worth of living expenses.

The *only* appropriate investment for short-term money is one that does not risk your capital, such as bank savings accounts and certificates of deposit (CDs), money market accounts, or short-term bonds that mature when you expect to need the cash.

Money for midterm goals can be in low-risk accounts or stocks (or a combination of the two), depending on how much time you have and how much risk you are comfortable with. As the time for the expenditure draws near, you simply switch cash from stocks to a low-risk investment. So if Junior is fifteen, you might move the cash for his freshman-year college tuition out of stocks and into a bond that matures in three years. Of course, you have some flexibility here. Lots of folks will leave the money in the market until Junior is dragging his footlocker down the stairs, but we don't advise taking chances with essential expenses. You could get hit with a bumpy market year and find your tuition fund 20 percent short. Years like that aren't predictable, but they hit often enough to keep us on our toes and out of the market with our must-have money.

For long-term money, such as retirement savings, we think that there is only one good place: stocks held directly or through a mutual fund. Let's not get ahead of ourselves, though.

Here's a summary of the most common short-term savings vehicles:

SHORT-TERM SAVINGS VEHICLES

- **Savings account:** Often the first banking product people use, savings accounts earn a small amount in interest (anywhere from 2 percent to 4 percent, often less), making them little better than that dusty piggy bank on the dresser.

- **Money market funds:** Money market funds are a specialized type of mutual fund that invests in extremely short-term bonds. Unlike most mutual funds, shares in a money market fund are designed to be worth $1 at all times. Money market funds usually pay better interest rates than conventional savings accounts but usually below what you could get in certificates of deposit.

- **Certificate of deposit (CD):** This is a specialized deposit you make at a bank or other financial institution. The interest rate on CDs is usually about the same as that of short- or intermediate-term bonds, depending on the duration of the CD. Interest is paid at regular intervals until the CD matures, at which point you get the money you originally deposited plus the accumulated interest payments. CDs offered by banks are usually insured.

Short-term savings tend to fall into two categories: emergency savings and planned expenses.

EMERGENCY SAVINGS

Think of your emergency fund as a "credit card defense fund"—money to defend yourself against the seductive call of the plastic when you get in a bind. Binds happen—might as well plan for them.

Questions to Ask Yourself

What would it take for you to survive financially if you lost your job? What would you do if your ten-year-old furnace broke down on the coldest day of the year? A rule of thumb is to have three to six months' worth of expenses saved up for emergencies. If you don't want to figure out exactly how much you spend each month, multiply your monthly income (after taxes) by three or six. Voilà! Instant emergency fund goal!

PLANNED EXPENSES

Unlike your emergency savings, this bucket is for money you know you're going to have to spend sometime in the foreseeable future (which we define as the next three to seven years). Got a kid starting college in a few years? Buying a house? Need a new (or newer) car? How about a vacation? New carpet? Remember, these things won't happen unless you plan for them or are willing to go into debt for them (boo, hiss!).

CAN YOU COUGH UP ENOUGH CASH IN A PINCH?

We'll make this quick. Two questions:

1. How much do you absolutely need to spend each month?

Forget the Blockbuster rentals and the daily Krispy Kremes. What do you *need* to get through the month? Food, of course, is on that list. Clothes? Not likely.

2. How long might you need to rely on emergency funds should you lose your job or become unable to work because of an accident?

For most people, the answer to this question is somewhere between three and six months. Multiply that number by your monthly expenses, and that should at least give you a ballpark figure to start with.

One tip: Don't confuse your emergency savings with mad money. A trip to Cancún is *not* an emergency. Nor is that fabulous Italian suit, even if it is on sale. At some point, your emergency savings could be all that stands between you and financial disaster.

SHORT-TERM SAVINGS GOALS WORKSHEETS

These worksheets will help you organize your short-term saving plan.

Your Emergency Fund

1. Enter the minimum amount that you need to meet all of your essential monthly expenses. There are items that keep a roof over your head, food in your tummy, and sanitary indoor plumbing. For a quick recap, refer to the line items listed in the accompanying chart that you figured out for your Bit-by-Bit Budget in Chapter 2.

2. Enter the number of months you feel you may need to rely on your emergency fund.

3. Voilà! You now have a rough estimate of the amount you need for your emergency fund.

Emergency = **Essential Monthly** × **Number of**
Fund   **Expenses**   **months needed**

$_____ × _____ (usually 3 to 6)

= $_____

Expenses	Cost per Month
Room and board:	
Rent/mortgage	
Electricity	
Water	
Oil/gas	
Telephone	
Cell phone	
Trash removal	
House maintenance	
Real estate taxes	
Improvement/furnishings	
Insurance	
Groceries	
Dining out/take-home food	
Transportation:	
Car loan payment	
Insurance	
Gas and oil	
Maintenance	
Other/commuting costs	
Other Expenses:	
Medical/dental expenses	
Disability insurance	
Total	

SHORT-TERM SAVINGS GOALS

1. Enter your short-term goals in the first column of the Short-Term Savings Worksheet.

2. How much dinero do you need to fund that goal? Put that amount in the "Amount Needed" column, and record any money you've already saved toward the goal in the "Amount Already Saved" column.

3. Subtract the amount saved from the amount needed and record your result in the "Need to Save" column.

4. So when do you want to achieve that goal? Yup, there's a place for you to write down the date. Now figure out how many months you have until that date and put it in the aptly titled "Number of Months to Date" column.

5. Divide the amount in the "Need to Save" column by the number you wrote down in the "Number of Months to Date" column. You end up with the amount of money you need to save per month to reach each goal. Record your answer in the "Need to Save per Month" column.

Start saving, Fool!

WHERE TO GET SHORT-TERM SAVINGS ACCOUNTS

There are three places to shop for short-term savings accounts:

• **Banks and Credit Unions.** Check the ads in your local paper or let your fingers do the walk-

WORKSHEET: SHORT-TERM SAVINGS GOALS

Short-Term Goals	Amount Needed	Amount Already Saved	Need to Save	Date Needed	Number of Months to Date	Need to Save per Month
Emergency fund	$	− $	$			$
	$	− $	$			$
	$	− $	$			$
	$	− $	$			$
	$	− $	$			$
	$	− $	$			$
	$	− $	$			$
	$	− $	$			$
	$	− $	$			$
	$	− $	$			$

ing (or typing, if you're online). See what the banks are offering and whether they offer perks for having more accounts or assets with them. Online, www.bankrate.com and www.banx.com offer listings of the highest-yielding investments at the banks in your area and in cyberspace.

- **Brokers.** Many brokerage firms offer some sort of "cash management" account, which often marries the convenience of a checking account to the return of a money market fund. Plus, they offer a wider choice of investments.

- **Mutual funds.** All the big fund families offer money market funds with attractive yields. Plus, if you need to build up your stake a little bit at a time,

amounts as small as $50 can be automatically transferred to the fund each month. Shop online or look in the newspaper to find the highest-yielding options available.

LONG-TERM INVESTMENT VEHICLES

Now let's turn our attention to the fun stuff. (Not that certificates of deposit aren't a blast for some folks.) When you've got a longer time frame to make your money grow, you can take advantage of a few more exciting (to Fools, at least) investment options:

- **Bonds.** Bonds are known as "fixed-income" securities because the amount of income the bond

WORKSHEET: CHOOSING THE RIGHT SAVINGS ACCOUNT

Use this worksheet to record and compare short-term savings options as you shop.

Financial Institution	Investment	Return (as of . . .)	How Accessed	Minimum Balance	FDIC Insured (Yes or No)	Term	Fees and Commissions
Big Bones Bank	Money Market	4% (7/5/03)	Checks, transfers	$10,000	Yes	N/A	None

generates each year is "fixed," or set, when the bond is sold. From an investor's point of view, bonds are very similar to CDs, except that they are issued by the government or by corporations instead of banks. Bonds generally have a set "maturity"—that is, a date at which investors will get their money back. The longer the maturity, the more interest the bond will pay. Therefore, long-term investors who want to invest in bonds should look for intermediate- and long-term bonds or bond mutual funds.

- **Stocks.** Stocks are a way for individuals to own parts of businesses. A share of stock represents a proportional share of ownership in a company. As the value of the company changes, the value of the share in that company rises and falls. Fools are partial to investing in stocks, simply because stocks have historically given the highest return on one's money.

ORDER! ORDER!

In what order should you start saving and investing? Here are some guidelines:

1. Build up your emergency fund. This should be your top priority. Obviously, if you are starting from scratch, you can't build it up overnight. It might even take you a few years. Accumulate it as quickly as possible because you shouldn't be socking away money for a vacation or a new carpet until you have this safety net in place.

2. Put some money away for retirement. We Fools believe that saving for retirement goes neck-and-neck with saving for an emergency. If possible, put enough into a corporate 401(k) to collect any matching funds your company may offer. Then take advantage of Uncle Sam's gift to us: the IRA (Individual Retirement Account).

3. Start stocking money away for your other savings goals. It's a good idea to save for these goals very specifically. It's much more satisfying to earmark your money, either by saving in different accounts or by tracking your deposits so that you know exactly how much is in the new-car fund.

So the general rule is to direct 50 percent of your savings to your retirement accounts and 50 percent to your emergency fund until it has reached the ideal size for you. Then start funneling funds to your short-term goals. As with any rule, though, there's room for personalization. If, for example, your jalopy has three wheels in the grave, you may want to put some of your savings toward a new car. However, do not forsake your emergency fund entirely, and do all you can to contribute to your employer-provided retirement plan at least to the extent that you receive the full match.

A REALLY, REALLY EASY WAY TO INVEST IN THE STOCK MARKET

Buy shares in an index mutual fund.

Now, on to the next topic!

Oh, you're still here. We gather you'd like a little more information about so-called index funds and why we Fools are so fond of them. We'll back up for a moment.

If you have decided that you want to invest in stocks for the long term (we hope that we've been convincing on this point), your choice of how to begin is very easy. Look for an *index mutual fund*.

An index mutual fund. Sounds simple enough, right? Let's break it down.

First *mutual funds* are companies set up to receive investors' money and then, having received it, to make investments with that money. When you buy shares in a mutual fund, you are a shareholder in—an owner of—that fund, but you are also an indirect owner of the companies that the fund has invested in.

An *index* is a set of securities that represent a specific market, economy, or industry. The most famous stock index is the Dow Jones Industrial Average, which is a group of thirty stocks that the editors of *The Wall Street Journal* think represents the overall U.S. economy.

Another well-known index is the Standard & Poor's 500 index, which most folks consider to be a good indicator of how the overall U.S. stock market is doing. It is also the index that most *index funds* attempt to match by buying each stock in the S&P 500, rather than hiring a manager to pick the stocks. Index funds do not even attempt to beat the stock market; they simply seek to come as close as possible to matching it.

S&P 500 index funds enable investors to participate in the successes and failures of the five hundred leading companies in America. If you buy an index fund, you own a piece of every company that makes up your fund's index. In case you're curious, the S&P 500 includes companies such as AOL Time Warner, Boeing, Cisco, Coors, Disney, Exxon Mobil, Ford, Gillette, Hershey, Intel, Johnson & Johnson, Lockheed Martin, Marriott, McDonald's, Motorola, Oracle, PepsiCo, Pfizer, Safeway, Sara Lee, Charles Schwab, Sears, Texas Instruments, Toys "R" Us, Wal-Mart, Walgreen, Waste Management, Wells Fargo, Wrigley, Xerox, and Yahoo! And that's just a small part of its holdings. Most major American companies that you can think of are part of this massive index.

That makes for some powerful cocktail-party patter when you wow them with the list of companies in which you own shares.

WHY NOT JUICE YOUR RETURNS WITH A PROFESSIONAL FUND MANAGER?

The crucial thing that distinguishes an index investment from a managed mutual fund is that the index investment simply owns shares of all the stocks that make up the index rather than attempting to pick the best stocks. Its goal is to match the performance of the index, not beat it. Index investments, with their firm ambition to match, not beat, the market, are, ironically, better performers than most actively managed mutual funds and thus better choices for most investors.

Why? Because most mutual funds over the long term can't beat the overall stock market, which also means that most mutual funds can't beat an index fund. In fact, if you invest in an index fund, you will likely outperform 70 to 80 percent of all other stock mutual funds.

This occurs for many reasons, but possibly the biggest reason is lower costs: an index fund doesn't pay a team of managers and analysts to pick the investments. This significantly lowers the costs of operating the fund, which means more of the money goes to the fund's shareholders—including you!

An index fund should certainly be the first stop for all investors—an investment that could also be the last. It's pretty much the one-stop shop for a lifetime of successful investing, the closest thing yet devised for getting the full value of the stock market into every man, woman, or child's investment account.

THE PROS AND CONS OF INDEX FUNDS

PROS

• Over the long term, they outperform the vast majority of managed mutual funds.

• They typically have no sales commissions, so you can add small amounts to your holdings regularly without paying sales fees.

• They have low annual expenses.

• You can authorize a regular automatic withdrawal from your bank account and the money will go straight into your fund. You don't even have to lick a stamp.

CONS

• Not all index funds are available from every broker or fund company.

• Some index funds charge high maintenance fees and/or commissions (loads). Just avoid those funds. There are plenty of pretty much identical funds with very low fees.

• A handful of actively managed mutual funds do consistently beat the market, and thus outperform index funds.

HOW TO INVEST IN AN INDEX FUND

There are many types of investment accounts—"baskets" in which you hold your investments—you can use to buy an index fund.

1. RETIREMENT PLANS

Start by looking at your retirement plans [e.g., IRA, 401(k), 403(b), SEP]. We'll give you the straight talk in detail in Chapter 6, which dwells on the topic ad nauseum.

2. MUTUAL FUND COMPANIES

Most of the cost-efficient, no-load (i.e., commission-free) mutual fund providers offer an index fund. If you're interested, consider contacting the company that started the whole indexing craze: the Vanguard Group.

3. BROKERAGE ACCOUNTS

These are regular traditional investment accounts that you can open with just about any financial-services firm (including many banks). One benefit of brokerage accounts, as far as index investing is concerned, is that you're not limited to investing in mutual funds. You can also invest in creatures known as exchange-traded funds (ETFs). ETFs are index funds that trade just like stocks. They have all kinds of scary names, like Spiders (officially known as SPDRs—Standard & Poor's Depositary Receipts—which track the S&P 500) and VIPERs (which attempt to match the performance of the entire stock market). Because of this flexibility, we're partial to brokerage accounts, and to *discount* brokerage accounts in particular. In fact, we're so partial to them that we're going to explain how to open a discount brokerage account right now.

OPENING A BROKERAGE ACCOUNT

Oh, brother, that title looks pretty daunting, eh? Well, it's not that tough. Let's race through it.

Opening a brokerage account is very much like opening a checking or savings account at a bank. You stumble down to a discount broker (or click over to the online site), fill out some paperwork, and deposit your money. You can often take care of all the paperwork by mail, without going anywhere in person, if you're lazy and there's a good rerun of *Welcome Back, Kotter* on cable. Some discount brokerages will even let you write checks against money in your account, and some have credit cards tied to the accounts. So they can be extremely similar to regular bank accounts.

Cash you do not invest initially, or that is doled out to you in dividend payments, will probably be dropped into a *money market savings account,* which will earn you small interest on that cash. And when you make investments—say, buying ten shares of Dell Computer or shares in an S&P 500 index fund—the brokerage will transfer money out of the interest-bearing savings account and into your investment.

TAKE SIXTY SECONDS AND JUST DO IT!

We told you we were going to race through this. In the next sixty seconds, we'll usher you through the five major steps in choosing and setting up a discount brokerage account. Start your stopwatches, Fools!

0:57 Decide how much you'll invest.

Will it be $500, $5,000, or $50,000? Some discount brokers require a minimum initial deposit of $2,000. Others require $500. And some require no minimum or accept smaller initial deposits to open an IRA. Your first step is to figure out how much dough you plan to start with.

0:50 Consider what you'll be investing in.

While we're partial to index funds, you may also want to invest in other mutual funds, bonds, or certificates of deposit (CDs). Not every online broker will offer all of these, so make sure you can buy what you want through your broker.

0:38 Compare broker fees and services.

Check out and compare how much different brokers will charge in commissions and fees. Hey, you can do that easily at www.broker.Fool.com! For extra credit, visit other brokerage sites to see what they bring to the table. Of course you'll want to find out information about trading commissions, but also compare account maintenance fees, IRA custodial fees, and other costs.

But don't simply judge online brokers by how much they charge. Some have a lot more to offer. Eyeball this checklist to help decide what additional services interest you:

- Phone trades
- Research products
- Local offices
- Check-writing capabilities
- ATM access
- A free Koosh ball

0:21 Do the paperwork and sign the check!

Setting up an account is usually as easy as downloading the application forms, signing them, and folding them nicely into an envelope with a check to fund your account. You'll receive confirmation of your ability to start trading in pretty short order. Voilà! (Even easier is transferring your loot from your old brokerage account to a new one. The broker does all the work!)

0:03 Revel publicly.

You're now "in the know." Memorize a few key lines to drop at the next office cocktail party: "I'm in the market for the long haul. Still, I couldn't help but click over to my discount brokerage account twice today." Or "I'm only a few trades away from owning an island next to that tow truck driver."

Whew! Done in just under fifty-seven seconds. Congratulations, Fool! You've just taken a giant step toward controlling your financial future.

· · ·

ACT!

Check the appropriate items below: Among the important weapons that are potentially in my investing arsenal, I will check into the following:

_____ Work retirement plans

_____ IRAs

_____ Discount brokerage accounts

_____ More about investing at www.Fool.com or *The Motley Fool Investment Workbook*

Answer: We wanna see a lot of check marks there. Four check marks, to be exact.

HOW NOT TO FREAK OUT WHEN THE MARKET'S FEELING FRISKY

To be a successful long-term investor, you need to be a *long-term* investor. For an index investor, the secret of success is: *Do nothing*. The market tanks? *Do nothing*. The market zooms up beyond all rational expectation? *Do nothing*. Your daughter dyes her hair green? *Do nothing.* (Trust us. It will drive her crazy, but better her than you.)

Doing nothing is *very hard.* The inability to do nothing has probably been responsible for just as many wrong moves as all the boiler-room shysters on Wall Street put together. But doing nothing is the secret to successful index investing. Your friends and coworkers might call you an idiot and you may even feel like an idiot at times, but doing nothing works every time. Doing something rarely does.

One of the hardest things for some new investors to learn is patience. But patience is *the* critical skill. Next is learning to ignore those friends and coworkers—especially that guy who sold and went to cash the last time the market was higher than it is now. He will rub it in.

In the short term, the stock market can go up and down in a heartbeat. But history shows us that the overall long-term trajectory of the stock market has been upward. Investors who have ridden out all the previous storms have been well rewarded.

DEALING WITH PAPER LOSSES

Panicking and selling when your account is down is the one sure way to turn a "paper loss" into a real loss. (A paper loss is when your holdings have fallen in value but you haven't actually lost any money because you haven't sold anything. Until you sell, you don't have a real loss.) The first time you go through a market retreat is the worst. After you experience the recovery, the next time isn't so bad. So here are some tips to get yourself through your first big market drop.

Focus on the long term. Ask yourself: What is the "real" consequence of my S&P 500 index fund being worth $20,000 this year instead of the $30,000 it was worth last year?

- Am I likely to lose my home?
- Will my car be repossessed?
- Will my dog scorn me because I have a paper loss? (If so, check the local pound. Lots of lovely pooches are waiting to give you a warm

face licking no matter how much your brokerage account is worth!)

While we don't mean to trivialize the real pain that can come with a paper loss, a successful investor has to keep investing in perspective. If your loss is in a specific Internet penny stock that just went bankrupt, well, yes, you do have a real loss on your hands. With an index fund that mirrors the return of the S&P 500 or the total market, you won't have the same potential for upside return as you would with some of the high flyers, but you also won't have the same downside risk. And that's the *whole point* of starting out your investing career with an index fund.

Your index fund holding may be worth $20,000 now after being worth $30,000 last year, but remember, what really matters is what it's worth *when you sell it,* which should be many years down the road. At that point, it might be worth $40,000 or $50,000 or even a lot more. Investments rarely go up in a straight line. Expect some slumps.

Remember, since 1926, the U.S. stock market has posted an average annual return of 11 percent. During that time we've had major and minor depressions, inflation and deflation, wars both hot and cold, political turmoil, natural and manmade disasters, and Pee-wee Herman. The market managed to survive and thrive through all of that, even if it wasn't thriving every moment or every year.

So while your account is in the paper loss territory, remember that life and economic growth go on, your very real life is unaffected in any way by paper losses (you weren't counting on this money for the mortgage payment, right?), and you have every reason to realistically expect the paper losses to turn into paper gains. So stop checking the ticker on a daily basis and get on with the business of living a Foolish life.

NINE HOT INVESTMENT TIPS

We don't want to end this chapter on a sour note. But we are going to end it on a cautionary one. Before you race off through the rest of this workbook, consider the following nine points. These are common mistakes many people make when considering what to do about investing.

1. **Doing nothing.** There is no guarantee that the market will go up the first day, month, or even year that you invest in it. But there is one guarantee: doing nothing at all will not provide for a comfortable retirement.

2. **Starting late.** Postponing your investing career is second only to not investing at all on the list of investment sins. You already know that the earlier you start the better off you are. (Take another look at the compound return charts.) If you're already past those formative twenties (you don't look a day over thirty-two to us), we'll reword this first pitfall to read "Not starting now."

3. **Investing before paying down credit card debt.** If you have money in your savings account and you have revolving debt on your credit card, pay the debt off. Many credit cards have an annual interest rate of 16 percent to 21 percent. Let's say you have $5,000 to invest, but you also have $5,000 debt on your credit cards with an average annual interest rate of 18 percent. It doesn't take an astrophysicist to figure out that you're going to have to get an 18 percent return after taxes just to break even on that $5,000. Pay the debt off first, then think about investing.

4. **Investing for the short term.** There are appropriate places for short-term funds that you're actually going to need in the short term. Invest money in the stock market that you won't need for at least five years or longer. If you'll need your cash next year for a down payment on a house or for the family Caribbean cruise, use one of the shorter-term, safer havens for your cash, such as money market funds or CDs.

5. **Turning down free money.** You'd never turn down a dollar if it was offered with no strings at-

tached. That's what you're doing if your company offers a 401(k) or similar retirement savings plan with an employer match and you're not participating. Take advantage of all tax-advantaged, employer-matched savings programs.

6. **Playing it safe.** If you're young, most of your investing dollars should be in the stock market—specifically, an index fund. You have enough time to weather any dips in the market and to reap the rewards of long-term gains. Although you may want to transition into bonds later in life as you depend on your investments for income, stocks should make up a large portion of the portfolio of every investor.

7. **Playing it scary.** Not every investment is for everyone. Even if you're a daredevil, you shouldn't pour all of your money into something that could end up going down the drain.

8. **Viewing collectibles or lottery tickets as investments.** If old comic books, Barbie dolls, and abandoned exercise equipment could be used to fund retirements, do you think the stock market would exist? Probably not. Don't make the mistake of thinking your jewelry, Beanie Babies, or the lottery will provide for you in your latter years.

9. **Trading into and out of the market.** We believe the best approach to investing is the long-term one. Pick your investments well, and you'll reap rewards over the long term that you had never dreamed possible. Trade into and out of the market, and you'll be saddled with fees that chip away at your returns, and you'll potentially miss out on gains that long-term investors enjoy with much less effort.

YOUR BIT-BY-BIT BUDGET ENTRY

Now it's time to return to your Master Plan. *(Mwa-ha-ha-ha-haaaa!)* Despite the fact that we discussed short- and long-term investments, we're going to add just the amount you need to save for your short-term goals to your Bit-by-Bit Budget . . . for now. Why not long-term savings? Because, for most people, one of those goals is retirement, which we'll discuss in the next chapter. For other people, their long-term goals include college, a house, a car, or other big-ticket items—which just

happen to be the topics of Chapter 7. So we'll worry about how much you need to save for that Scottish castle later. Right now, fill in your Bit-by-Bit Budget with the results of your Short-Term Goals Worksheet on page 77. As you'll note, we've provided a special entry for "emergency fund accumulation." Your other short-term goals can go in the "Goal" entries at the top of your budget.

BIT-BY-BIT BUDGET

	AMOUNT FROM YOUR MONEY TRACKER WORKSHEET	BUDGETED AMOUNT	MONTH 1	MONTH 2	MONTH 3	MONTH 4	MONTH 5	MONTH 6
Short- and long-term investments:								
Emergency fund accumulation								

Now let's move on to Chapter 6, where we're going to make you a very attractive retiree.

CHAPTER 6

RETIREMENT PLANNING

SIXTY-SECOND GUIDE TO RETIREMENT PLANNING

You work hard—so one day you won't have to. Over the next sixty seconds, we'll show you how to save for that day when you tear up that punch card and skip with glee onto the shuffleboard court.

0:60 Picture your perfect retirement.

Start with where you want to be; then you can figure out how to get there. Begin with the most basic questions: When do you want to retire? How many years do you have to make that goal a reality?

0:55 Determine where the money will come from.

Estimate how much you can expect from Social Security, your pension, your savings, and other sources of retirement income. Throw it all into a pot and see what kind of retirement you'll be able to brew.

0:48 Invest early and often.

Invest on autopilot: have your contributions taken directly from your paycheck, and/or have money transferred automatically from your bank account to your retirement accounts. Don't delay another day!

0:40 Choose the best accounts.

Take advantage of accounts such as IRAs, 401(k)s, SEPs, XYZPDQs (we're kidding on this last one) that offer tax savings. Contribute the maximum allowable amounts that you can. If your employer matches contributions you make to your plan at work, make sure you grab that free money.

0:32 How much will you need?

Sure, it's easy to see yourself living the retirement high life. Figuring out what it will actually cost is another thing. Start pricing it so that you don't experience sticker shock when your heart isn't as healthy.

0:26 How much will you need to save to get that much?

Once you know how much it'll cost, you'll need to determine what you'll need to do to pay for it. In other words, how much do you need to invest on a monthly basis now in order to pay for your retirement?

0:19 Put the plan into action.

You know what you have to do; now go out and do it. Open an IRA, increase your contributions to your 401(k), cut back on your spending—whatever you think you need to do to retire in the style to which you aspire.

0:11 Rinse and repeat.

At least once a year, reevaluate your plan. Are you on track, or has your plan veered off course? Grip the wheel and get back onto the road.

0:05 Are you retiring within a decade?

If you're ten or fewer years from retirement (you lucky devil), you have a few extra considerations. In particular, start considering safer investments, withdrawal rates from your retirement accounts, and taxes.

• • •

Now that you have the overview, let's get down to the nitty-gritty so you can retire when you want. (Sounds appealing, doesn't it?)

DESIGN YOUR RETIREMENT PLAN

With a little planning and some foresight, you have the ability to choose the kind of retirement you'll live. There's nothing magic about selecting when you want to retire, as long as you have the answers to the following questions:

• How much income will you need each year?
• Where will it come from?
• How big must your investment pool be to generate that income?

• How will it be protected from the ravages of inflation?
• What's a safe withdrawal rate from investments to ensure that your money will last as long as you do?

Stop running for the door! We promise it's not as overwhelming as it sounds. We'll help you with the answers; all you have to do is decide what you want.

WHEN DO YOU WANT TO RETIRE?

The truth is that many of us have no idea what we want in retirement or when we expect it to happen (the ages of fifty-nine or sixty-two or sixty-five or ninety-nine are dimly in there, bouncing around like Ping-Pong balls in a lottery drawing).

But we're going to rub a crystal ball and imagine the future. By knowing what to expect, we can better use today's resources to meet those future needs.

First, take a stab at choosing the date you want to retire. Then figure out how much time you have before retirement.

Age when you want to retire: _____

− Age you are now: _____

= Years until retirement: _____

HOW WILL YOU PAY FOR IT?

Money is the most important practical key to a successful retirement. Certainly there are other issues involved, such as the fulfillment of a life's dream, self-satisfaction, and the pursuit of other activities. But without the cold, hard cash, successful retirement will be an elusive goal.

Retirement isn't cheap. Let's say you want to retire in twenty years and you expect your savings to provide you annually with $50,000 in today's dollars (i.e., not adjusted for inflation). How much money must you have socked away by the time you bid adieu to the boss, the water cooler, and the naps in the supply closet?

About two million bucks.

Fortunately, your nest egg probably won't be your only source of retirement nourishment. When all is said and done, there are five sources of retirement income and two things you have to know about each one:

1. Will it increase with inflation? Consider a $1,000 monthly income that fails to increase with the cost of living (assuming that inflation runs at 4 percent annually). In fifteen years, that $1,000 will buy only $555 worth of today's goods. To protect your purchasing power in the future, you must save enough today to be able to increase your income in retirement. Either that or cut back to 55.5 percent of the caviar and champagne you're tossing back each night.

2. Will it pass to a survivor when you die? Whether your source of income will pass to a survivor is important if you might be leaving behind someone who depends on your income. This usually means a spouse, but it might include an elderly or incapacitated relative. If your source of income will not pass to your heirs, they will have to plan accordingly.

We'll go into detail about each potential source of income in a minute, but the following table summarizes the must-knows about each income source.

Source of Income	Will It Keep Pace with Inflation?	Will It Pass to a Survivor?
Social Security	Will likely keep pace with inflation	May be payable to children and surviving spouse if deceased was primary breadwinner
Employer-provided pension	Depends on the plan itself, but most do not	Unless you specifically decline the option, it will always provide a continuing lifetime benefit to the surviving spouse
Personal investments (taxable accounts, 401(k)/403(b)/457 plans, IRAs, etc.)	Depends on how your assets are invested	Will always pass to heirs at your death
Work (wages)	Depends on your wages and raises	Not unless you can find a way to work from the grave
Other (gifts, inheritances, collectibles, homes, real estate, etc.)	Might keep pace with inflation	Depends on how you hold title or what you put in your will

"BROTHER, CAN YOU SPARE $41.68?"

Inflation can make a mountain of savings seem like a molehill. Take a look at the chart below to see what inflation has done—and might do—to your purchasing power.

Item	1966	1996	2026 (at 4% Annual Inflation)
Cup of coffee	$0.10	$0.75	$2.43
Luxury car	$3,000.00	$40,000.00	$130,000.00
Pair of sneakers	$5.00	$90.00	$290.00
Postage stamp	$0.05	$0.32	$1.04
Quart of milk	$0.27	$0.80	$2.60
Gallon of gas	$0.30	$1.39	$4.51
Movie ticket	$1.00	$7.50	$24.00

From Retire Rich, *by Bambi Holzer. Note: Though this is useful information, we included it mostly so we could cite work by someone named Bambi. There's no word on Thumper's contribution, but we strongly recommend that the author's mother stay out of the woods during hunting season.*

DETERMINING YOUR SOURCES OF INCOME

As we work through each source of income, you should be working along to determine where your money will come from. You'll compile all of the data into a Master Sources of Retirement Income Worksheet on page 90. For each source of income you should indicate:

- Whether it's part of your plan (e.g., you may not want to include 100 percent of your Social Security income, or maybe you don't have a pension)

- Whether it will keep pace with inflation
- Whether it will pass to your survivors
- Its current value

You'll probably have to do a little legwork to complete this chart. Use the worksheets on the following pages to do some calculations, and then enter the final number in your Master Sources of Retirement Income Worksheet on page 90.

You'll also notice that there are three columns in which to input the value of your income. This will enable you to come back in the future and track any changes.

SOCIAL SECURITY

You may not believe that Social Security will be there when you become eligible to collect it. We won't promise you that it will. However, we won't say you should exclude it from your plans. Fools know who votes in federal elections (think of those over the age of fifty), and we also know that our fearless leaders can count. Therefore, we tend to believe that Social Security is here to stay.

But we also recognize that the system will almost assuredly give future recipients less than it promises today. Here's what the Social Security Administration has to say: "In 2015, we will begin to pay out more in benefits than we collect in taxes. By 2037 . . . the payroll taxes collected will be enough to pay only about 72% of benefits owed." That doesn't sound too heartening, but it also doesn't sound as though the program will be penniless. Perhaps a prudent method of estimating future benefits is to expect just 50 to 70 percent of what the Social Security Administration says might be your benefits.

Another important factor in your Social Security benefit is the age at which you'll retire. Will you be at least of age to receive full Social Security benefits? That is age sixty-five for those born in 1937 or earlier. If you were born later, the age at which you receive full benefits will increase progressively. (Consult the Social Security Administration's Web site—www.ssa.gov/retirement/—for your full re-

WORKSHEET: MASTER SOURCES OF RETIREMENT INCOME

Don't get freaked out by this table. In the next few pages, we'll help you fill out the whole thing.

Source of Income	Are You Including It in Your Plan? (Circle one)	Will It Keep Pace With Inflation? (Circle one)	Will It Pass to a Survivor? (Circle one)	Current Annual Value (from Retirement Income Worksheets) (Date)	Value as of (Date)	Value as of (Date)
Social Security	Yes No	Yes No	Yes No			
Employer-provided pension	Yes No	Yes No	Yes No			
Personal investments	Yes No	Yes No	Yes No			
Work income (wages)	Yes No	Yes No	Yes No			
Other income	Yes No	Yes No	Yes No			

tirement age.) If you retire before full retirement age, you will receive a reduced benefit for the rest of your life. On the other hand, put retirement off to age seventy and you'll receive a larger benefit—$500 to $1,000 more per month than sixty-two-year-old retirees—for the rest of your days.

WILL IT KEEP PACE WITH INFLATION?

Social Security will likely keep pace with inflation. Congress has never failed to increase benefits each year to reflect changes in the cost of living. That's not to say someday it won't do so, just that over the past four decades it never has.

WILL IT PASS TO A SURVIVOR?

Upon your death, Social Security benefits may be payable to your children and your surviving spouse, depending on their ages and, in the case of your spouse, whether you were the primary wage earner.

FIGURE OUT YOUR SOCIAL SECURITY INCOME

You should receive a benefits statement from the Social Security Administration each year. If you have your statement, insert your estimated annual income directly from your statement into the "Current Annual Value" column in the Master Sources of Retirement Income table.

If you do not have your Social Security statement, you can request one from the Social Security Administration by visiting its Web site or calling (800) 772-1213. In the meantime, you can estimate it by using a calculator on the SSA Web site: www.ssa.gov/planners/calculators.htm.

If you don't have your Social Security statement, record the inputs you used in the Social Security calculator below and then note the results.

EMPLOYER-PROVIDED PENSION

Employer-provided pensions, otherwise known as defined-benefit plans, are rapidly becoming an endangered species as employers switch to defined-contribution plans [e.g., 401(k) or 403(b) plans] or hybrid vehicles such as cash balance plans. By eliminating the traditional pension plan, the employer shifts all investment risk to the employee and avoids having to guarantee an income upon the employee's retirement. This puts more importance on personal savings as a major source of retirement income—which makes your need for retirement planning more important. (Aren't you glad you bought this book?)

WORKSHEET: SOCIAL SECURITY

INPUTS	RESULTS
Your age by the end of this year _____	Retirement age _____ Annual benefit amount (monthly benefit × 12)
Your earnings in the current year $ _____	Year in which you will reach age 62: _____ $ _____
Select to see your benefit estimate in: (circle one) Today's dollars Inflated future dollars	Year in which you will reach full retirement age: _____ $ _____
	Year in which you will reach age 70: _____ $ _____

Depending on the age at which you plan to retire, enter one of the resulting numbers in the "Current Annual Value" column for Social Security in the Master Sources of Retirement Income Worksheet.

WILL IT KEEP PACE WITH INFLATION?

Perhaps. That depends on the plan itself. Be aware that most do not. And even those that do rarely provide a full cost-of-living adjustment. Instead, the increase is typically limited to one half of the annual inflationary increase as measured by a common index such as the Consumer Price Index (CPI).

WILL IT PASS TO A SURVIVOR?

Unless you specifically declined the option, at death it will provide a continuing lifetime benefit for your surviving spouse.

FIGURE OUT YOUR EMPLOYER-PROVIDED PENSION INCOME

If you have a pension, fill out the Employer-Provided Pension Worksheet below. Run through the questions and then enter your projected income in the employer-provided pension "Current Annual Value" column.

PERSONAL INVESTMENTS

As you'll soon see, a large portion of your retirement income will have to come from your personal savings. We covered some strategies for accumu-

WORKSHEET: EMPLOYER-PROVIDED PENSION

If you will receive a pension, fill out the following information.

Do you have an employer-provided pension? (circle one)   Yes   No

What is your vesting period?   _____ years

Will the value of your pension depend on the age at which you retire? (circle one)   Yes   No

What will your projected annual income be? $ _____

Write this number in the "Current Annual Value" column for employer-provided pension in the Master Sources of Retirement Income Worksheet.

lating the most money you can in Chapter 5. But for now, let's determine how much you have devoted to retirement right now.

WHAT KINDS OF SAVINGS ARE WE TALKING ABOUT?

We're talking about money that you're putting away exclusively for retirement—money you're not planning to touch for several years, perhaps

even decades. This excludes such things as your monthly spending money, the money you've put aside to buy a new car, and your children's college funds.

What's included:

- Traditional and Roth Individual Retirement Accounts (IRAs)
- An employer-provided retirement plan, such as a 401(k) or 403(b)
- Annuities

WORKSHEET: PERSONAL INVESTMENTS INCOME

Since the annual benefit you'll receive from your savings depends on many factors, just enter the total value of your savings in the "Current Value" column in the Master Sources of Retirement Income Worksheet.

ACCOUNT INFORMATION (FINANCIAL INSTITUTION, ACCOUNT NUMBER)	TYPES OF INVESTMENTS/SAVINGS (STOCKS, BONDS, MONEY MARKET ACCOUNTS, CDs, ETC.)	MONTHLY CONTRIBUTION	CURRENT VALUE	NEED TO MAKE A CHANGE?
Employer plan [401(k), 403(b), 457, Keogh, SEP plan, profit-sharing plan, employee stock purchase plan]				
IRAs				
Brokerage accounts				
Mutual fund accounts				
Bank accounts (savings, checking)				
Annuities				
Other (Treasuries, trusts, sugar daddies, etc.)				
TOTAL VALUE OF PERSONAL SAVINGS		$	$	$

- Any other assets that will not be spent until retirement

WILL IT KEEP PACE WITH INFLATION?

Your assets may or may not keep pace with inflation. That, dear Fool, is a function of how you invest. Keep the investments largely in fixed-income vehicles, and chances are strong that the nest egg will not maintain its purchasing power over the years.

WILL IT PASS TO A SURVIVOR?

Savings will pass to whomever you choose. That will probably be your heirs, though you may decide that your favorite charity should receive a large portion of your estate. Whatever you decide, make sure that you make your intentions clear by writing a will.

FIGURE OUT YOUR PERSONAL INVESTMENT INCOME

Let's start with the Personal Investments Worksheet on page 93. For now, fill in the following:

- Savings or investment account information
- The current value of your account
- Any contributions you currently make to that savings vehicle

After you have these filled in, tally up the total and enter that number in your Master Sources of Retirement Income Worksheet.

WORK (WAGES)

Will you work during retirement? There are many people who have had enough of the corporate grind by age sixty-five (or sometimes well before

that) but who like the idea of working in other environments for years to come. If you have a reasonable expectation of a postretirement income, there's no reason why you should not include that amount in your financial calculations. Just remember that you need to be conservative in your assumptions because it will be difficult to reenter the workforce at your old rate of pay.

Many folks think they will be forced to work just to survive. We hope you're not in that category. Instead, we trust you will work only as a means of providing yourself pleasure, to contribute your productivity to others, and/or to fill your waking hours with meaningful activity. We believe that Fools who plan ahead will work during retirement by choice, not by necessity. And you're a planner—or you wouldn't be reading this book.

WILL IT KEEP PACE WITH INFLATION?

When it comes to wages and other income, the issue of keeping pace with inflation becomes more difficult to pin down. You'll always be the judge of whether you're being paid fairly for your work.

WILL IT PASS TO A SURVIVOR?

Nope. If you are relying on your income to support your dependents, though, you should carry some life insurance.

FIGURE OUT YOUR RETIREMENT WORK INCOME

Complete the following Work Income Worksheet. If you decide that work might be part of your retirement plans, answer the questions to help you arrive at a projected annual income. Enter the amount in your Master Sources of Retirement Income Worksheet.

WORKSHEET: WORK INCOME

Do you plan to work in retirement? (circle one)   Yes   No

ADDITIONAL QUESTIONS TO CONSIDER:

Why do you want to work in retirement? (check all that apply)

____ For pleasure
____ To share your productivity with others
____ To fill your hours
____ Out of necessity
____ Because you're a glutton for punishment
____ Other _____

How many hours do you hope to work per week?   _____

Would you like to work for yourself? (circle one)   Yes   No

Do you want to do something related to your job before retirement or something completely new?
Don't expect to make as much as you do now if you switch career fields completely. (check one)

____ Something new
____ Something using my current skills
____ I don't know

What is your projected annual income after retirement? $ _____

Insert this amount in the "Current Annual Value" column for work income in your Master Sources of
Retirement Income Worksheet.

List some possible jobs you might be interested in after retirement:

1. _____

2. _____

3. _____

4. _____

OTHER INCOME

OK, we admit this is a broad category, but it includes all sorts of things, such as gifts, inheritances, and the collection of Bicentennial quarters you stole from under your sister's bed when you were eleven. However, we recommend that you be conservative in your estimates of how much you can receive from such sources. Gifts may not materialize, and estates have a way of disappearing in the wake of terminal illnesses, remarriage, and taxes.

It's tempting to think of collectibles as potential sources of income. While we don't ordinarily think of selling these items, they do have value and could be sold in a pinch. (Plus, who wants to spend their retirement dusting bottles of "Always Elvis" wine?) Again, though, we're going to be conservative and say you should ignore 'em.

For those who own their homes, we could also include home equity—meaning that you could take some money out from what you've paid in for your home. You can do this either through a loan or by selling your home. Both actions have advantages and disadvantages, a discussion of which is outside the scope of this book.

We could also include rental real estate. Many folks have properties that produce an income stream from rent. Again, such a discussion is outside the scope of these pages. If you have such property, we'll leave it up to you to decide how reliable the annual income from that property may be.

WILL IT KEEP PACE WITH INFLATION?

Other income, such as that coming from the sale of collectibles, may or may not keep up with inflation.

WILL IT PASS TO A SURVIVOR?

What passes to whom on your demise depends on how you hold title and what you've provided for in your last will and testament.

CALCULATING OTHER INCOME

As mentioned, we think it's a good idea to ignore this category, but if you want to add these things in, go ahead. Complete the worksheet below, then add the total to your Master Sources of Retirement Income Worksheet.

WORKSHEET: OTHER INCOME

As discussed earlier, we should simply ignore gifts or inheritances as a source of income in our retirement. But if you want to make a list of "other" sources of income you plan to have (your button collection or Mickey Mantle rookie card), be our guest.

OTHER SOURCES OF INCOME   APPROXIMATE ANNUAL VALUE

1. _____   _____

2. _____   _____

3. _____   _____

4. _____   _____

5. _____   _____

Enter the total in the "Current Annual Value" column for other income in your Master Sources of Retirement Income Worksheet.

BACK TO THE MASTER WORKSHEET

By now you should have your entire Master Sources of Retirement Income Worksheet filled in. Take a moment to look it over.

How does your retirement look? If you have faith in the Social Security system and you'll receive a generous pension benefit, things may be looking pretty good. On the other hand, if you think Social Security will go the way of the dodo and you won't receive a pension, you might be getting jittery.

It's time to focus on the source of retirement income over which you now have the most control. Sure, you can write your congressperson about Social Security, get a job with a good pension, and even contemplate spending your retirement working part-time at K-Wal-Target-Mart.

But right now, what you have the most control over is your personal savings; *you* decide how much you will save, and *you* decide how you will invest it.

LONG-TERM INVESTING . . . NOW!

As you start to add up your sources of retirement income (Social Security, your pension, possible wages, and all that "other" stuff), it becomes even clearer that a large portion of your retirement income will have to come from your own piggy bank.

The bottom line: Your savings are an integral part of this whole retirement thing coming out the way you want it to. Want an easy formula for increasing the number of bucks in that pork's belly? Here it is:

Invest early and often

There are thousands of examples that show you how important it is to start *right now*, or—if you're already saving—to *keep it up* or *increase it*. But we thought we'd throw in one of our own for emphasis.

You know that you should be squirreling away a certain portion of your hard-earned money for retirement. But where to begin? And how can you get the most bang for your retirement buck? From a traditional or Roth IRA? What about the plan at work? What about taxable accounts and annuities? Mutual funds or stocks?

Don't worry. We'll address those questions here.

THE VALUE OF STARTING EARLY

You may notice that throughout this chapter we encourage you to start saving *now*. That's because the longer money is invested, the more it'll be worth. Consider the chart on the next page before moving on.

Each person invested $5,000 a year for ten years, for a total of $50,000.

WHERE TO INVEST YOUR MONEY

You have many options when it comes to retirement accounts. Trying to decide which is best can be overwhelming. To help you out, we've listed the most important types in a general pecking order of where you should deposit your savings:

- Employer plan with a match
- Roth IRA
- Employer plan without a match
- Traditional IRA
- Taxable investments
- Annuities

Let's look more closely at each one.

EMPLOYER PLAN WITH A MATCH

If your employer matches your contributions to your company's defined-contribution plan—e.g., 401(k) or 403(b)—this should be the first place to devote every dollar that you can afford to lock

THE VALUE OF STARTING EARLY

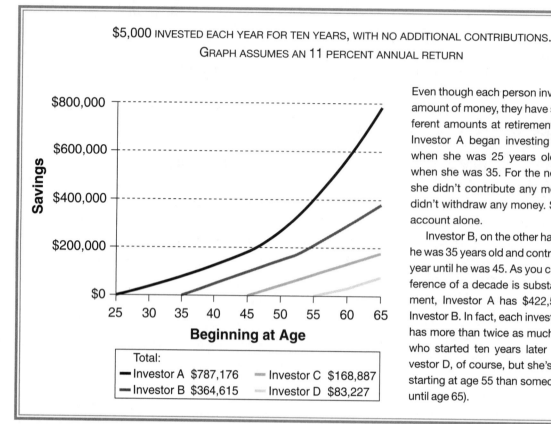

$5,000 INVESTED EACH YEAR FOR TEN YEARS, WITH NO ADDITIONAL CONTRIBUTIONS.
GRAPH ASSUMES AN 11 PERCENT ANNUAL RETURN

Total:
- Investor A $787,176
- Investor B $364,615
- Investor C $168,887
- Investor D $83,227

Even though each person invested the same amount of money, they have significantly different amounts at retirement. For example, Investor A began investing $5,000 a year when she was 25 years old and stopped when she was 35. For the next thirty years, she didn't contribute any more money and didn't withdraw any money. She just left the account alone.

Investor B, on the other hand, waited until he was 35 years old and contributed $5,000 a year until he was 45. As you can see, that difference of a decade is substantial. At retirement, Investor A has $422,561 more than Investor B. In fact, each investor in this graph has more than twice as much as the person who started ten years later (except for Investor D, of course, but she's a lot better off starting at age 55 than someone who waited until age 65).

away for the long term. Why? You're staring at free money, and you shouldn't just stare at free money—you should take it.

Other advantages of an employer-sponsored plan:

- **Tax deduction:** The money you contribute to the employer plan is not included in your income for tax purposes.

- **Tax deferral:** You don't pay taxes until you retire. That leaves more of your money to grow through the years.

- **Automatic investment:** The money is transferred directly from your paycheck to your account. There are no checks to write, no monthly reminders, no paper cuts to the tongue while sealing the envelope.

The contribution limits vary from plan to plan but generally are $12,000 in 2003, and will increase in $1,000 increments to $15,000 by 2006. Thereafter, the maximum contributions will be indexed to inflation.

Making your employer's plan the first stop applies only to those dollars you defer that are joined by matching dollars in your account. Check your plan. For instance, if the employer offers a match only up to the first $3,000 that you contribute annually but you're contributing $5,000, those two thousand unmatched dollars might well be put to even better use—namely, a . . .

ROTH IRA

The next place to turn after you've taken full advantage of the company match (i.e., free money) is a

Roth IRA, as long as you qualify. (Your ability to contribute to a Roth begins to phase out at a modified adjusted gross income of $95,000 for single filers and $150,000 for joint filers, reaching the ineligible stage at $110,000 and $160,000, respectively.) Why a Roth?

• **Tax-free growth:** While you won't get a tax deduction on contributions to a Roth IRA, you'll never have to pay taxes on the earnings when you begin withdrawals (assuming you follow the rules).

• **More control:** If you open your account with a discount broker, you can purchase individual stocks, bonds, and any index investment offered through that broker. This is an advantage over the limited selection offered by most employer-sponsored plans.

• **No mandatory distributions:** With employer-sponsored plans and traditional IRAs, you must begin withdrawing funds by April of the year following the year in which you reach age 70½, even if you don't need the money. Not so with a Roth. If you don't need the money, it can keep growing on its merry, tax-free way.

The contribution limit for a Roth (and for a traditional IRA as well) is $3,000 for 2003 and 2004; $4,000 for 2005 through 2007; and $5,000 for 2008. Thereafter, the $5,000 maximum allowable contribution will be indexed to inflation in $500 increments.

EMPLOYER PLAN WITHOUT A MATCH

We still like defined-contribution plans for your retirement savings even after you've reached the matching limit. The money that you contribute to the plan comes regularly out of your paycheck without your having to do anything at all, and you still get a tax deduction by contributing pretax money.

However, the investment options in your plan might not be all that great. If you're staring at a bunch of underperforming managed mutual funds as your only choices, you might want your money going into a better account, such as a . . .

TRADITIONAL IRA

If your income level is too high for you to start or to continue contributing to a Roth IRA, you can nonetheless make a contribution to a traditional IRA. The contribution limits are the same as for the Roth, and those limits apply to total annual IRA contributions; in other words, you can't contribute $3,000 to a Roth and $3,000 to a traditional IRA (at least until contribution limits reach $6,000 a year).

A traditional IRA grows tax-deferred, and is taxed as ordinary income upon withdrawal. Plus, contributions are tax-deductible if (1) your employer doesn't offer a retirement plan, or (2) your modified adjusted gross income is below certain limits. Those limits change occasionally, but for reference, in 2002 the entire contribution to a traditional IRA was tax-deductible for single filers with a modified AGI below $34,000, and for married joint filers with a modified AGI below $54,000. Contributions were partially deductible for single filers with a modified AGI up to $44,000, and for married joint filers with a modified AGI up to $64,000. After those AGI limits, contributions were not tax-deductible—but they still enjoyed tax-*deferred* growth, which is powerful stuff indeed!

TAXABLE INVESTMENTS

After you've maxed out the tax-advantaged vehicles at your disposal, only then should you put your retirement savings dollars into taxable accounts. However, if you don't like the investment options available in your employer-provided plan, you might move taxable investments up higher on this list, ahead of your unmatched defined-contribution plan.

ANNUITIES

For most people, annuities are a last-resort investment because they are too expensive, offer mediocre insurance coverage, restrict the owner's investment choices, and lack liquidity. They are most suitable for investors who:

- Have contributed the maximum to their defined-contribution plans and IRAs and desire further tax deferral on investment gains
- Prefer investing in mutual funds as opposed to individual securities
- Will keep the annuity for at least fifteen to twenty years
- Are in a 27 percent or higher income tax bracket today but expect to be in a lower income tax bracket in retirement
- Don't need the annuity proceeds prior to age 59$\frac{1}{2}$
- Are unconcerned that their heirs will have to pay ordinary income taxes on any appreciation
- Desire a "guaranteed" income for life in retirement

EVALUATE AND REARRANGE

Take a look at your Personal Investments Income Worksheet! Are your retirement savings going into the right types of accounts? If not, write down the actions you need to take in the "Need to Make a Change?" column—then make those changes!

THE CAVEAT AND THE STICK

As you can tell, we love tax-advantaged retirement accounts. However, keep this in mind: Money that you are saving for retirement should be money that you definitely won't touch until your retirement. Sure, you can get money out of a 401(k) or IRA before your retirement age if you absolutely have to, but in general there's a penalty—and some taxes to boot—attached to doing so. The best thing to do is to repeat after us: "Retirement savings are for retirement."

HOW MUCH WILL RETIREMENT COST?

OK, now it's time to get down to the nuts and bolts of retirement saving, namely, how much you will need and how much you will have to save to have enough by the time you retire.

Let's start with the first question: How much will all your retirement savings have to be worth before you can exchange the briefcase for the traveling bag?

To answer that question, take a step back and ask this question: How much income will you need in each year of retirement? The rule of thumb here is that you'll need 80 percent of your preretirement income. Why? Because many costs you have today might disappear in retirement, such as:

- Social Security taxes
- Job-related expenses
- Retirement plan contributions
- Child-related expenses
- Education and professional development expenses
- Disability and life insurance premiums
- Your mortgage (depending on how long you've owned your home)
- Any other expenses that you have now but will disappear by the time you retire

SPENDING AND DEMOGRAPHICS

Financial writer Harry S. Dent has built an entire investment strategy on birthrates and spending habits. In his book *The Roaring 2000s*, Dent says the spending of the average American family peaks at age forty-seven. After that, expenses drop because the kids have left home, there's no need to buy and furnish a bigger house, and many other big-ticket items have already been bought. Vacation/retirement homes might be purchased, and leisure and medical expenses will rise, but the average sixty-five-year-old spends less than the average forty-seven-year-old. That's another reason why you should be able to enjoy a peachy retirement on a fraction of your preretirement income.

However, some costs may increase as you retire and as you age, such as:

- Travel expenses
- Medical insurance and care
- Long-term care and/or long-term care insurance
- Costs of retirement hobbies and pastimes

So the "80 percent of preretirement income" rule is handy—but it's not hard and fast. When deciding on how much you'll need in retirement, keep these points in mind:

- You will possibly be retired for a couple of decades, perhaps even more. Your life—and the world—will change a lot over those years. After all, how many people who retired a decade ago would have factored the cost of a computer and Internet access into their budgets? Give yourself a cushion so dramatic life changes won't destroy your finances.

- The term "preretirement income" usually refers to the income received right before retirement. Of course, if you are a long way from the big day, you don't know yet what your preretirement income will be. In that case, it might be best to start with your current income and adjust it upward or downward according to whether you expect your lifestyle in retirement to cost more or less.

- If you are close to retirement (say, ten years or less), you probably have a good feel for what you'll be spending, at least for the first few years. It might be more useful for you actually to create a retirement budget, omitting the costs you'll no longer

incur and adding the new expenses you'll take on, as mentioned above.

THE REALLY IMPORTANT NUMBER

Knowing how much you'll need each year in retirement is nice, but it's only a step to answering another, perhaps more important question: How much must you have socked away to guarantee your income for a long time—in fact, from the time you retire to the time you expire?

Rob Bennett, a Fool community member who's considered to be an expert on retiring early, uses the "Multiply by 25" rule for a quick assessment of lifetime expense. He explains:

"I took each expense in my monthly budget (from books to electricity to vacations), multiplied it by 12 to get an annual expense figure, and then multiplied by 25 to get the lifetime cost of that item. The reason I multiplied by 25 is because I presume a 4 percent real rate of return on my savings. If you assume a 3 percent rate, you need to multiply by 33; 5 percent would have you multiplying by 20."

We'll explain this and then give an example.

> First you figure out what the real rate of return (i.e., the return above and beyond inflation) on your savings will be (Rob chose 4 percent).
> Dividing 4 percent (0.04) into 1.00 gives you 25.
> Multiply your annual expenses by that number to arrive at the "lifetime expense."

EXAMPLE

Let's say you want to retire tomorrow and you'll need $50,000 a year in income. Get out your calculator and multiply $50,000 by 25. (Click . . . click . . . tap . . . tap . . . your eyes widen . . . you fall on the floor . . .)

Yep, it's $1.25 million.

That money earning 4 percent (above inflation) will provide the necessary annual income, and you won't have to touch your principal. When you die, your kids will shed a few tears . . . but then they'll cheer up because they'll get the principal with which you started (provided the government doesn't tax it away).

As implied earlier, you don't have to choose 25 as the multiplier. If you think you can earn 5 percent above inflation instead of 4 percent (either because of your investing acumen or because you think that inflation will be low), then choose 20 as the multiplier. This will result in a smaller amount that you'll need to cover your retirement expenses.

BITE OFF A MONTH-FULL

"Great," you're thinking, "all I have to do is come up with more than a million smackers and I can retire. Know anyone willing to pay a lot for a slightly used kidney?"

The news isn't quite that bad. As we said earlier, you'll have sources of income other than your savings accounts. And, with enough time and investing, you might be able to build up quite a stake (so take your kidney off the eBay auction block).

So let's put it all together and figure out the *most* important number when it comes to retirement planning: how much you need to sock away each month to meet your retirement objectives.

This won't be as hard as it looks. No square roots or root canals or any of that stuff. Just a little addition, subtraction, multiplication, and division. That's it, we promise. Follow the steps beginning on page 103, entering your answers in the Retirement Savings Worksheet on page 107.

WARNING!

Let's make something perfectly clear: It's very difficult to estimate exactly how big your nest egg will have to be in retirement, especially if you're a couple of decades away from the big day. There are too many shifting factors: your current income, your retirement income, the rate of return on your investments, medical expenses, inflation, and Viagra.

The Retirement Savings Worksheet that you are about to complete will spit out a high number, relative to other ways of calculating how much you need to save. Why? Well, if you can manage to save the amount indicated by the worksheet, you'll have a very good chance of getting the retirement income you want—without ever touching your principal.

But to give you an idea of how a seemingly small change in one factor can drastically affect the amount of required retirement income, let's look at an example.

Meet Scooter, a forty-year-old who wants to retire at age sixty-seven. Here's what we know about him (dollar amounts are not adjusted for inflation):

- Current income: $60,000
- Desired retirement income: $50,000
- Estimated Social Security benefit: $18,744
- Estimated pension benefit: $12,000
- Life expectancy: 97 (retired 30 years)
- Savings: $30,000 in a 401(k) (he contributes $3,000 a year) and $15,000 in a Traditional IRA (he'll begin contributing $2,000 a year to a Roth IRA)
- Return on investments: 8% before and after retirement

The Retirement Savings Worksheet assumes that inflation will average 4 percent. Running Scooter's numbers though the gauntlet, we learn that he will have to save about $12,169 a year. Wow—that's more than 20 percent of his pretax income!

But if we assume that inflation is just 3 percent a year, then Scooter would need to save just $6,216. That one-percentage-point difference in inflation cut his required savings in half!

Now, let's look at what a few retirement calculators found at some prominent Web sites have to say about Scooter's savings requirements:

Calculator #1: Need to save $1,713 a year
Calculator #2: Need to save $4,900 per year
Calculator #3: Need to save $9,960 per year

Look at that. We put the same numbers in different retirement calculators, and we get very different results, and none as high as the number spit out by our Retirement Savings Worksheet. Why the disparities? Each calculator has different assumptions and emphasizes different aspects of the retirement-planning process. And most assume that retirees will spend part of their principal.

Thus, we have two lessons for ya:

1. Our Retirement Savings Worksheet is looking to give you the best chance of meeting your retirement goals. It assumes you will not use any of your principal to cover your expenses. This is ideal, but it may not be realistic.

2. Go online and try many calculators. If you can't afford to save as much as the Retirement Savings Worksheet suggests, then consider averaging the results of a few calculators. (Of course, we have a retirement calculator at Fool.com, as does any financial Web site worth its weight in hyperlinks. But you can also enter the words "retirement calculator" in any Internet search engine and you'll be offered many choices.)

1. **Find how much you'll need to withdraw from your savings each year** by subtracting from your target retirement income the following:

- Your annual pension (if you will receive one)
- Your projected annual Social Security benefit
- Your projected income from postretirement wages
- Your projected income from other sources

Note: You may want to be conservative with your Social Security projection, especially with benefits you'll receive twenty-plus years from now. Perhaps count on just 50 to 70 percent of what the Social Security Administration says you'll receive.

2. **Find your "lifetime retirement expense"**—the amount you need to fund your retirement indefinitely in today's dollars—by multiplying the number above by 25. (Remember the "multiply by 25 rule"? Here it is in action.) Remember, too, that you can use 20 as the multiplier instead, if you think

Years to Retirement	Inflation Factor (4%)
40	4.80102
39	4.61637
38	4.43881
37	4.26809
36	4.10393
35	3.94609
34	3.79432
33	3.64838
32	3.50806
31	3.37313
30	3.24340
29	3.11865
28	2.99870
27	2.88337
26	2.77247
25	2.66584
24	2.56330
23	2.46472
22	2.36992
21	2.27877
20	2.19112
19	2.10685
18	2.02582
17	1.94790
16	1.87298
15	1.80094
14	1.73168
13	1.66507
12	1.60103
11	1.53945
10	1.48024
9	1.42331
8	1.36857
7	1.31593
6	1.26532
5	1.21665
4	1.16986
3	1.12486
2	1.08160
1	1.04000

you can earn 5 percent above inflation instead of 4 percent.

3. Find your "lifetime retirement expense" with an adjustment for inflation by multiplying the number above by an inflation factor found in the previous table.

The number you figured out above is in today's dollars and is perfectly fine if you will retire in the next few years. However, if that's not the case, you'll have to account for inflation. To factor in 4 percent inflation, multiply your lifetime retirement expense by a factor that corresponds to the number of years you have until retirement.

4. Find the projected size of your current assets in retirement by multiplying your current savings by your savings factor.

Multiply the total of all your retirement accounts—the amount in the "Personal Investments" row of your Master Sources of Retirement Income Worksheet—by your savings factor. The table below provides a factor by which to multiply current savings, based on expected return and years until retirement.

For example, if you have $100,000 in your 401(k), you'll retire in twenty years, and you expect to earn 8 percent annually, multiply $100,000 by 4.66096, resulting in $466,096.

Years Until Retirement	Expected Returns				
	4%	6%	8%	10%	11%
40	4.80102	10.28572	21.72452	45.25926	65.00087
39	4.61637	9.70351	20.11530	41.14478	58.55934
38	4.43881	9.15425	18.62528	37.40434	52.75616
37	4.26809	8.63609	17.24563	34.00395	47.52807
36	4.10393	8.14725	15.96817	30.91268	42.81808
35	3.94609	7.68609	14.78534	28.10244	38.57485
34	3.79432	7.25103	13.69013	25.54767	34.75212
33	3.64838	6.84059	12.67605	23.22515	31.30821
32	3.50806	6.45339	11.73708	21.11378	28.20560
31	3.37313	6.08810	10.86767	19.19434	25.41045
30	3.24340	5.74349	10.06266	17.44940	22.89230
29	3.11865	5.41839	9.31727	15.86309	20.62369
28	2.99870	5.11169	8.62711	14.42099	18.57990
27	2.88337	4.82235	7.98806	13.10999	16.73865
26	2.77247	4.54938	7.39635	11.91818	15.07986
25	2.66584	4.29187	6.84848	10.83471	13.58546
24	2.56330	4.04893	6.34118	9.84973	12.23916
23	2.46472	3.81975	5.87146	8.95430	11.02627
22	2.36992	3.60354	5.43654	8.14027	9.93357
21	2.27877	3.39956	5.03383	7.40025	8.94917
20	2.19112	3.20714	4.66096	6.72750	8.06231
19	2.10685	3.02560	4.31570	6.11591	7.26334

YEARS UNTIL RETIREMENT	EXPECTED RETURNS				
	4%	6%	8%	10%	11%
18	2.02582	2.85434	3.99602	5.55992	6.54355
17	1.94790	2.69277	3.70002	5.05447	5.89509
16	1.87298	2.54035	3.42594	4.59497	5.31089
15	1.80094	2.39656	3.17217	4.17725	4.78459
14	1.73168	2.26090	2.93719	3.79750	4.31044
13	1.66507	2.13293	2.71962	3.45227	3.88328
12	1.60103	2.01220	2.51817	3.13843	3.49845
11	1.53945	1.89830	2.33164	2.85312	3.15176
10	1.48024	1.79085	2.15892	2.59374	2.83942
9	1.42331	1.68948	1.99900	2.35795	2.55804
8	1.36857	1.59385	1.85093	2.14359	2.30454
7	1.31593	1.50363	1.71382	1.94872	2.07616
6	1.26532	1.41852	1.58687	1.77156	1.87041
5	1.21665	1.33823	1.46933	1.16051	1.68506
4	1.16986	1.26248	1.36049	1.46410	1.51807
3	1.12486	1.19102	1.25971	1.33100	1.36763
2	1.08160	1.12360	1.16640	1.21000	1.23210
1	1.04000	1.06000	1.08000	1.10000	1.11000

5. **Find your savings gap,** the amount you'll have to generate with future investments, by subtracting the above number (the future value of your savings) from your Lifetime Retirement Expense.

Now for the moment of truth . . .

6. **Find the amount you'll have to save monthly to hit your goal** by multiplying your savings gap by your savings gap factor.

The table on page 106 provides a factor by which you multiply the size of your requisite nest egg, resulting in the amount you need to save monthly. For example, if you plan to retire in twenty years, need $250,000, and expect to earn 8 percent annually on your investments, multiply $250,000 by 0.00168. To meet your goal, you should invest $420 each month.

If your current savings will be worth *more* than your lifetime retirement expense, you've already saved enough.	If your current savings are *less* than your lifetime retirement expense, you have a little more work to do. Continue reading on to see how much you'll have to save to hit your goal.

	YEARS				
RETURN	1	3	5	10	15
2%	0.07616	0.02622	0.01559	0.00474	0.00338
3%	0.07578	0.02583	0.01520	0.00709	0.00438
4%	0.07540	0.02544	0.01481	0.00672	0.00403
5%	0.07502	0.02505	0.01443	0.00637	0.00371
6%	0.07464	0.02467	0.01406	0.00604	0.00341
7%	0.07427	0.02429	0.01370	0.00571	0.00313
8%	0.07389	0.02392	0.01334	0.00540	0.00286
9%	0.07352	0.02355	0.01299	0.00510	0.00262
10%	0.07315	0.02319	0.01265	0.00482	0.00239
11%	0.07278	0.02282	0.01231	0.00455	0.00217
12%	0.07241	0.02247	0.01198	0.00429	0.00198
13%	0.07205	0.02212	0.01165	0.00404	0.00180
14%	0.07168	0.02177	0.01134	0.00380	0.00168
15%	0.07132	0.02142	0.01103	0.00358	0.00149

	YEARS				
RETURN	20	25	30	35	40
2%	0.00338	0.00256	0.00202	0.00164	0.00136
3%	0.00303	0.00223	0.00171	0.00134	0.00108
4%	0.00271	0.00193	0.00143	0.00109	0.00084
5%	0.00242	0.00167	0.00120	0.00088	0.00065
6%	0.00215	0.00143	0.00099	0.00070	0.00050
7%	0.00190	0.00123	0.00081	0.00055	0.00038
8%	0.00168	0.00104	0.00067	0.00043	0.00028
9%	0.00148	0.00088	0.00054	0.00034	0.00021
10%	0.00130	0.00075	0.00044	0.00026	0.00016
11%	0.00114	0.00063	0.00035	0.00020	0.00012
12%	0.00100	0.00053	0.00028	0.00015	0.00008
13%	0.00087	0.00044	0.00023	0.00012	0.00006
14%	0.00076	0.00037	0.00018	0.00009	0.00004
15%	0.00066	0.00030	0.00014	0.00007	0.00003

WORKSHEET: RETIREMENT SAVINGS

Enter your desired annual income in retirement. (If you are going the "80% of income" route, multiply your income by 0.80.)   _____

Subtract the following:

Your projected annual Social Security benefit   − _____

Your annual pension (if you will receive one)   − _____

Your projected income from postretirement wages   − _____

Your projected income from other sources   − _____

How much you'll need from your savings each year   = _____

Multiply it by 25 (or 20)   × 25 (or 20)

This is your Lifetime Retirement Expense in today's dollars   = _____

Multiply by the inflation factor (table on page 103)   × _____

This is your Lifetime Retirement Expense, accounting for inflation   = _____

How much will you have to save?

Current savings (total of all retirement accounts)   _____

Multiply by the savings factor (table on page 104)   × _____

Projected size of your current assets in retirement   = _____

If your current savings will be worth more than your "Lifetime Retirement Expense," congratulations! That means you've already saved enough.

However, if that's not the case,

Subtract the future value of your savings from your Lifetime Retirement Expense   − _____

Your savings gap   = _____

Multiply by your savings gap factor (table on page 106)   × _____

Adjusted amount you'll have to save until retirement   = _____

Amount you'll have to save monthly to hit your goal   = _____

PLAY WITH YOUR PLAN

After running through the worksheet—and perhaps giving a retirement calculator or two a whirl—you should have an idea of where your current path will lead. If you need to take evasive action to avoid disaster, the time to improve your lot is *now*.

Start with these questions:

- Can you cut down on your current expenses to save more now?
- Can you live on less than your projected retirement income?
- Can you put your retirement off for a few years?

- Are you being too conservative with your investments?
- Are you taking advantage of available tax-advantaged accounts?

Go back to your worksheets and do some tweaking. Will you reach your goals if, for example, you retire two years later, save $200 more a month, and live on $200 less a month in retirement? Keep playing with the plan.

FROM PLAN TO ACTION

OK, Foolish cartographers, it's time to draw a map. We're going to record where you are, where you're going, and what you need to do get there.

YOUR PLAN SUMMARY AND ACTION STEPS

WHERE YOU ARE		WHERE YOU'RE GOING	
Total amount of retirement income from "guaranteed" sources (Social Security, pension, other) $ _____	Total sum of your personal investments right now $ _____	Amount of personal investments you need before you retire $ _____	Amount you must save monthly to meet your retirement goal $ _____

Make changes to existing retirement accounts.

Examples: Increase contribution amount, change investments

Action: _____   Due date: _____

Action: _____   Due date: _____

Action: _____   Due date: _____

Open and fund a new retirement account.

Examples: Sign up for company plan, open a Roth IRA

Action: _____   Due date: _____

Action: _____   Due date: _____

Action: _____   Due date: _____

Reduce current costs in order to invest more for retirement.

Examples: Track expenses, eat out less often, forgo cable TV

Action: _____ Due date: _____

Action: _____ Due date: _____

Action: _____ Due date: _____

TEN TIPS ON SAVING FOR RETIREMENT

1. Save early and often. Save early and a lot. Save early and as much as possible.

2. Take advantage of tax-friendly accounts, namely, employer pension plans and IRAs. You'll save a whole bunch on taxes now and have a lot more for retirement.

3. Get an employer match, if it's provided. That's an instant, guaranteed return on your retirement investment.

4. If you have changed jobs and left money in your old employer's retirement plan—or you plan to change jobs—you will usually be better served by transferring the assets in the old plan to your new plan or, better yet, an IRA. Whatever you do, make sure it's a "direct transfer," which means that the old plan provider sends the money to the new account. You do not want the check sent to you because, unless you put it into another retirement account within sixty days, you will have to pay penalties and taxes.

5. Manage your own investments as much as you can. This has always been a Foolish mantra, but it's particularly important when it comes to your retirement money. Why? Because if other people handle your money, you'll have to pay them 1 to 3 percent of the value of your investments.

You are essentially transferring that money from your nest egg into someone else's pocket. Add that up over a period of decades, and you will have paid tens of thousands of dollars for those services.

6. Leave your retirement money alone. It's tempting to tap your accounts in times of need or covetousness, but you'll be shortchanging your future—and paying loads in taxes and penalties.

7. Make your retirement saving automatic. Besides having your 401(k) contributions taken out directly from your paycheck, sign up for an automatic transfer program into your IRA. The money is taken out of your bank account and invested in the security of your choice, without your having to lift a finger (and the money is socked away before you can put a finger on it).

8. Social Security will not be—and was never meant to be—a sufficient source of income on its own. The average recipient receives about $11,000 a year. That won't buy a lot of cruises or fishing trips, or even decent room and board. And you can count on benefits being reduced in the future.

9. If your children or grandchildren have earned income, they can open an IRA. And the money that goes into the account doesn't necessarily have to come from them. So if little Jocelyn earns $500 from her paper route, she can open an IRA and you can deposit up to $500 for her. By the time she retires, that one deposit could be worth tens of thousands of dollars. What a gift!

10. Never retire. When you're ready to leave the full-time rat race, take a job you've always been curious about and do it for only as long as you want. Perhaps you'd like to try teaching, being a part-time librarian, or putting your carpentry skills to work. You'll broaden your horizons, bring in extra income, and possibly fulfill some lifelong aspirations.

YOUR BIT-BY-BIT BUDGET ENTRY

Combine the knowledge you garnered from the Personal Investments Worksheet and the Retirement Savings Worksheet and decide on how much should be contributed to what kind of retirement account. Then add that amount to your Bit-by-Bit Budget. Onward, Fool!

BIT-BY-BIT BUDGET

	AMOUNT FROM YOUR MONEY TRACKER WORKSHEET	BUDGETED AMOUNT	MONTH 1	MONTH 2	MONTH 3	MONTH 4	MONTH 5	MONTH 6
Retirement:								
Employer-provided plan(s)								
IRA(s)								
Other								

CHAPTER 7

BUYING BIG-TICKET ITEMS

SIXTY-SECOND GUIDE TO BUYING BIG-TICKET ITEMS

Throughout your life, there will be times when you lay down some serious cash all at once. Rare is the person who plunks down a Visa card to purchase a house. Chances are no one can pay Junior's college tuition with the change jangling around in his pockets. Here's the best way to prepare for big purchases like these, and to soften their impact.

0:60 Look into the future.

You don't need a crystal ball (though you'd be a hit at Halloween parties and at the track). Just think about what pricey items or services might be on your horizon. Start with the goals you've listed on your Bit-by-Bit Budget.

0:50 What will happen if you don't plan ahead?

If you don't plan ahead and just hope you'll have the money when the purchase is upon you, be ready for disappointment . . . or debt.

0:40 Break the expense down month by month.

When you know how much you will need, when you will need it, and what kind of return you can get on your savings, you can break your goal down into monthly savings goals.

0:30 When it comes to a house, should you buy or rent?

There are advantages to both, but if you decide to own a piece of the American Dream, understand the financial ins and outs.

0:20 Saving for college? Let Uncle Sam help.

It's no secret that the costs of an education are rising. But there are some very smart ways to save for that piece of paper on the wall.

0:10 Best car-buying advice: Don't do it!

Everyone likes a little appreciation, but do your best to avoid *depreciation*, that is, the quick decline of value. That's what happens to a car right after you buy it: the value of the asset begins a quick descent. And you still have all those monthly payments to make!

. . .

BIG PURCHASES

Every day, you make purchasing decisions: Should I buy lunch? Is that a reasonable price for a pair of jeans? Which gas station should I pull into? Should I get a grande or mucho-grande superskim latte?

Though we applaud you for watching your pennies, these types of transactions won't make or break you. However, as you flitter, flutter, and flicker through life, you will encounter many big-ticket expenses that will have a significant effect on your finances. These expenses may be annual events (such as Christmas and the family vacation) or once-in-a-lifetime events (such as your daughter's wedding or college education). Whatever their frequency, you will always be better off planning ahead for these expenses as much as possible.

That's what this chapter is all about. It will answer a very important question: How much do I have to save every month to pay for a future big expense?

We'll move from the generic (saving for any old large outlay) to the specific (saving for a house, a car, or a college education). If none of those specific expenses is on your horizon, you can skip that part of the chapter. But everyone should read the first part. In fact, Allen Greenspan* read it and said, "If I had read this when I was a younger man, I would be much better off today." And don't forget to complete the Bit-by-Bit Budget exercise for this chapter on page 139.

ANY BIG-TICKET EXPENSE

What are we talking about? First, we're talking about your pricier goals. You've written your goals

* Allen Greenspan—not to be confused with Alan Greenspan, the chairman of the Federal Reserve—is often asked by telemarketers if he's "that short guy on TV who has something to do with money."

down in a few places in this workbook—you'll probably see a few big-ticket items on your list of what's really important to you. However, we're also talking about any expense that, if not planned for, would compromise your goals, or cause you to take on imprudent debt. Here are some examples:

- A new porch or revamped kitchen
- Extensive dental work
- A wedding
- A house boat
- A vacation
- A family reunion
- Holiday gift giving
- A hair transplant
- Any financial goal you have

WHY BOTHER?

We have three good reasons for why you should anticipate your big expenses as much as possible:

1. **You'll get what you want.** Makes sense, doesn't it? If you plan to sock away a little bit at a time now, you're more likely to have the money when you need it.

2. **You won't take on debilitating debt.** Some forms of debt are better than others. We covered all that in Chapter 3, but suffice it to say that it's more reasonable to take on debt for an appreciating asset (e.g., a house) than a depreciating one (e.g., a car). And unless it's necessary, it's hardly ever reasonable to assume more credit card debt.

3. **You won't waste money.** As discussed in Chapter 2, unless you take control of your money, it'll slip through your fingers without a trace. On the other hand, if you actively direct your funds to your priorities, you will ensure that those priorities will be funded first, your frivolities second.

So how can you plan for a big expense? Start by determining three factors: (1) How much you will need, (2) when you will need it, and (3) what kind of return you can get on your savings in the meantime. Then plug all that into this formula:

$$\underline{R} = \underline{Si}/[(\underline{1} + \underline{i})^n - \underline{1}]$$

This tells you how much you need to save each month (R) in order to accumulate a certain amount of money (S) by a certain number of months in the future (n) while your money earns a particular rate of interest (i).

Uh . . . yeah.

Don't worry, we'll make it easier on you.

HOW MUCH YOU NEED TO SAVE FOR ANY EXPENSE

Consult the following table and follow these steps:

1. Choose the column that most closely corresponds to the number of years until you need the money.

2. Follow that column down to the row that corresponds to the return you expect to earn on your savings. That will lead to a number we'll call the return factor.

3. Multiply that return factor by the amount of money you'll need. The result is the amount you should save each month to meet your goal.

A couple of notes:

- These calculations ignore the harmful effect taxes will have on your earnings. Also, they don't account for inflation, so if your goal is more than a few years away, plan on having more money than you'd need for that goal today.
- If you want a confirmation of your number, or you want a quick way of playing with different scenarios, visit the calculators at www.Fool.com/calcs/calculators.htm.

RETURN FACTOR

	YEARS				
RETURNS	1	3	5	10	15
2%	0.07616	0.02622	0.01559	0.00474	0.00338
3%	0.07578	0.02583	0.01520	0.00709	0.00438
4%	0.07540	0.02544	0.01481	0.00672	0.00403
5%	0.07502	0.02505	0.01443	0.00637	0.00371
6%	0.07464	0.02467	0.01406	0.00604	0.00341
7%	0.07427	0.02429	0.01370	0.00571	0.00313
8%	0.07389	0.02392	0.01334	0.00540	0.00286
9%	0.07352	0.02355	0.01299	0.00510	0.00262
10%	0.07315	0.02319	0.01265	0.00482	0.00239
11%	0.07278	0.02282	0.01231	0.00455	0.00217
12%	0.07241	0.02247	0.01198	0.00429	0.00198

(continued)

RETURN FACTOR, continued

	YEARS				
RETURNS	20	25	30	35	40
2%	0.00338	0.00256	0.00202	0.00164	0.00136
3%	0.00303	0.00223	0.00171	0.00134	0.00108
4%	0.00271	0.00193	0.00143	0.00109	0.00084
5%	0.00242	0.00167	0.00120	0.00088	0.00065
6%	0.00215	0.00143	0.00099	0.00070	0.00050
7%	0.00190	0.00123	0.00081	0.00055	0.00038
8%	0.00168	0.00104	0.00067	0.00043	0.00028
9%	0.00148	0.00088	0.00054	0.00034	0.00021
10%	0.00130	0.00075	0.00044	0.00026	0.00016
11%	0.00114	0.00063	0.00035	0.00020	0.00012
12%	0.00100	0.00053	0.00028	0.00015	0.00008

Now that you've figured out how much you'll have to save, is it a realistic amount? If not, here are your options:

1. **Scale down your goal.** Perhaps you should aim for a rowboat instead of a motorboat.
2. **Move your target date back.** Will the goal be more attainable if you put off the purchase and save for another year or two?
3. **Spend time looking for cheaper options.** While you're socking money away, spend the time investigating ways to save money on your purchase.
4. **Don't do it.** Maybe it's not worth the time and effort.

WHERE TO PUT THOSE SAVINGS

So where should you squirrel away your money until you need it? You know what we're going to say: It depends. In this case, it depends on your tolerance for risk and your time horizon. But we do have some general guidelines. For more specifics, review Chapter 5.

Expenses Less than Five Years Away These are considered short-term goals, so stay out of volatile investments such as stocks and even long-term bonds. Stick with money market accounts, certificates of deposit, Treasury notes, and short-term bonds. A few pages back we provided some guidance on shopping for a safe account that'll give you the best return.

Expenses Between Five and Ten Years Away Depending on how comfortable you are with investments in the stock market, you might consider putting some of your money into equities. However, as you move closer to your goal, more of your money should be shifted to safer investments.

Expenses More than Ten Years Away The longer your time horizon, the more you mitigate the risk of being in stocks. And history shows that over most ten-year periods, the stock market has been the best place to be. (Don't make us pull out that compounding chart again!) Again, though, as you near the time when you will need the money, move toward safer havens.

ACQUIRING YOUR CASTLE

There's nothing like owning the roof over your head and the floor beneath your feet. Having a bunch of walls in between is even better. (Though some people prefer the loft lifestyle.) But purchasing that mass of lumber, pipes, wires, and glass—and possibly the surrounding land and airspace—is a huge financial endeavor. If you have a yen to become part of the landed gentry, the first question you should ask yourself is: Should I? (Don't ask too loudly, or people will point.)

This chapter will not try to tell you all the ins and outs of getting a mortgage, finding a real estate agent, finding your dream house, and negotiating a purchase price. There are plenty of other places to get that information (including the Home Center at Fool.com).

What this chapter will do is introduce you to some of the financial considerations of buying a house and help you decide if you should borrow tens (if not hundreds) of thousands of dollars to do so. So let's first address the renting-versus-purchasing question.

WHY YOU SHOULD RENT

1. **You don't think you'll be in the same city for more than three years.** The thousands of dollars of up-front costs related to buying a house (lawyers, brokers, agents—they all get a cut) will be wasted if you move within a short time.

2. **You don't want to worry about making repairs.** When the toilet explodes, it's the landlord's problem, not yours.

3. **You don't want to take on a mortgage.** Most people have to borrow tens of thousands of dollars

to purchase a home. That can put a lot of limits on you for a long time. However, if you rent, you're free of that enormous debt.

Of those points, the first one is the most important. If you're the ramblin' type—moving from town to town, breaking hearts along the way—buying a home may not be worth the time and money.

Now let's look at the other side of the housing coin.

WHY YOU SHOULD BUY

1. **Your monthly housing payments will line your pockets, not a landlord's.** A house is (usually) an appreciating asset; that is, your house will probably increase in value. That means you may make a profit when you sell the house. Also, you can use the equity in your house for tax-deductible loans. And speaking of taxes . . .

2. **You get a sizable tax deduction.** Uncle Sam likes homeowners—they make for a more stable country, or something like that. Anyway, to encourage ownership, Uncle Sam allows homeowners to deduct the interest on their mortgages and other related costs from their income taxes.

3. **Your housing payments are fixed.** Assuming you get a fixed mortgage (which is the most popular kind), your housing payments will not change for as long as you own the house. If your mortgage is $1,200 a month now, it'll be $1,200 a month fifteen years from now. On the other hand, if you're renting your residence, your rent will probably increase every year, to where it could be 30 to 50 percent more fifteen years down the road.

4. **You love worrying about repairs.** When the toilet explodes, there goes your Saturday (after you explain to your kids that flushing Fluffy down the john is not a proper burial for a deceased hamster).

5. **You own the place.** Put Velcro on the ceiling. Carpet the bathtub. Prune your bushes into the

shape of candy canes. Hang so many pictures that no one can guess the walls' paint color. Go crazy—it's your house!

HOW MUCH HOUSE WILL FIT YOUR BUDGET?

If you have decided that buying is for you, the next step is figuring out how much you can afford to spend. Let's start by examining what goes into buying a house. First, there are some up-front costs:

1. **Down payment.** Ideally, you should have 20 percent of the house's purchase price ready to hand over on the day you close the sale. That way, you'll have a good chunk of equity in the house. But more practically, you also won't have to pay for private mortgage insurance (see monthly costs, below), which will cost hundreds of dollars a year.

2. **Closing costs.** These will entail all kinds of expenses, such as title insurance, survey fees, escrow fees, property taxes, and appraisal fees. You'll get the complete laundry list (and feel as though you've been taken to the cleaners) from your mortgage company. For now, just know that these costs run 3 to 6 percent of the purchase price of the house. Also know that you can sometimes get the seller to pay some of these costs or roll the costs into the mortgage.

3. **Home inspection and termite inspection.** Before you purchase the house, you want to make sure that the roof isn't about to collapse and the walls aren't infested. This will cost $300 to $600.

Now let's look at the ongoing monthly costs of home ownership:

1. **Mortgage.** Unless you have enough cash to buy a house outright, you'll have to borrow some money. (If you do have enough cash to buy it out-right, are you single? Plunking it all down at once is probably not the best financial move.) That loan is known as a mortgage, and each payment consists of some principal and some interest.

2. **Taxes.** Each year you will pay property taxes, usually to your county. Taxes run about 1.5 percent of the value of the house nationwide, but you should check with your local tax authority to get your exact local tax rate. Keep in mind, however, that the interest on your mortgage is tax deductible, and your local property taxes are deductible on your federal income tax return. So, most people's overall tax situation improves from home ownership.

3. **Homeowner's insurance.** This will protect your house and your valuables from damage, theft, and assorted other perils. To get an idea of how much this will cost, call a few insurance providers with the zip codes of some of the prospective areas in which you'd like to live. For more info on homeowner's insurance, go back to Chapter 4.

4. **Private mortgage insurance (PMI).** If your down payment is less than 20 percent of the value of the house, your mortgage company will require you to pay PMI to protect it from your skipping town. PMI will cost approximately $35 a month for a $90,000 mortgage on a $100,000 home; $80 a month for a $140,000 mortgage on a $150,000 home; $110 for a $190,000 mortgage on a $200,000 home; and $140 a month for a $240,000 mortgage on a $250,000 home. Note that, unlike mortgage interest, PMI is *not* tax deductible. (Just one more reason to put 20 percent down on your house, if you can.)

5. **Maintenance.** Remember Fluffy and the toilet? You are responsible for fixing, and paying for, any exploding furnaces or belching refrigerators. Of course, you don't know exactly how much household upkeep will cost from month to month. However, a good rule of thumb is that you'll spend

1 to 2 percent of the value of the house a year on maintenance, depending on the condition of the house and appliances.

Given all those expenses, how much do you think you could afford to pay on a monthly basis for housing? Start with your current housing expenses, and then work up (or down) from there. If you add the aforementioned costs, what do you come up with? And is that number manageable—without shortchanging your retirement or other important goals?

YOU DECIDE HOW MUCH TO BORROW

Before you borrow $90,000, $200,000, or whatever you need for your mortgage, figure out whether you can really afford it. Just because the bank will loan it to you doesn't mean that you will live your life in such a way as to be able to pay it back. Are you planning to have a big family? Would you rather replace your Chevy Cavalier with a new Mercedes? Are you saving enough for retirement? Your house payment is just one piece of your financial puzzle. What might you need to give up to make that house a reality, and are you *really* willing to do it?

GET THE GOING PRICE ON MORTGAGES

To figure out how much your monthly mortgage could be, start by finding out the general interest rate on a thirty-year fixed mortgage (there are other types of mortgages, but this is the most popular form, and we're just looking for a ballpark figure for now). Different lenders will offer different rates, but they'll all be in the same neighborhood. You can find the general going rate by visiting any finance-related Web site, such as Fool.com or www.bankrate.com, looking in the business section of the newspaper (listed among other financial stats or even in ads from lenders), or just calling your bank. Then find the rate column in the table below that corresponds to the prevailing thirty-year fixed mortgage rate. Follow that column down to the row that is closest to the monthly payment you think you can afford. Now go to the far-left-hand

ESTIMATED MONTHLY MORTGAGE PAYMENT (30-year fixed rate)

Loan Amount	6%	6.50%	7%	7.50%	8%	8.50%
$50,000	$307	$316	$333	$350	$367	$384
$75,000	$450	$474	$499	$524	$550	$577
$100,000	$599	$632	$665	$699	$734	$769
$125,000	$749	$790	$831	$874	$917	$961
$150,000	$899	$948	$998	$1,049	$1,100	$1,153
$175,000	$1,049	$1,106	$1,164	$1,223	$1,284	$1,346
$200,000	$1,199	$1,264	$1,330	$1,398	$1,468	$1,538
$225,000	$1,349	$1,422	$1,497	$1,573	$1,651	$1,730
$250,000	$1,499	$1,580	$1,663	$1,748	$1,834	$1,922

(continued)

ESTIMATED MONTHLY MORTGAGE PAYMENT (30-year fixed rate), continued

LOAN AMOUNT	9%	9.50%	10%	10.50%	11%	11.50%	12%
$50,000	$402	$420	$439	$457	$476	$495	$514
$75,000	$603	$630	$658	$686	$714	$742	$771
$100,000	$804	$840	$877	$915	$952	$990	$1,029
$125,000	$1,006	$1,051	$1,097	$1,143	$1,190	$1,238	$1,286
$150,000	$1,206	$1,261	$1,316	$1,372	$1,428	$1,485	$1,543
$175,000	$1,408	$1,471	$1,536	$1,601	$1,667	$1,733	$1,800
$200,000	$1,609	$1,682	$1,755	$1,829	$1,905	$1,980	$2,057
$225,000	$1,810	$1,891	$1,975	$2,058	$2,143	$2,228	$2,314
$250,000	$2,012	$2,102	$2,194	$2,287	$2,381	$2,476	$2,572

column. That's the approximate amount you could borrow.

Did you get all that? Let's go through an example to make sure everything is clear.

Let's say the prevailing interest rate on a thirty-year fixed mortgage is about 8.15 percent and you're currently paying $950 a month in rent. However, you think you could afford to pay $1,300 on a mortgage. Since 8.15 percent is close to 8.00 percent, we'll look down that column in the table above until we find an amount that approximates $1,300. Ah, there's $1,284. Looking to the far left, we find $175,000. Voilà—that's roughly the size of a mortgage you think you can afford.

Remember: That's the size of the *loan,* not the price of the house. So factor in the other costs mentioned on page 116 (down payment, closing costs, insurance, etc.).

CLOSING COSTS

On the big day when the house becomes yours, you will meet at the office of a real estate agent or attorney and sign *lots* of papers. You will also have to fork over a lot of dough. Here are some of the costs you will incur on the day you close the deal.

• **Points or loan origination fee.** This is an up-front payment of the interest that you owe your lender. The range that you'll have to fork over is anywhere from nothing to about 3 percent of the loan. Remember, the more points you pay, the lower your overall interest rate should be, and vice versa. If you're strapped for cash, you can get a loan with no points, but you'll pay a higher amount of interest over the life of your loan. Another option is to have the seller pay these costs for you.

• **Escrow fees.** These are the fees that are charged to process all of the paperwork and keep the money in a safe place while you and the seller dicker over things. Depending on the cost of your home, this can amount to a few hundred to a couple of thousand dollars.

• **Homeowner's insurance.** We discuss this in detail in Chapter 4. For now, though, know that you should expect to pay between $500 and $2,000 depending on the value of your home and your coverage. You must get this insurance before your lender will release the funds for your house.

- **Title insurance.** What would happen if, six months after you move into your new house, you discover that the person who sold you the house didn't really own it? Arrgh! While it's a remote possibility, it does happen. Luckily, there's protection against this very problem. Your lender will want you to get title insurance to take care of this situation should it arise. Based on the value of your home, expect to pay between $500 and $2,000.

- **Property taxes.** Depending on when your purchase actually closes, you may owe the previous owners for taxes that they've already paid. For example, say the old owners paid their taxes from January through June. You buy the house in April. Well, they've already paid the taxes for May and June. You need to reimburse them for this expense. In addition, you may need to prepay some taxes.

- **Private mortgage insurance.** If you have a loan that requires it, count on paying at least a few months' premiums in advance. Some lenders will want you to pay for an entire year in advance. You can nix this if you can come up with a 20 percent down payment.

- **Notary.** Yes, someone has to swear that you are who you say you are. Expect to pay about $50 for the privilege.

- **Other fees.** These can include document preparation fees, appraisal fees, tax service fees, survey fee, and state recording fees.

- **Irving.** At every closing there's this guy named Irving. He always wants anywhere from $20 to a couple of thousand dollars just for the trouble of showing up. Sometimes he doesn't even show up. He just sends a letter saying "Pay me now or you can't have your house!" Irving may represent the municipal tax office, which says you have to pay an obscure tax for buying a blue house on Tuesday. Or he might represent the courier company demanding payment to rush some last-minute document across town. In any case, expect Irving to come up with some other off-the-wall charge that you haven't anticipated. To anticipate this, bring your checkbook to the closing.

TAX SAVINGS ON YOUR HOME PURCHASE

We've all heard it before: Buy a home and save a *ton* of money on your income taxes! While it may sound enticing, it's not always true—at least not as true as some people would have you believe.

While you can deduct any interest you pay on your mortgage, as well as points you pay at settlement, that deduction will do you good only to the extent that those expenses exceed the standard deduction.

Huh?

Remember that itemized deductions are applied against your adjusted gross income (AGI), thereby allowing you to arrive at a lower taxable income and thus a lower income tax (yippee!). But itemizing your deductions is something that you're *allowed* to do, not necessarily something that you *must* do.

If your situation is such that you have itemized deductions *greater than* your standard deduction, you can report your itemized deductions. But if you don't have any or many itemized deductions, you're allowed to take the standard deduction. You get the standard deduction simply for being you— an enriched and happy Fool.

So it's your choice, your decision. You basically compare your itemized deductions to your standard deduction and use the larger of the two results to reduce your taxable income. For 2001, the standard deduction for folks married and filing jointly amounted to $7,600. For single filers, the standard deduction was $4,550. If you qualify for head of household status, your standard deduction is $6,650. And those of you who are married and filing separately can look forward to a standard deduction of $3,800.

(Please note that we are using tax year 2001 standard deduction amounts for illustrative purposes only. The standard deduction amounts change each year, so make sure you use the most current ones—found on your most recently filed Form 1040.)

So let's say you're married, are in the 27 percent tax bracket, and paid $10,200 in interest on your mortgage. From that amount, subtract the amount of the standard deduction of $7,600, then figure the 27 percent tax rate on the difference in order to determine your buyer's net tax savings: $10,200 − $7,600 = $2,600 × 27% = $702 in actual tax savings.

However, there's another benefit. It's very likely that you will have some other itemized deductions—such as donations to charity—that were of no tax consequence in prior years (because you didn't itemize). These deductions now become very important. Check Chapter 8 for a complete list of deductible expenses.

THE MORTGAGE

Taking out a mortgage can be a hassle. The bank will want to ask you all sorts of nosy questions about your income and savings (or lack thereof) and then might not even lend you as much as you need. The nerve!

There is a reason for this. Put yourself into the bank's shoes: If you were going to lend people money, what would you want to know about them? Basically, you'd like to know (1) if they make enough money to pay you back, (2) if they've been trustworthy in the past, and (3) if they have something of value that you can seize should they be unable to pay you back.

Congratulations: in financial parlance, you've just been introduced to the concepts of income, creditworthiness, and collateral. Let's look at each one and how it affects what you can afford.

1. **Do you make enough to pay the lender back?** Your lender will want to know not only how much money you have but how much you will likely make over the next thirty years. Also, what are your other debts? Do you owe money for college loans or credit card charges? Do you have any other as-

sets? Investments such as stocks or mutual funds and personal property such as a boat or car are also considered in figuring out how much a bank will lend you.

The lender will also plug your income numbers into a couple of formulas: the front-end ratio (having to do with your mortgage payments) and the back-end ratio (having to do with your debt).

Let's say your gross income is $4,000 a month and you have $400 a month in debt payments. The rule of thumb is that the bank will allow you to pay 29 percent of your gross income toward your mortgage payment every month. This is known as the front-end ratio. In this example, 29 percent of $4,000 is just under $1,200 a month—so they'll reason that you can put $1,200 toward your mortgage payment.

Your debt ratio, or back-end ratio, on the other hand, is $400/$4,000, or 10 percent. That's not bad. They don't want more than 41 percent of your gross income going to total debt—mortgage, credit card interest, and other payments—and in this case you'd be paying 39 percent toward that purpose. (These ratios can vary somewhat; the ones given here are just examples.)

2. **Have you been trustworthy in the past?** What is your credit rating? The three major credit reporting agencies are Experian, Equifax, and Trans-Union. You can request credit reports individually from each agency—or order one from all three agencies in one easy step at www.truecredit.com.

3. **Do you have any collateral?** The house you buy will generally be considered the collateral for your mortgage. As a result, in case you can't repay the loan, the bank can decide to do something really nasty: foreclose on the mortgage and repossess the house. You will find yourself out on the street—with your dog, your La-Z-Boy, your collection of unpublished poetry, a couple of suitcases, and your toiletry kit. Your house now belongs to the bank, and it is unlikely that anyone will ever loan you money again. Hot tip: *Avoid this scenario at all costs.*

SEEK THE BANK'S APPROVAL

You've found the perfect neighborhood, the cutest little house with the greatest backyard, and you think you can afford it. It has everything you ever wanted. You've spent a couple hundred hours finding your little treasure, you've spent a couple hundred dollars on fees and property inspections, and you have scrounged up your courage to make an offer. Your heart is so set on it that you've even started telling your friends your new address.

Then the bank calls. Your mortgage application has been denied.

Arrrghhh!

How could you have saved yourself from this heartache? With a preapproval for a mortgage. In fact, we heartily recommend you get one before you go any further in the home-finding process.

What is preapproval? It's basically a quick-and-dirty look at your creditworthiness by a lending institution. With a preapproval or prequalification letter in your hand, you're immediately in a stronger negotiating position with any seller.

There are two types of "pre" letters:

- **Prequalification** is an informal agreement between you and your lender. The bank gives its opinion on how much it thinks it will be able to lend to you based on information that you have provided to it. Your bank doesn't do any background checks at this point. It relies solely on your portraying an accurate picture of your circumstances. Because this is more like a friendly handshake, the lender can decide not to give you the loan if it later finds out that you have been less than candid. There is no charge to do this, and you are under no obligation to get a mortgage with this lender if you find a better deal later.

- **Preapproval** is more serious. The bank will actually check your credit history, employment information, assets, and liabilities. The only thing it won't check is the property that you plan to buy, because, of course, you haven't found it yet! If you're concerned that you might not qualify for a mortgage, we highly recommend that you go for preapproval. It will put your mind at ease while you search for your new home and make the entire experience much less worrisome. Some lenders charge for a preapproval. If you decide to go with one that charges for this service, make sure you're really going to buy a house soon or you'll just be throwing money away.

ANATOMY OF A MORTGAGE

What exactly is a mortgage? Simply put, it's a loan from a financial institution to you. In return, you pay interest on the amount loaned. The lender also has first dibs on your house in case you neglect to pay back the loan.

Francophiles and wordsmiths will recognize the root word "mort" in there. No, that's not your Uncle Mort; that's the French word for "dead." The idea is that you're going to kill off that loan by paying back the money you borrowed. You amortize the loan over time. Yes, it's a slow death, but it must be carried out.

A loan has three facets:

1. **Size: How many dollars you need to borrow.** This one is self-explanatory (although there are choices you can make about the down payment, as we've mentioned earlier).

2. **Term: How long it will take to pay off the loan.** The most common term for a fixed-rate mortgage is thirty years, with fifteen years the next most common.

A thirty-year-versus-fifteen-year mortgage debate rages, but one thing is sure: You will pay much more interest over the term of the loan (in most cases twice as much) on a thirty-year mortgage. On the flip side, a thirty-year mortgage offers lower monthly payments. You'll be getting a tax write-off for the interest portion of your payments, which could be substantial. On the other hand, in the first fifteen years of your loan, you will be un-Foolishly lining someone else's pocket with interest, while not building up significant principal for yourself.

Example: Let's say you buy a $150,000 home. You put down 20 percent, or $30,000, which leaves you $120,000 to finance. If you get a thirty-year loan at 8.5 percent, your payments will be $922.70. After five years of payments, your balance owed will be $114,588. If, on the other hand, you obtain a fifteen-year mortgage at 8 percent (rates are lower with shorter-term loans), your payments will be $1,146 ($224 more each month). After five years in this loan, however, your balance owed will be only $94,000. That's quite a difference when it comes time to sell.

In sum, a thirty-year loan is good for long-term stability. If you can afford a fifteen-year mortgage, you will build principal faster. Another option would be to pay what would be equal to the fifteen-year payment on a thirty-year loan, enabling you to pay it off in about fifteen years (slightly longer due to the higher interest rate), while still having the ability to make the lower payment should money problems arise.

3. **Rate: The charge for borrowing the money.** Your mortgage lender will charge you a certain amount of interest for using its money. That rate of interest can be fixed (the rate never changes), variable (the rate fluctuates according to prevailing interest rates), or combination of the two (the rate is fixed for a few years, then adjusts).

Which is better? Choose a fixed-rate mortgage if you like the stability of knowing exactly how much you'll pay each month. Adjustable-rate mortgages (a.k.a. ARMs) often begin at a rate (otherwise known as the teaser rate) that is generally a couple of percentage points below the market rate. There is also an upward limit above which the interest rate isn't allowed to go—this is called the cap. If your teaser rate is 4 percent and you have a five-point cap, the highest your interest rate can go is 9 percent. Also, the amount that the interest rate can rise each year is limited, usually to one or two percentage points per year.

If you're considering an ARM, think about the worst-case scenario: What if interest rates go up, and your ARM adjusts to its maximum? What will that maximum be, and when will it kick in? Will you be able to afford the payments?

LOSING, OR AVOIDING, PMI

Over the years, private mortgage insurance will cost you thousands of dollars. However, you don't have to pay it forever. You can usually cancel it after you have at least 20 percent equity in the home. (Contact your loan servicer to find out the procedure for doing this.) Typically, you'll be required to get an appraisal on the property. This will cost money—about a few hundred dollars—but could be worth it in the long run.

Some lenders may have fancy ways to allow you to avoid PMI while still putting down less than 20 percent. For example, they might offer you a second-tier mortgage to make up the difference. The interest on the second loan will be higher, but it will be tax deductible, whereas PMI is not. As always, it pays to do your homework and explore as many options with your lender as you can.

WHERE CAN YOU GET A MORTGAGE?

Regardless of what type of mortgage you're interested in, you also need to figure out where you'll get it from: a bank or a mortgage broker.

Mortgages are offered by several types of lenders. You can get a loan from a mortgage broker, a mortgage banker, a bank, a credit union, or a savings and loan. In most cases, the lender earns origination fees and, in the case of a mortgage broker, a broker's fee. The servicer is the company where you, the borrower, make your payment. Here's a breakdown of the major mortgage providers.

• **Mortgage brokers.** Mortgage brokers are much like independent insurance agents. They have access to many lenders and many different programs. In some cases, especially when your credit history is flawed, a mortgage broker can find funding for you. Mortgage brokers are compensated on commission, and they will have higher closing fees. Brokers are sometimes compensated by the lenders.

- **Banks and mortgage bankers.** The term "mortgage banker" can refer either to a loan officer who works at a bank or to the bank itself. A mortgage banker generally sells the underlying loan to an investor but continues to service the loan. One place to check is your local bank. This can result in a reasonably good deal for the qualified customer. In many other cases, the bank will not have a program that fits your needs, or you may fall outside the guidelines of its lending ability. Once you have visited your bank, look in the real estate section of your local paper for the rates at other banks or visit www.bankrate.com. It's a good idea to start the legwork on your own before bringing in a mortgage broker, so that you'll (1) avoid the hard sell from the get-go, and (2) have a better idea of what you could find on your own.

- **The Internet.** The Web lets you comparison shop right from the comfort of your own computer. Not only that, but you don't have to hunt down a hundred different banks—certain aggregator sites have done that for you. As we mentioned before, www.bankrate.com has a good search engine that can help you shop for the lowest mortgage rates around the country. There are others out there, too, so just fire up a search engine and input "mortgage rate comparison" to see what pops up. By the way, there is no reason why you shouldn't take out a loan with a bank in California if you live in Virginia, or vice versa.

- **Real estate agents.** You might well find the cheapest rates in town (or in the country) on the Internet. If, however, you end up working with a real estate agent, you might feel more secure with a lender that has a relationship with your agent.

SHOULD YOU BORROW TENS OF THOUSANDS OF DOLLARS OVER THE WEB?

How does shopping for a mortgage online differ from getting one from a bank? Let us count the ways . . .

Advantages

1. You can comparison-shop several loans at once, as we have noted before. This is similar to the services a mortgage broker might offer you. In addition, because the information is on the Internet and laid out neatly, you can more easily compare apples to apples. This is more difficult when you're going from bank loan officer A to bank loan officer B.

2. You can do it whenever you want, even in the dead of night (should you be so inclined). Since you have a wide range to choose from, you're not limited by the mortgages from one particular bank.

3. You may like the impersonal nature of the inquiry: you don't have to go and stare across the table at a loan officer.

Disadvantages

1. You don't get to go and stare across the table at a loan officer. That is, you may find it a bit impersonal for your taste.

2. Similarly, if you're not comfortable using the Web, you probably won't be comfortable exploring mortgages by clicking hither and yon. If need be, though, we suggest you find someone who's Web-savvy to give you a hand—if only to arm yourself with information for when you go in to your local bank or mortgage broker's office. If you're afraid of security or identity theft, simply use a made-up name when getting information.

3. If you have special circumstances, either related to you personally or to the specific kind of

loan you might need to have tailor-made, you're probably better off speaking to a real live human being. Keep in mind, though, that most online loan aggregators have personal representatives who will work with you over the phone. It's just that they may not be as experienced in more complicated loan situations.

LENDER INFORMATION

Make copies of the list below and fill it out each time you talk to a potential mortgage lender. Then, when you've talked to a few or checked 'em out online, compare:

Your down payment	$
Amount of loan	$
Lending institution	
Contact person	
Telephone number or Web site	
Interest rate	
Is interest calculated annually or semiannually?	
Amortization period	
Term of loan	
Fixed or ARM?	
Monthly payment	$
Prepayment penalties	$
Fees	$

PAYING FOR COLLEGE

In this book, we will focus mostly on how to save for college. We will mention some tips concerning financial aid, getting scholarships, and taxes. Some

will serve you well if you're saving up for private school or graduate school. But we'll predominantly be concerned with how sending your bundle of joy to college in a few years should affect your monthly spending now.

HOW MUCH IS THAT DIPLOMA IN THE WINDOW?

You've probably read about the rising costs of a college education and that you'll have to forgo a few of life's luxuries (such as food) to send Junior to school. Well, yes . . . and no. Here's some information from the College Board (the nonprofit association of educational institutions that is best known for creating the SAT):

The Bad News

• Educational costs have risen far more quickly than the rate of inflation for several years.

• For the 2001–2002 academic year, the average cost of a four-year private education was $17,123 (up 5.5 percent from the previous year). In the year 2008 it is estimated that the average cost will rise to $25,747.

• For the 2001–2002 academic year, the average cost of a four-year public education was $3,754 (up 7.7 percent from the previous year). In the year 2008 it is estimated that the average cost will be $5,645.

The Good News

• There is more than $74 billion worth of financial aid available. That's up from less than $40 billion in 1990.

• Because of all that financial aid, what students actually pay is very different from a school's stated price tag. More than 40 percent of students attending four-year schools pay less than $4,000 a year for tuition and fees, and almost 70 percent of students attending four-year schools pay less than $8,000.

- The average college graduate earns 81 percent more than the average high school graduate. That gap could add up to $1,000,000 over a lifetime.

HOW MUCH WILL IT COST?

That depends on the school your kid chooses and the financial aid he or she is awarded. Let's look at those two factors.

The School

As noted previously, a private college education costs about five times as much as an education at a public university. Is an Ivy League education better than a degree from State U.?

The debate over whether an education at an elite school translates into higher lifetime earnings rages on. Some studies have claimed that the cost of a highly selective and challenging school is justified by higher earnings. Others have found flaws in those studies' methodology. (Academic debate—don't you love it?)

One of the best studies looked at students who were accepted at prestigious schools but chose to go somewhere else and compared them to students who did attend Ivy League schools (so the study was looking at students with the same qualifications). The choice of school didn't affect earnings at all except for those at the low end of the income scale. Students from lower-income families saw a small increase in lifetime earnings if they attended a more prestigious school, presumably because of better social networking opportunities. For most students, however, there was no difference.

An interesting exercise is to have your child interview five to ten adults he or she admires, asking where they went to college and how they think their college choice made a difference in their careers.

Your child might also look over the following lists of people and the schools they attended, to see that successful people have gone to all kinds of schools:

PUBLIC SCHOOLS

Warren Buffett	University of Nebraska
Bill Cosby	Temple University
Stephen King	University of Maine
David Letterman	Ball State University
Steven Spielberg	California State College
Oprah Winfrey	Tennessee State University

PRIVATE SCHOOLS

Madeleine Albright	Wellesley College
Carly Fiorina	Stanford University
Ruth Bader Ginsburg	Cornell University
Steve Jobs	Reed College
Denzel Washington	Fordham University
Tiger Woods	Stanford University

So it looks as though you *can* go to a public school and still become successful, especially if you want to build an entertainment empire or be a billionaire investor (like Warren Buffett, who's pretty entertaining as well).

If the fruit of your loins has a career firmly in mind, perhaps he or she should first consider the top schools in that field. In many cases, the best schools are public schools. If you can get the best training for a public college price, what a deal!

FINANCIAL AID

The good news is that most college students receive some form of financial aid. The not-so-good news is that most of that financial aid is in the form of loans. Most financial professionals will tell you that taking on debt in order to earn a degree is a prudent move, and in general we agree. (Remember: College grads earn 81 percent more than their high school grad peers.) However, those loans will be a burden on your kid as she starts off her professional career. Here's an excerpt from an e-mail we received at the Fool:

A friend of my wife's is a schoolteacher and makes about $30,000 a year. She is a single mom with two kids, 6 and 2. Her youngest is profoundly deaf and will, of course, need extra financial support throughout his life. Her problem is that she has about $40,000 in college loans that are just beginning to come due. She is realizing that she will never be able to save anything and she will be burdened with these payments for a long time. Of course a house, decent car, etc., will also be out of her reach.

It's an extreme example, to be sure, but it does demonstrate how much of a burden school loans can be.

So should you eschew school loans? Absolutely not. If it's the only way your progeny will be able to go to college, a loan could be a great investment. And it's not such a bad idea to ask kids to be responsible for financing a portion of their education, whether through work-study programs, scholarships, or school loans. The point is that taking on any form of debt should never be done lightly. If the difference between going to one school over another means assuming tens of thousands of dollars' worth of loans, factor that prominently into your decision process.

SO HOW MUCH WILL IT *REALLY* COST?

Following are two tables that project the annual costs of attending a college or university. One table projects just the increases in tuition; the other tuition *and* room and board. Here is how we came up with these tables:

• We started with the average public school and private school tuitions for the 2001–2002 school year. Then, in the middle, we started with a "reasonable target" of $8,000. Why? Because 70 per-

COLLEGE COSTS: TUITION ONLY

Year	In-State Public University	Reasonable Target	Private University
2001	$3,754	$8,000	$17,123
2002	3,979	8,480	18,150
2003	4,218	8,989	19,239
2004	4,471	9,528	20,394
2005	4,739	10,100	21,617
2006	5,024	10,706	22,914
2007	5,325	11,348	24,289
2008	5,645	12,029	25,747
2009	5,983	12,751	27,291
2010	6,342	13,516	28,929
2011	6,723	14,327	30,665
2012	7,126	15,186	32,505
2013	7,554	16,098	34,455
2014	8,007	17,063	36,522
2015	8,487	18,087	38,713
2016	8,997	19,172	41,036
2017	9,536	20,323	43,498
2018	10,109	21,542	46,108
2019	10,715	22,835	48,875
2020	11,358	24,205	51,807
2021	12,040	25,657	54,916
2022	12,762	27,197	58,211
2023	13,528	28,828	61,703
2024	14,339	30,558	65,406
2025	15,200	32,391	69,330
2026	16,112	34,335	73,490
2027	17,078	36,395	77,899
2028	18,103	38,579	82,573
2029	19,189	40,893	87,527
2030	20,341	43,347	92,779

COLLEGE COSTS: TUITION, ROOM, AND BOARD

Year	In-State Public University	Reasonable Target	Private University
2001	$11,976	$16,000	$26,070
2002	12,695	16,960	27,634
2003	13,456	17,978	29,292
2004	14,264	19,056	31,050
2005	15,119	20,200	32,913
2006	16,027	21,412	34,888
2007	16,988	22,696	36,981
2008	18,007	24,058	39,200
2009	19,088	25,502	41,552
2010	20,233	27,032	44,045
2011	21,447	28,654	46,687
2012	22,734	30,373	49,489
2013	24,098	32,195	52,458
2014	25,544	34,127	55,605
2015	27,077	36,174	58,942
2016	28,701	38,345	62,478
2017	30,423	40,646	66,227
2018	32,249	43,084	70,201
2019	34,184	45,669	74,413
2020	36,235	48,410	78,877
2021	38,409	51,314	83,610
2022	40,713	54,393	88,627
2023	43,156	57,657	93,944
2024	45,745	61,116	99,581
2025	48,490	64,783	105,556
2026	51,399	68,670	111,889
2027	54,483	72,790	118,602
2028	57,752	77,158	125,719
2029	61,218	81,787	133,262
2030	64,891	86,694	141,257

cent of college students paid $8,000 or less for tuition for the 2001–2002 school year. So we felt that was a fair target. However, if you've already decided the public-versus-private dilemma, feel free to use those numbers. We essentially followed the same procedure for room and board.

• Since 1971, college costs have grown an average of 7.7 percent a year. However, since that figure includes the high-inflation 1970s and early 1980s, we assumed that college costs will grow 6 percent a year.

Here's how to figure out a monthly savings target for future college expenses:

1. Add up the costs for the four years your child will be in college.

2. Using that number, an expected rate of return on your savings, and the number of years until Junior enrolls, consult the Return Factor table on page 113.

3. Fall on the floor.

DON'T GET SCARED OUT OF SAVING

Sometimes when people see such astronomical price tags attached to a college degree, they . . . do nothing. They figure there's no way to save that much without shortchanging other goals, so they cross their fingers and hope Albert Jr. will win large scholarships or join an antieducation cult.

Don't fall into this trap. If you start soon enough, you can have a large chunk of higher education money when your pride and joy is ready to enroll in P.U. If as soon as their kid is born, a couple starts investing $100 a month and earns 8 percent per year, they'll have almost $50,000 in eighteen years (assuming they utilize a tax-friendly savings vehicle, which we'll discuss presently). That's $50,000 less that you or your kid will have to borrow.

Whatever you do, do whatever you can. Really, every little bit helps.

UNCLE SAM WANTS YOUR KID TO GO TO COLLEGE

The government recognizes the benefits of an educated public and the fact that the price of an education can be mighty steep. Therefore, good ole Uncle Sam is willing to give you some tax breaks to offset those high costs. These breaks come in the form of tax-friendly savings vehicles and in the form of tax deductions and credits. Let's start with the former—where to put your college savings.

Coverdell Education Savings Accounts

Our friend the Education IRA has recently been given a new moniker: "Coverdell Education Savings Account" (or Coverdell ESA). This was done in memory of the late Senator Paul Coverdell, Republican of Georgia, when someone realized that the Education IRA had nothing to do with retirement; so why call it an IRA?

Any individual may contribute a maximum of $2,000 a year to a Coverdell ESA for the benefit of any person under age eighteen. But the contribution limit is phased out incrementally for contributors with a modified adjusted gross income between $95,000 and $110,000 for single persons and between $190,000 and $220,000 for married people filing jointly. In other words, if you're married and file jointly and you make $205,000 a year (halfway between $190,000 and $220,000), you will be able to contribute only $1,000 because that is half of the normal limit. You have until the due date of your tax return (not including extensions) to make that contribution and still have it apply to the previous year.

But if you exceed those income limits, don't worry. Just give the money to the kid and let him open the Coverdell ESA himself. For example, let's say Heather, a single mom, wants to establish a Coverdell ESA for her favorite little guy, Spanky. But Heather's AGI is $130,000. Her maximum contribution to little Spanky's Coverdell ESA would be . . . ahem . . . *zero*, because of the income limitation rules. But there is no reason why

Heather can't make a $2,000 gift to Spanky, who can then open his own Coverdell ESA with $2,000, since he's well under the income limitations (assuming his lemonade stand doesn't rake in more than $95,000 a year). It's as simple as calling up a discount broker and asking it to send you the proper forms to fill out.

Virtually all reasonable expenses for both higher education and elementary/secondary education will be eligible for the tax-free treatment afforded Coverdell ESA distributions. Under the new law, "qualified elementary and secondary education expenses" are defined as:

- Expenses for tuition, fees, academic tutoring, special needs services (in the case of a special needs child), books, supplies, and other equipment that are incurred in connection with enrollment or attendance of the child as an elementary or secondary school student at a public, private, or religious school.

- Expenses for room and board, uniforms, transportation, and supplementary items and services (including extended day programs) that are required by a public, private, or religious school.

- Expenses for the purchase of any computer technology or equipment or for Internet access and related services if the technology, equipment, or services are to be used by the child and the child's family during any of the years that the child is in school. But there is a specific exclusion for any computer software designed for sports, games, or hobbies unless the software is educational in nature.

If you invest your Coverdell ESA in stocks or mutual funds, you might be in for a very unpleasant surprise. Most brokers and mutual fund companies charge an annual fee to maintain a Coverdell ESA account. That fee could be as much as $35. If you invest $2,000, a $35 administration fee is almost equivalent to a 2 percent charge. Ouch! That means that you'll have to make at least a 2 percent return on your contribution just to break even. Depressed yet? Don't be. There's a (relatively) new way of saving for college . . .

529 Plans

Another tax-smart way to fund a college education is through a Qualified Tuition Program (QTP). You may also know this kind of plan as a "Section 529" plan (so called because these plans are discussed in Section 529 of the Internal Revenue Code) or even as a Qualified State Tuition Program (QSTP). No matter what you call it, a rose by any other name is still a rose. And if you're concerned about saving for college, this might be the most beautiful rose that you've ever sniffed.

529 plans come in two aromas: prepaid tuition plans and college savings plans. Prepaid tuition plans are just what they sound like. Your investment buys a given number of tuition credits at a public college or university at today's prices. Thus, regardless of what increases occur in tuition rates in the future, the number of quarters/semesters/years purchased today is guaranteed for the future. The state agrees to pay those costs later at whatever price that might be.

College savings plans are basically investment programs. Unlike a prepaid tuition plan, a college savings plan does not lock in future tuition costs at today's prices. Instead, it affords an opportunity for investments to grow through the years at rates that equal—or better yet, exceed—future inflationary increases in college costs.

Here's the real kicker: Distributions used to pay for qualified higher education expenses will be completely tax free. Yowza! You read that right. Distributions from a qualified tuition program will be completely excluded from income as long as that distribution is used to pay for qualified higher education expenses (generally tuition, fees, books, supplies, and equipment required for the enrollment or attendance of the student at an eligible institution). If the distributions exceed the qualified higher education expenses, a portion of the distribution must be included in your taxable gross income.

(Note: The law that made distributions from a 529 plan tax free will "sunset" in 2010 unless Congress chooses to extend the law. In other words, if Congress does nothing, distributions after 2010 will not be tax free, but the assets will still grow tax deferred. Will Congress extend the law? We don't know, but permitting the law to sunset will not garner many votes.)

Anyone may contribute to a Section 529 plan for the benefit of a child. While the contribution is not deductible for federal income tax purposes, a number of states do permit a deduction for state income tax purposes. Earnings are allowed to accumulate untaxed within the account until used to pay for the costs of the child's higher education.

You don't even necessarily have to live in the state of the plan that you choose. You could live in New Mexico and contribute to a plan based in Maine for your grandchild who lives in Oregon and who ends up going to college in Michigan.

The 529 plans allow you to sock away huge sums of money—much more than $200,000 in some cases—versus the annual $2,000 Coverdell ESA contribution. Most of these plans have no age or income limitations, so higher-bracket taxpayers can also participate. Heck, if you're thinking of going back to school, you can even set up a 529 plan for yourself.

Unlike a custodial account, the assets in a 529 plan remain in your control. With only a few exceptions, your kids can't grab the money and run off to Europe when they reach the age of majority. Instead, you're in complete control. You decide when distributions are made and what the funds will be used for.

ESTATE PLANNING, ANYONE?

There are some great estate-planning aspects, since making a large contribution to a 529 plan reduces your taxable estate much more quickly than the $11,000 annual gift exclusion. That's because you can make a substantial gift in one year and treat it as if it had been made over a five-year period. That means that you could fund your child's 529 plan with $55,000 ($110,000 for couples) and have no gift tax problems because the gift would be considered to be $11,000 ($22,000 for couples) annually made over a five-year period. (Note that the annual gift exclusion will be adjusted for inflation, so you'll be able to contribute more, without paying gift taxes, as the years go on.)

POTENTIAL PITFALLS

As with most things, you've gotta take the good with the bad, and there are some minor drawbacks to 529 plans. First, if you remove the earnings from the 529 plan and decide not to use them for higher education expenses, not only will you have to pay taxes on those earnings, but you'll get zapped with a 10 percent penalty. That being the case, many folks are concerned that if their child decides to skip college, there will be a tax and penalty problem. However, you are able to change beneficiaries to a 529 plan without penalty. So if your older child decides not to attend college, you can transfer the 529 plan account to a new beneficiary who is related to the old beneficiary.

Note that the tax-free rollover treatment won't apply to any transfer that occurs within twelve months from the date of any other transfer to a QTP for the benefit of the same child or beneficiary. If you have more than one rollover within a twelve-month period, the second one will be deemed a taxable distribution. But if you make a rollover *and* change the beneficiary, the twelve-month rules don't apply.

Additionally, the funds in the 529 plan account are handled by the 529 plan administrators and not by you, though you often have a choice among investment options.

IS THAT ALL THERE IS?

Far from it. The information above only scratches the surface. You have a cornucopia of options when dealing with 529 plans. Would you like to

COLLEGE SAVINGS PLANS COMPARISON CHART

	COVERDELL ESA	529: PREPAID TUITION	529: SAVINGS PLAN
Highlights	An investment account available to contributors who earn less than $110K (for single filers) and $220K (for joint filers)	Contributions today are guaranteed to cover tuition costs in the future	A state-sponsored investment account for the benefit of anyone—your child, your cousin, your neighbor, yourself
Offered by . . .	Brokerages, mutual fund companies, banks	States	States (usually with help from financial services companies)
Contribution limit	$2,000 per student per year	Depends on plan and age of student	Depends on plan—varies from $100,000 to $305,000
Tax treatment of withdrawals	Tax-free if used for qualified expenses	Tax-free if used for qualified expenses	Tax-free if used for qualified expenses
Qualified expenses	Tuition, room, board, fees, supplies, and special needs related to the attendance of a qualified elementary, secondary, or post-secondary institution	Tuition at a college within the plan (some plans will also cover room and board)	Tuition, fees, room, and board at qualified higher education institutions

	COVERDELL ESA	529: PREPAID TUITION	529: SAVINGS PLAN
Tax-deductibility	None	Some states allow contributions to be partially or completely deductible	Some states allow contributions to be partially or completely deductible
Investment flexibility	Assets can be invested in stocks, bonds, mutual funds, and cash equivalents. Investments can be bought and sold as often as desired	Plan administrators invest all assets	Assets are professionally managed. Depending on the plan, participants can choose from 2 to almost 30 mutual fund–type investments. Investment choice may be changed once every 12 months
Ability to transfer account	Account may be transferred to other brokerage or mutual fund, or to a 529 plan, subject to fees and penalties	Depends on plan	May transfer to another 529 plan once every 12 months
Interaction with Hope and Lifetime Learning Credits	Credits can be claimed in the same year as tax-free withdrawal provided that the distribution is not used for the same expenses for which a credit is claimed	Credits can be claimed in the same year as tax-free withdrawal provided that the distribution is not used for the same expenses for which a credit is claimed	Credits can be claimed in the same year as tax-free withdrawal provided that the distribution is not used for the same expenses for which a credit is claimed
Effect on financial aid	Considered to be an asset of the student, which means a large portion of the assets will be considered in the financial aid calculation	Considered to be the student's resource and thus reduces financial aid dollar-for-dollar	Assets are considered to be property of the account owner, which—unless the owner is also the beneficiary—means only a small portion of the assets will be considered in the financial aid calculation
Control of the account	In most states, account assets become property of the student at age 18	In most states, control of account will always remain with contributor	In most states, control of account will always remain with contributor
Must use funds by . . .	Age 30	Varies by plan	Varies by plan
Assignability to other relatives	Immediate family, including cousins, step-relatives, and in-laws	Immediate family, including cousins, step-relatives, and in-laws	Immediate family, including cousins, step-relatives, and in-laws
Penalty for nonqualified withdrawals	Earnings are taxed as ordinary income to contributor, plus a 10% penalty	Earnings are taxed as ordinary income to contributor, plus a 10% penalty	Earnings are taxed as ordinary income to contributor, plus a 10% penalty
Contribution deadline	Tax-filing deadline for the year of the contribution	Depends on the plan	Depends on the plan

learn more about them? Then go directly to www.Fool.com/csc or www.savingforcollege.com.

WHAT TO DO WHEN YOU START LATE

So you haven't saved enough to pay for your kid's college? Well, if it's any consolation, you're not alone. A study by Sallie Mae, the country's largest source of funds for higher education, found that parents of high schoolers applying for college had saved less than half of what they needed to cover their expected expenses. What's more, *one in five* hadn't saved anything at all.

So what's a Foolish mom and dad to do? Well, it's never too late to get smart.

• **Make sure Junior is really ready to go to college.** An astounding 38 percent of all college students quit school for at least one semester before the end of their sophomore year. Before plunking down (or borrowing) $10,000, make sure that this is really something your child wants. A year off in the real world, waiting tables or delivering pizza, may be just the ticket to convince him that college might be worth it after all. Also, if he is expelled from school for academic reasons, it will be very difficult to get more financial aid. And you have to start paying those loans back right away.

• **Choose a cheaper school.** Weigh carefully the true benefits of a private school against the cost savings offered by a larger state school. A college degree is an investment. Will a psychology degree from Snooty U. really be more valuable than a psychology degree from State U.? Will it be worth taking on six more years of repaying debt to pay for it? Only you and your child can answer that. But the burden of debt after school is a compelling argument.

• **Choose a school close to home.** As an in-state student at a public institution, your child will not only pay a reduced tuition but will also probably be eligible for financial aid earmarked for locals.

Also, travel expenses and long-distance phone bills add up, especially during the first year, when homesickness may be more pronounced than later (when your kid realizes that he doesn't really miss you that much after all).

• **Think creatively.** Why shouldn't your child go to a community college for the first year to get the more generalized courses out of the way at cost savings of 50 percent? Or take some classes online? Hundreds of colleges and universities now offer classes over the Internet, and most charge in-state tuition whether you're a resident of that state or not.

• **Look for co-op/intern programs.** Many schools offer co-op programs in which Junior can go to school for a semester and then work in his field for a semester. It may take him a little longer to finish his degree, but when he gets out he'll have experience in what he studied. He'll also have some money in his pocket and possibly a job offer from the company where he interned.

FINANCIAL AID TIPS

• **Don't sell any securities for a profit in the year before you apply for aid.** Any profits you make from sales of securities will be counted toward your income, the first item that goes into determining need on financial aid forms.

• **Reduce your income as much as possible.** If you have losses from a business venture gone wrong, now is the time to take them. Reducing your income will help increase your eligibility for financial aid.

• **Have your child classified as "independent."** The good news is that your child will be judged on his own savings and income when the school assesses the need for financial aid. The bad news is that you won't be able to claim him as a dependent for tax purposes anymore and he'll have to fend for himself for a year before the benefits of this strategy kick in.

- **Look for unorthodox sources of scholarships.** Millions of dollars in scholarships are given away each year to deserving students. The problem is that everyone is vying for the same scholarships. Look for the out-of-the-way treasures. Find out if any fraternal societies or religious groups that you belong to offer scholarships.

Student Loan Interest Deduction

If your income is below $65,000 for single taxpayers or $130,000 for married folks, you can deduct from your federal income tax the interest you pay on your school loan. And this is an "above-the-line" deduction; that is, you don't have to itemize your deductions in order to take a deduction for student loan interest paid. So if you qualify otherwise, you can claim the student loan interest deduction even if you use the standard deduction.

Higher Education Expense Deduction

This allows for a deduction of up to $3,000 for qualified higher education expenses that you pay for yourself, your spouse, or your family members. This $3,000 deduction comes into play in 2002 and 2003. In 2004 and 2005, the deduction will be increased to $4,000. But as with virtually all of the other education provisions, there are income limitations. You can kiss this deduction good-bye if your income exceeds $65,000 ($130,000 for marrieds filing jointly) in 2002 and 2003. Those income limitations will increase to $80,000 ($160,000 for marrieds filing jointly) in 2004 and 2005.

What will happen in 2006? Unless legislation is passed to make this provision in the law permanent, it will be automatically repealed at the end of the 2005 tax year. You'll have to be careful if you plan to use this new deduction, since there are restrictive provisions that will not allow for the deduction if you also claim a Hope or Lifetime Learning Credit in the same year for the same student. There are also restrictions if you take distributions from a Qualified Tuition Plan. So make sure that you clearly understand the rules and don't trip yourself up.

Employer-Provided Education Assistance

Your employer can pay for up to $5,250 of your qualified education expenses (undergraduate or postgraduate education) and you don't have to treat any of the payments as compensation or taxable income.

The Hope Scholarship and Lifetime Learning Credits

Two major education provisions introduced by the 1997 Taxpayer Relief Act are the Hope Scholarship Credit and the Lifetime Learning Credit.

The Hope credit may allow you to convert part of the higher education expenses you pay for yourself, your spouse, or your dependents into tax savings.

The maximum Hope credit a taxpayer may claim is $1,500 per year per student for the first two years of undergraduate education at an eligible educational institution. The credit equals the sum of:

- 100 percent of the first $1,000 of qualified tuition and related expenses paid, plus
- 50 percent of the next $1,000 of qualified tuition and related expenses paid

The maximum Hope credit amount will be adjusted for inflation beginning in 2002. Also, it's available for only the first two years of undergraduate education at an eligible educational institution. So this credit isn't for everybody.

While the Hope credit is available only to students in the first two years of postsecondary education, the Lifetime credit (as the name implies) is available to all qualified students for all qualified education, regardless of whether the education is taken for an advanced degree or not. In addition, there is no limit on the number of years for which the Lifetime credit can be claimed. (Woo hoo!)

The taxpayer may claim a Lifetime credit equal to 20 percent of up to $5,000 in qualifying tuition and related expenses. This credit applies to qualified expenses paid by the taxpayer for the taxpayer, his or her spouse, or any dependent. Therefore, the maximum Lifetime credit that may be claimed is $1,000 (20 percent of $5,000). Starting in 2003, the maximum amount of qualified tuition and expenses that may be taken into account in determining the Lifetime credit for a tax year will increase to $10,000. The maximum credit after 2002 will be $2,000 (20 percent of $10,000). You should know that these expense limits will not be indexed for inflation (at least not according to the way the law is currently written).

Those are the highlights of the tax-friendly ways of saving for college. There are many other technical issues embedded within each of the benefits, so if there is something you read that perks up your ears, make sure to get even more information on those specific changes and how they will affect you and your family.

BUYING A CAR

Here's our Foolish advice when it comes to buying a car:

Don't do it!

Yes! You read it here first, folks: a car-buying process that first counsels its readers *not* to buy a car! Utter Foolishness!

Why? Because, no matter what mystical incantations a car salesperson may whisper in your ear, *a car is not an investment.* Go ahead, say it with us—even if there are children in the room—all together now: A CAR IS NOT AN INVESTMENT!

Vehicles are *depreciating assets.* Yup, that's right: all that iron, glass, and plastic *loses value* over time.

How big a bite does this depreciation take? On average, cars (and trucks, too) lose more than 20 percent of their value in the first year. Some vehicles lose as much as 40 percent. The second year isn't much better, as they disintegrate another 15 percent or so in value.

If you pay $20,000 for a new car, after two years of driving it might be worth $13,000. Yes, ma'am, $7,000 has vaporized into the thin air of depreciation. That's $3,500 per year. Almost $300 a month! What if the $100,000 house you moved into just two years ago was now worth $65,000? How would that make you feel?

The average age of cars in the United States is somewhere between seven and eight years. Since most families have two or more of them, this means they end up buying one every three or four years.

From the foregoing issues comes our first really big piece of fully Foolish advice:

Don't do it!

Ask yourself these two questions each time you consider a vehicle purchase:

1. Do I really need a vehicle change?
2. Why?

Answer them truthfully, each time, and you will come away with a much better understanding of what your needs really are.

Sit down with a sheet of paper in front of you and write down that first question. "Do I really need a vehicle change?" Or could I just use an oil change? If you feel that you really do need a new car, write down the second question, "Why?" You might find that you have more than one answer. That's fine. In fact, keep asking yourself "Why?" until you run out of responses.

The choice to buy a car, of course, is up to you, so you're the one who ultimately has to judge whether your reasons are valid. However, here are what we think are good and not-as-good reasons for buying a car.

GOOD REASONS TO BUY A CAR

- Your current set of wheels is dead, kaput, finished (e.g., an accident has turned your leather-topped Cadillac into a convertible subcompact).
- Your current hot rod is unsafe beyond repair (e.g., your car is such an "antique" that it predates seat belts).
- There's a drastic change in the type of car you need (e.g., your Volkswagen Beetle won't accommodate your four kids).

NOT-SO-GOOD REASONS TO BUY A CAR

- You're bored with your current car.
- Everyone else in your neighborhood has a BMW.
- Your car needs $1,000 in repairs, and it's worth only $2,000.

That last one surprises some people. Why pour so much money into a car that has seen better days? Because you should be comparing the costs of repairs to the costs of replacing the car, not to the car's current value.

For example, let's say your trustworthy mechanic tells you that you can expect to pay $1,000 a year on your old beater for the next few years. Wow, you think, that's a lot of money to spend on a car that's been around since the Carter administration. But let's compare that to the cost of buying a $15,000 car and borrowing $13,000 of the cost at a 6 percent interest rate over thirty-six months (which translates into a monthly payment of $395). Let's compare those costs over three years.

	OLD CAR'S ANNUAL COST	NEW CAR'S ANNUAL COST	CUMULATIVE DIFFERENCE
Year 1	$1,000	$4,740	$3,740
Year 2	$1,000	$4,740	$7,480
Year 3	$1,000	$4,740	$11,220

At the three-year point, your payments on the new car stop, so the cumulative difference starts shrinking. But by putting off that purchase for three years, you would accumulate more than $11,000—even after paying $1,000 in repair bills each year. Even if you paid $2,000 in repair bills each year, you'd still come out ahead by $8,220. That's money that could be put toward other goals or saved up for when you eventually purchase a new car, at which time you would not have to borrow as much.

This assumes that your old jalopy can last another three years. Cars do eventually reach the point of no return. But if you can extend your car's life by a few years—and your kids can endure the shame of being seen in a pea green station wagon—you can save thousands of dollars.

IF YOU DO DECIDE TO BUY

If after all this you decide to boldly go where lots of others have gone before and buy a car, here's our Foolish strategy for navigating the shark-infested waters of the car-buying process: stay out of the water. That is to say, the best way to negotiate a new-vehicle deal is to stay out of dealerships.

Staying away keeps you in control of the negotiation process and gives you your most effective tool in new-car negotiations—the Foolish same-apple principle. You're going to pit the piranhas against one another!

You are going to accomplish this task by using your fax machine. If you don't have one, consider borrowing a friend's, or improvise by using e-mail or regular old snail mail.

1. **Get the fax numbers of all the dealers within a hundred miles of you** that sell your number one vehicle choice. If a fax number isn't listed, call the dealership and ask for the fleet manager's name and the fax number. The person who answers may say, "We don't have a fleet manager." Your response should be a polite "Oh, do you have a specific person who handles house sales?" If the person continues to claim ignorance, just ask for the sales

manager's name and fax number. It'll help you avoid some extra costs.

2. **Create a detailed listing of your vehicle on a single sheet of paper.** Work up a detailed list of the base vehicle and the options you're looking for.

You would include this with the letter faxed to the dealer. Don't just list the specific make, model, and year but an exact option package, sport package, radio, and wheel type. The permutations and combinations can be mind-boggling. If you're not sure you want a particular option, list it as an extra add-on that the dealer can quote or ignore. Often the dealer will throw one in for free in the hope that you'll go with his quote.

If color doesn't matter to you, then tell the dealer. Remember, an in-stock vehicle that meets your option goals will carry the lowest price. Color exactness may eliminate that low-price deal.

3. **Create a generic fax cover sheet**, on which you will introduce yourself and lay out your buying strategy to the various dealerships. We've created an example—a Foolish fax letter—to aid you in your fax-a-thon:

[date]

Dear [fleet manager's full name]:

I am looking to buy a new car this week. On the second page of this fax, please find a listing of the specific vehicle features that I am interested in having included with the vehicle when I make my purchase.

Over the next three days I'll be taking bids from any local dealers interested in my business. After selecting the most attractive bid, I will formally secure financing for purchase within one week.

If you bid, please include all costs, and itemize these costs specifically to the options that I have listed on the next page. The bid should also include an itemized listing of all other fees and tax liabilities, including dealership preparation fees, title

costs, and licensing fees. Any bid that is incomplete or not per the option listing will not be considered in my purchase decision. If you have an option package alternative or other changes, please list these as a separate bid and note the exact specifics of the changes in the bid.

I have not "shopped" your dealership in more than one year and have had no sales contact with any employees operating in the dealership's interest during that time. Because of this please consider this bid to be a "house sale." In addition to that, I will accept no bids after [time] on [date].

I thank you for your time and interest. If you choose to bid, please fax your fully itemized bids to [your first name] at (XXX) XXX-XXXX.

Again, thank you in advance for your time, and I look forward to doing business with you.

[Your signature]
[Your name printed here]

You may have noticed that we put "Dear ____:" at the top of our cover sheet. Why not just make it truly generic and put "Dear Sirs"? We've found that the more personal you make these inquiries, the more effective they will be. If you have the fleet manager's or the sales manager's name up top, he figures you're not "spamming" the entire marketplace, and when he sees your detailed vehicle listing on the second page, he knows you're a serious buyer. Nothing excites a sales manager as much as a serious buyer, so be personal when possible.

There are a couple of other items for the fax cover sheet: let the recipients know you're a serious buyer by saying "I'm looking to buy a new car this week." Also, since it's to your advantage to put a time limit on the bidding process (this helps prevent your inquiry from going to the bottom of the pile) you might add something such as "Over the next three days, I'll be taking bids." Make it a reasonable amount of time; if you say "I'll give you three hours to respond" then you're asking to have zero responses. Notice also the word "bid"—this lets the dealer know you're shopping your dream vehicle around town. Again, let the piranhas fight among themselves; there is nothing wrong with dangling a juicy leg of beef in the water!

4. **Review the faxed bids.** More than likely the fax bids will start rolling in after twenty-four hours or so. Some of these bids will not be bids at all; instead, they will be a nice little form letter inviting you to "Come on down" to the best dealership on the planet, where it will be happy to beat any bid you receive. Ignore these. It either doesn't have the vehicle you're looking for or it figures it can switch you or perform some other dealer prestidigitation on your wallet. Put these bids in your "No Way" folder, the perfect place to save them until you need some starter fuel for your fireplace.

As the real bids with real numbers start to come in, look each one over closely. Sometimes a dealer will leave off a thing or two from your model listing. Obviously, when it forgets to include a retractable sunroof and a trunk-mounted ten-CD changer, the price of the vehicle is going to be a few dollars lower. For any bid that deviates from the model listing, you should circle the problem areas in red and insert the bid into the "Possibly Redo" folder.

The bids that are exactly as you requested should be placed in your "Top Priority" folder. After the bidding period is over (don't accept any late bids), start with your "Top Priority" folder and line up all the bids by price, arranged from lowest (on top) to highest (on bottom). You may be amazed at the variations in these prices, particularly given the fact that they are all for the same type of car!

If one bid is significantly lower than all the others—and we mean *significantly* (such as 15 percent)—then, Fool, drop everything: your ship has come in! (Just make sure that all your specifications have been accounted for on the bid.) Get on the phone and call the nice people over at Car Sales by Tina, and tell them you'll be happy to accept the bid that they recently faxed to you. Be prepared to talk delivery and other paperwork, but when you finally get off the horn it'll be time to pat yourself on the back for a job well done. If you have a significant other, now's the time to demand that special something—a back rub, a belly dance, coupons redeemable for golf dates or kitchen cleanups, an all-expenses-paid trip to Aruba—you've just saved a pile of loot!

5. **Get ready for Round Two of faxes.** More often than not, you'll find yourself with a host of bids that are below MSRP but still some distance from what you think you should pay. If this is the case, then prepare for phase two of the Foolish Fax-a-thon. But first take a peek at your "Possibly Redo" folder. Perhaps by adding and subtracting the various extras or missed items you will find a bid for a more reasonable price. Send a second fax to this dealership asking it why they added or left off a particular option. Allow it an opportunity to requote the vehicle, making sure it complies with the model listing. Give it a shorter time period to rebid, say twenty-four hours; in the meantime create a second list of dealers within 100 to 200 miles.

For this second listing, use the same cover letter, only add in big letters, "LOWEST BID $ _____ from the first set of dealerships, CAN YOU BEAT THIS?" Be truthful here; put down the best price you've received, or use the low bid that had something missing but add in the invoice price of the missing option(s). You're hoping that one of the farther-out dealers has a vehicle that matches your dream car but has been on the lot for some time. It might discount the vehicle several hundred dollars below the "low bid" in order to move it off the lot. Getting $500 off your lowest bid is certainly worth the extra hundred-mile drive. (Of course, you'll have to weigh that savings against the possibility that you might have to return the car to the dealer for repairs.)

6. **Make a decision.** Eventually you have to stop the fax-a-thon and decide what you're going to do. If you're not comfortable with the bids you received, step back and reconsider—perhaps you've mistimed the market or you've miscalculated. Whatever the reason, it's best to reevaluate your fi-

nancial and "needs" issues before accepting any bids. On the other hand, if there are bids you're comfortable with, it's time to take the two best and start negotiating.

To do this, lay the best two bids out in front of you, call the second-highest bidder, and talk to the person who sent you the fax. Make a *firm* offer to buy the car at a price of, say, $250 below the lowest bid. If he or she accepts the bid, request that the dealer immediately fax such a bid to you and arrange for a paperwork session and a delivery time. If instead he or she counters with a slightly higher price, say thank you and immediately hang up. At this point your next move is to call the best-bid dealer and congratulate it on winning your business. Your job, Fool, is now nearly complete.

WHEN THIS METHOD DOESN'T WORK

There are circumstances in the vehicle retail market that from time to time align themselves to work against buyers. The fax-a-thon may come up short at the "low supply and heavy demand" end of the business. This tends to occur with new models, high-end (expensive) small-lot production vehicles, and models that aren't even on the market but have created a buzz via the automotive press and the automaker's publicity machine. Generally speaking, this applies to the sports car niche. If you determine you need a vehicle like this, be prepared to keep the dealer smiling, because the cash will be flowing from your wallet. Then again, it might be time to reconsider the "don't do it" advice we set forth earlier.

You may also have to go farther afield if you live in a remote location. You need ten or more unique dealerships bidding against one another for such a system to have a fighting chance.

Generally speaking, it is best to start your fax-a-thon about one week before the end of the month. Why? Well, most, but not all, dealer incentives and allotments are on a monthly basis, so dealerships are more eager to move inventory at the end of the month. Starting a week before the end of the month gives you the required time to perform the fax-a-thon while still allowing for the maximum use to your advantage of the inevitable pressure the regional sales manager is placing on the dealerships.

What about all those dealerships from which you received bids but that didn't win your business? You may receive follow-up faxes and phone calls. Let the other dealerships know that you've taken your business elsewhere. A simple one-page "Thank you for your time" fax should put the kibosh on the fax traffic. Just be sure to wait until your best offer is in the bag.

HOW ARE CARS PRICED?

The main thing to remember when you look over vehicle prices is that "MSRP" stands for "manufacturer's *suggested* retail price," and you should focus on the word "suggested."

It's far from the actual cost of the vehicle and, in most cases, is well above the price you should actually pay.

Here's how the system typically works. The manufacturer ships a bunch of Schnauzer 900XZs to the dealership. The dealership is billed at and pays the invoice price. Once a Schnauzer is sold, the manufacturer deposits a certain percentage of the vehicle price into a kitty for the dealer. This is the "holdback" percentage, which varies but is usually between 2 and 5 percent. You'll find the holdback percentage for any particular vehicle listed on many of the auto Web sites. (Here is a bunch of good Web sites: www.edmunds.com, www.autobytel.com, www.carpoint.msn.com, www.autoweb.com, www.autosite.com, www.thecarconnection.com.)

Regularly, perhaps once per quarter, the manufacturer clears out the kitty and sends the dealer a check. This holdback system permits the dealer to swear to you that he's paying a certain invoice price for the vehicle, while not mentioning that he gets a certain percentage of that price back. On a $20,000 car, a 3 percent holdback comes to $600—and it's an amount you don't have to surrender in full to the dealer.

There are additional incentives for dealers that you can learn about by doing a little digging online or in trade magazines such as *Automotive News*. As a very rough example, imagine that you're looking at a vehicle with an invoice price of $20,000 and an MSRP of $22,000. A dealer might tell you that he'll give it to you for just $20,500, fully $1,500 off the MSRP. But he might not mention that he's getting a $600 holdback, plus a special factory-to-dealer incentive of $1,000. (Some special dealer incentives amount to several thousand dollars.) In other words, the $20,000 car is really costing him $18,400 and he's asking $20,500 of you. Naturally, car salespeople have to earn a living, but that doesn't give anyone the right to speak half-truths.

With a bit of research under your belt before you approach a salesperson, you can negotiate a win-win result, with the dealer netting a modest profit and you not getting taken to the car wash.

YOUR BIT-BY-BIT BUDGET ENTRY

By now you know the drill. Now's the time to plug your big-ticket items into your Bit-by-Bit Budget. A few of these items may be the same as the goals you came up with in Chapter 1. Hey, at least you're consistent! Just transfer the duplicates to this part of your Bit-by-Bit Budget and carry on. (Just make sure you're not saving twice as much as you need for a goal!)

Again, use pencil. Later on, when you tally up all of your must-pay expenses, you'll come up with the amount left over to put toward these goals. By using some of the money-saving tips you learned in this chapter—and others—you'll be able to decrease the price of some of these big-ticket items and find more money in other parts of your budget to funnel toward them.

BIT-BY-BIT BUDGET

	Amount from Your Money Tracker Worksheet	Budgeted Amount	Month 1	Month 2	Month 3	Month 4	Month 5	Month 6
Big-Ticket Purchases:								
Goal 1:								
Goal 2:								
Goal 3:								

CHAPTER 8

INCOME TAXES

SIXTY-SECOND GUIDE TO INCOME TAXES

A glance at your paycheck will reveal that taxes take a huge bite out of your bacon. And we all know that preparing your income tax return can take a bite out of your April. Learning about the ways of the IRS can save you lots of money—and perhaps your sanity.

0:60 Know the operation.

To exploit the tax system to your advantage (legally, of course), you have to understand how the system works. Let's start with the basics.

0:49 Lay it on the tables.

Do you know what your tax bracket is? And do you know how it is used to determine your tax bill using those tables in the IRS tax booklets? We'll give you a hint: if you're in the 27 percent tax bracket, 27 cents of every dollar you make does *not* go to Uncle Sam.

0:37 Be a record holder.

To file an accurate tax return, you need to keep accurate records. Your auditor will appreciate it.

0:30 Deduct your due.

The IRS gives you plenty of opportunities to reduce your taxable income. We're sure you're a good citizen and loyal American, but there's no need to pay more taxes than necessary. You can take deductions for things such as charitable contributions, medical expenses, theft losses, foreign taxes paid, mortgage interest paid, and so on—if the expenses qualify.

0:19 Let Uncle Sam give you some credit.

Although tax deductions are great, tax credits are even better: They reduce your tax bill dollar for dollar. Make sure you get all the credit you deserve.

0:08 Know how to calculate capital gains.

Whenever you sell a qualifying asset for a profit, the government wants to share in your good fortune. But there's more to capital gains than the difference between the purchase price and the sale price.

• • •

If there's one thing most of us don't want to think about, it's taxes. (Well, taxes and dental work.) However, the wonderful world of taxes has got a bad rap. Once you sink your teeth into it a bit, you'll find that it's not nearly as stupefyingly dull as you might expect. Better still, take a little time to learn about taxes, and you might find that you'll encounter fewer tax hassles for the rest of your life. You might save thousands—or hundreds of thousands—of dollars, too.

There's so much to say about taxes that you could write a whole book about it (and hey—we did!). So please understand that this chapter will cover only a handful of key income tax concepts. Once your appetite for tax information is whetted, you'll find that Fooldom offers much more tax guidance at www.Fool.com/taxes.

HOW THE TAX PROCESS WORKS

It all begins with income, which for most of us is automatically reported to the IRS by our employers, banks, and brokerages. Sometimes you'll have additional income to report, such as tips, gambling winnings, business income, rental income, and alimony income. Total all your income for the year, and you'll be looking at what's called your gross income.

Now you'll make adjustments, subtracting things such as IRA contributions, alimony payments, qualified moving expenses, and qualified student loan interest paid. Once you've made all your adjustments, you'll be left with a very important sum: your adjusted gross income, or AGI. The AGI is used throughout your tax return, for exam-

ple, in determining the limitations on a number of tax issues, including exemptions, IRA contributions, and itemized deductions.

You now claim your exemptions and make your deductions. You can take either an itemized deduction or the standard deduction—whichever is greater.

You're entitled to one exemption for yourself, plus one each for your spouse and/or dependents, if you have them. The exemption is a set amount that you're permitted to deduct from your income, reducing the sum on which you're taxed. Exemption levels are tied to inflation and change from year to year, usually increasing. Once you've taken your exemptions and deductions, you're left with your taxable income. It's this number that determines your tax.

You're not done yet, though. Now take the tax due on your taxable income, add any other taxes (such as self-employment taxes and taxes on qualified retirement plans), and subtract any credits (perhaps for children, the elderly, the disabled, adoptions, or foreign taxes paid). The end result is your total tax—what Uncle Sam will demand of you.

Depending on how much you've already paid through withholding at work or quarterly estimated tax payments, either you'll owe more money or you'll be due a refund. That's it!

Below is an example of how the process works, in a nutshell. Don't worry if you don't understand the words "exemption" or "standard deduction" yet. We'll get to those eventually.

Gross income	=	$45,000
Adjustments	−	$2,000 (contribution to retirement account)
Adjusted gross income	=	$43,000
Exemptions	−	$2,900
Deductions	−	$4,500 (standard deduction)
Taxable income	=	$35,600
Tax on taxable income	=	$6,556 (determined from the IRS tax tables)
Credits	−	$500 (one child credit)
Other taxes	+	$300 (penalty tax on an early IRA distribution)
Total tax	=	$6,356
Withheld taxes	−	$7,000
Estimated tax payments	−	$0
Refund or payment due	=	$644 to be refunded

SAVE FOR RETIREMENT, SAVE ON TAXES

One of the best ways to turn your gross income into a much smaller adjusted gross income is by contributing to a retirement account, whether through a plan at work—such as a 401(k) or a 403(b)—or a deductible traditional IRA. In other words, by saving for retirement, you build a bigger nest egg for tomorrow while paying fewer taxes today. (And if your employer matches your contributions, even better!)

But wait—there's more! IRAs, 401(k)s, and their ilk are tax-deferred accounts, which means you don't pay taxes on the earnings on the investments in the account until they are withdrawn. That leaves more of your money to grow during your working years, resulting in more money for your golden years.

Note: Contributions to a Roth IRA do not reduce your taxable income, but you won't pay *any* taxes on the earnings—an even better deal for some people.

SAMPLE TAX TABLE

TAXABLE INCOME	TAX
Up to $26,250	15% of the taxable income
Over $26,250 but not over $63,550	$3,937.50 plus 28% of the excess over $26,250
Over $63,550 but not over $132,600	$14,381.50 plus 31% of the excess over $63,550
Over $132,600 but not over $288,350	$35,787 plus 36% of the excess over $132,600
Over $288,350	$91,857 plus 39.6% of the excess over $288,350

Here are three sample taxable incomes. See if you can figure out what tax the tax table would specify.

	TAXABLE INCOME	TOTAL TAX
The Huffnagels	$36,000	$ _____
The Wigglesworths	$65,000	$ _____
The Hoplamazians	$142,000	$ _____

[Answers: (1) $6,667.50; (2) $14,831; (3) $39,171.]

THE TAX TABLES

Chances are, if you've prepared your own taxes, you've gone to the tax tables in the booklet that accompanies your forms, and you've looked up your tax by finding the number associated with your total taxable income.

If you've ever wondered where that number comes from, here's how it's calculated. Following is a table for a single person from a past year (the numbers change each year, so just use this for its instructive value, not to calculate your own tax for this year). And not only do the numbers change, but single people use a different tax table than do married people filing jointly. Head-of-household filers use yet another tax table. But for the purposes of our discussion here, let's just assume that this is a "universal" tax table for all folks.

If that exercise stumped you, here's how you'd do the first one: Start with the salary of $36,000. By looking at the table, you'll see that it falls into the second category, as it's between $26,250 and $63,550. Subtract $26,250 from $36,000, which gives you $9,750. Now, to take

28 percent of that, multiply it by 0.28, which gives you $2,730. Finally, add $2,730 to $3,937.50, to get $6,667.50.

WHAT'S YOUR TAX RATE?

When people speak about their tax rate, they're generally referring to their marginal tax rate, the rate of tax they pay on their last dollar of taxable income. Someone may say that he is in the 28 percent tax bracket, but that doesn't mean he paid 28 percent on all his income. That 28 percent is his marginal rate—but what's more informative is his *effective* rate.

To understand this better, go back to the exercise associated with the Sample Tax Table. The Huffnagels are in the 28 percent bracket because their next dollar of income would be taxed at 28 percent. That's their marginal rate. But divide their total tax by their taxable income, and you get an effective rate of 19 percent ($6,667.50 divided by $36,000 is 0.19, or 19 percent; this assumes that the Huffnagels don't end up reducing their tax due with any adjustments or credits). The effective rate is 19 percent because the first big chunk of their income was taxed at the lower rate of 15 percent, and the second chunk was taxed at 28 percent.

The marginal tax rate matters because it's the rate of tax on your next dollar of taxable income, which is important for future tax planning. The effective rate is important because it shows you what you're really paying overall.

RECORDS YOU SHOULD KEEP

One way to make tax preparation time less of a nightmare is to prepare for it throughout the year by putting aside investment-related records and any other records you might need at tax time. Following is a worksheet that can help you. After each one is some space where you can jot down any notes or reminders. (For example, next to records of improvements made to your house, you might list any such improvements you can think of. Then

dig around for the supporting paperwork.) The checklist is long, but it isn't comprehensive. Basically, you should keep a record of each and every investment-related expense and anything else that will relate to your tax return.

USE YOUR COMPUTER (OR PHONE)!

If you haven't tried it yet, you should consider trying one of the inexpensive software packages that can help you prepare your returns. In fact, you can even bypass the software and prepare them directly on the Web for a modest fee. With these programs, you end up printing filled-out tax forms, which you sign and then mail in, perhaps with a check attached. If you love filling out questionnaires and answering questions, you might actually enjoy preparing your taxes this way. They have many advantages:

• You don't have to gather any forms; they're all in the program already.

• You can revise and revise and revise, without making a mess with Wite-Out or an eraser. Enter your information, see what your tax liability is, and then you can make adjustments, playing out different scenarios to see which is most cost-effective. (You might, for example, see that it's smart to realize some capital gains this year.)

• The software can assist you with decisions. It will ask you questions and either make decisions for you (regarding which forms to use, for example) or offer you some information and ask you to make a choice.

• You can pay less attention to details. Once the program has certain information, it will make sure that it's carried over to all required places. You don't have to worry about that.

• Carryovers from year to year are taken care of automatically—if you used the same program to prepare your return last year.

WORKSHEET: RECORDS TO KEEP FOR TAX TIME

Confirmation reports of stock purchases and sales, including the execution prices and trade dates.

_____

_____

_____

All statements and reports sent to you by your brokerage, mutual fund company, or other investment services company, and by other sources. Perhaps most important are 1099 forms, which show your proceeds from sales of securities (1099-B) and other capital assets, as well as interest income (1099-INT), state tax refunds and other government payments (1099-G), dividend income (1099-DIV), Social Security earnings (1099-SSA), and distributions from IRAs, pensions, and annuities (1099-R).

_____

_____

_____

Records of how you acquired any securities (such as through purchase, inheritance, etc.) and your cost basis.

_____

_____

_____

If you participate in a dividend reinvestment plan for stocks and/or mutual funds, keep track of the dividends you receive and how many shares they have purchased at what price. This information is necessary to help you calculate the new cost basis of your shares.

_____

_____

_____

Records of contributions to IRAs and other retirement plans. If you make nondeductible contributions to an IRA, make sure you declare these on IRS Form 8606 so that you don't end up paying a second tax on them down the line. You should have year-end account statements as well as receipts for your contributions.

_____

_____

_____

Documentation relating to any securities that have become worthless, especially something that includes the date on which it became worthless.

_____

_____

_____

Records relating to interest expense and how you used any loaned funds. This is an advanced topic, but it's an important one. For more information, consult IRS Publications 535 and 550.

_____

_____

_____

Records relating to any travel or meal expenses that you plan to deduct. Keep records of exactly what the trip involved. Know, though, that many trips are not deductible, such as travel to attend a shareholder meeting or an investment seminar. IRS Publications 463 and 550 will give you more details.

_____

_____

_____

Records of improvements made to your home. These can be added to your basis price, decreasing your taxable gain when you sell the home.

_____

_____

_____

Records of expenses related to selling your home. These can also be deducted from your capital gains.

_____

_____

_____

Records of charitable donations and the day of the donation. If you donated stock, record the cost basis of the shares, and their fair market value.

_____

_____

_____

Records of any stock that you've given away—including what you gave, the day of the gift, the cost basis of the shares, and their fair market value.

_____

_____

_____

Records of expenses for professional help, such as tax preparers and advisers, legal counsel, and so on.

_____

_____

_____

Electronic tax return preparation has its disadvantages, though. The main one is that you have to trust the software, even though you're still the one responsible for filing a correct return. There's always a small chance that the software will cause an error—or that you will provide an incorrect number and generate the error yourself. (Of course, even manually prepared returns may contain errors.)

ITEMIZED DEDUCTIONS

You probably know that tax deductions are things you should cherish, but you may not know exactly how they work and what deductions are available to you.

Itemized deductions are applied against your adjusted gross income, thereby allowing you to arrive at a lower taxable income . . . and a lower income tax (woo hoo!). But itemizing your deductions is something you're *allowed* to do, not necessarily something you *must* do. If you have itemized deductions greater than your standard deduction, you can report your itemized deductions. If you don't have any or many itemized deductions, you're allowed to take the standard deduction. It's your choice. You basically compare your itemized deductions to your standard deduction and use the larger of the two results to reduce your taxable income.

Don't fall prey to some common misconceptions about itemized deductions. Many people believe that they shouldn't bother itemizing their deductions unless they're homeowners paying large amounts of deductible interest expense. Not true. When smaller deductions are added together, you may well find yourself "over the top" of your standard deduction. Each and every year you should take at least a few minutes to review Schedule A and see if your circumstances will allow you to itemize your deductions.

(Note that you can itemize deductions only if you file Form 1040. Itemization is not permitted with Form 1040A or 1040EZ.)

KINDS OF ITEMIZED DEDUCTIONS

Here's a brief overview of some of the major miscellaneous itemized deductions. Itemized deductions can be divided into six major categories:

- Medical expense deductions
- Tax deductions
- Interest deductions
- Charitable contribution deductions
- Casualty and theft loss deductions
- Miscellaneous deductions

Here's a quick (and partial) rundown of some of them. You'll most definitely need to learn more about any that you believe apply to you. To do so, visit the following Web address: www.Fool.com/taxes. Most of these categories have a bunch of rules explaining the circumstances under which you might qualify to take a deduction and what exactly is allowed. As you read through the list, check off any items that you want to learn more about.

MEDICAL DEDUCTIONS

_____ Medical expenses of dependents

_____ Prescription drugs and insulin

_____ Medical service providers

_____ Institutional care

_____ Lodging that's "primarily for and essential to medical care"

_____ Birth control

_____ Cosmetic procedures necessary to ameliorate certain deformities

_____ Laser eye surgery

_____ Counseling

_____ Treatment for drug, alcohol, and smoking problems

_____ Special diets

_____ Medically necessary weight-reduction programs

_____ Membership in health clubs or fitness centers, in certain circumstances

_____ The costs of attending a special school (or receiving special education) for a mentally or physically handicapped individual

_____ Legal expenses incurred to establish the right to proceed with a course of treatment

_____ Capital improvements and expenses primary to the medical care of you, your spouse, or your dependents

_____ Transportation that's primarily for, and essential to, medical care

_____ Long-term care services

_____ Insurance covering medical care and transportation for medical care, and the cost of qualified long-term care insurance contracts

DEDUCTIONS FOR TAXES PAID

_____ Real estate property tax

_____ Real property refunds and rebates

_____ Co-op mortgage interest and property taxes

_____ Special assessments

_____ State income tax

_____ Personal property taxes

DEDUCTIONS FOR INTEREST PAID

_____ Mortgage interest

_____ Home equity loan interest

_____ Points

_____ Home improvement loan points

_____ Seller-paid points

_____ Refinance points

_____ Home equity line of credit points

_____ Construction loans

_____ Timeshare-related interest

_____ Boat and motor home interest

_____ Prepaid mortgage interest

_____ Seller-financed loans

_____ Investment interest and margin interest

CHARITABLE CONTRIBUTIONS

_____ Money contributed to qualifying organizations

_____ Stock contributed

_____ Travel related to charitable activities

_____ Volunteer expenses

_____ Expenses incurred while hosting an exchange student

_____ Delegate expenses

CASUALTY AND THEFT LOSS DEDUCTIONS

Rules governing deductions for stolen or destroyed property are very particular, so you'll need to do more research.

MISCELLANEOUS ITEMIZED DEDUCTIONS DEDUCTIBLE IN FULL

_____ Gambling expenses (to the extent of gambling income)

_____ Job-related expenses for handicapped people

_____ Estate taxes already imposed on the same taxable income (income with respect to a decedent)

_____ Unrecovered costs of an annuity (on a decedent's final return)

_____ Repayment of income (in some cases)

MISCELLANEOUS ITEMIZED DEDUCTIONS, DEDUCTIBLE IF THEY SURPASS THE 2 PERCENT FLOOR IN TOTAL

_____ Unreimbursed job costs and expenses

_____ Education costs

_____ Investment expenses

_____ Legal fees for investment or employment purposes

_____ Business-related travel and entertainment

_____ Business use of home

_____ Appraisal fees (for charitable donations or casualty losses)

_____ Clerical assistance to maintain investments

_____ Depreciation on business assets

_____ Expenses to collect interest or dividends (collection fees)

_____ Hobby expenses—to the extent your hobby produces income

_____ Work clothes and uniforms required by your employer and not suitable for outside wear

_____ Tax preparation fees and/or other tax assistance expenses

_____ Legal fees for collecting or producing taxable income, keeping a job, or obtaining tax advice

_____ Professional fees for obtaining investment advice

_____ Investment expenses in general and some investment travel

_____ Job-hunting expenses

_____ Cost of a home safe to retain tax/investment papers

_____ Small tools and supplies used in your trade or business

_____ Retirement custodial fees paid directly (IRA, Keogh, SIMPLE, etc.)

_____ Job-related educational expenses

_____ Medical examinations required by your employer

_____ Professional and union dues

_____ Repayment of income (in some cases)

_____ Service charges on dividend reinvestment plans

_____ Trust administration fees

_____ Long-distance business calls

_____ Books, magazines, and other publications dealing with investments or taxes

_____ Legal fees for the collection of alimony

_____ Office-in-home deduction for an employee (self-employed folks are treated differently)

_____ Job dismissal insurance

_____ Cost of an extra phone installed in your home for business use

_____ Cleaning and maintenance of work clothes (if done professionally)

_____ Business-related travel and entertainment

Remember that the list above is not comprehensive—and that for each item, you'll need to learn more.

Here's a list of items that, contrary to popular opinion, don't qualify as miscellaneous itemized deductions:

- Personal living expenses
- Commuting expenses
- Funeral expenses
- Home repairs and improvements on your personal residence
- Legal fees for divorce (other than for tax planning)
- Parking tickets and other fines that are payments for illegal activities
- Political contributions
- Sales tax (except when added to the cost of a business asset)
- Telephone expenses of the first line for basic local residential service (even if a portion of the use is for business purposes).
- College tuition
- Education expenses that qualify you for a new trade or business
- Club dues (except for certain business or public service organizations)
- Gambling losses in excess of gambling winnings
- Licenses and fees (such as marriage licenses, animal licenses, drivers' licenses, etc.)
- Life insurance
- Losses from the sale of your personal residence
- Cleaning of your work clothes if you wash them yourself (not professionally)
- The cost of travel that is primarily a form of education
- Costs directly related to buying or selling an investment (such as broker purchase and sale commissions)
- Expenses and costs of attending investment seminars or conventions
- Expenses to attend a company's annual stockholder meeting—even if you own stock in that company (unless you're organizing a hostile takeover)
- Estates planning advice (except for the portion related to tax advice)
- Legal costs and expenses relating to child support and custody

BUNCH YOUR DEDUCTIONS

By bunching your deductions into one year rather than spreading them out over two years, you may be able to eke out a valuable deduction.

Consider combining as many of your taxes, medical expenses, charitable contributions, and any other itemized deductions you might have over a two-year period into one year. Doing this means that every other year or so, you may be able to claim a deduction. In alternate years, the standard deduction may be your best bet.

As an example, if you typically donate $2,000 per year to charities, you might give $2,000 in January and then give the following year's gift(s) in December of the same year. That way you've chalked up twice as much in possible deductions, by bunching.

Think for a few minutes and list any items you can think of that you might be able to bunch:

_____

_____

_____

_____

_____

_____

_____

_____

LIMITS ON ITEMIZED DEDUCTIONS

Various categories of itemized deductions have threshold (or "floor") limits. For example, there's a 7.5 percent threshold for medical deductions, a 10 percent floor for casualty losses, and a 2 percent floor for miscellaneous deductions. The floors are in respect to your adjusted gross income. Here's a Fool Lib that should demonstrate the concept of the floor (ask a friend for the called-for words and jot them down—then read the whole thing aloud):

The tax code also limits the amount of itemized deductions allowed to certain "high-income" taxpayers. The limit applies to you if your AGI is in excess of a certain specified level. (This changes from year to year, but to give you a general idea, it was roughly $137,300 last time we checked and roughly $68,650 for a separate return filed by a married individual). If you're subject to this limitation, you're required to reduce the overall amount of your allowable itemized deductions by the lesser of:

- Three percent of the excess of adjusted gross income over the applicable amount; or
- Eighty percent of the amount of otherwise allowable itemized deductions.

Imagine _____ , who is a _____ with an adjusted gross income of $40,000.
                    [your name]   [occupation]

His/her floor for miscellaneous deductions is 2 percent. This means that he/she can deduct only those qualifying items that exceed 2 percent of $40,000, or $800. His/her miscellaneous deductions include safe deposit

box fees at _____ bank, expenses for a uniform for a moonlighting job as a _____ , and
                 [name]   [occupation]

long-distance business calls to _____ and _____ . If _____ 's miscellaneous
                                        [a celebrity]   [another celebrity]   [your name]

deductions total $700, he/she's out of luck. If he/she has $900 of miscellaneous deductions, he/she can deduct $100—

the amount by which the deductions exceed the floor. The hurdle is higher for medical deductions. _____ will
                                                                                                           [Your name]

be able to deduct only those medical expenses that exceed 7.5 percent of his/her AGI—in this case, $3,000.

Of course, to make things more complicated, this limit doesn't apply to all deductions.

Deductions subject to the overall limit include taxes paid, interest (except investment interest), charitable contributions, job expenses, and most miscellaneous deductions. Deductions not subject to the overall limit include medical (and dental) expenses, investment interest expense, nonbusiness casualty and theft loss, and gambling losses (to the extent of gambling winnings).

YEAR-END STOCK TIPS

When the stockings are hung by the chimney with care, it's time to make some last-minute tax-reducing moves. Here are a few suggestions:

• **Make a contribution to your favorite charity.** If you have appreciated stock that you've held for more than one year, you might want to keep the cash in your pocket and donate the stock. You'll avoid paying tax on the appreciation but will still be able to deduct the full value of the stock. You win, your charity wins, and the only loser is Uncle Sam (but he doesn't really mind—which is why this tax break has been written into the law!). This little trick has merit only if you are planning to itemize your deductions on Schedule A (one of the main parts of your tax return). If you're a "standard deduction" filer, you should still keep charity in your heart, but Uncle Sam won't help you out with a tax deduction.

• **Use your credit card.** If you have year-end deductible expenses (such as business expenses, medical expenses, charitable donations, rental expenses, miscellaneous itemized deductions, or virtually any other allowable deduction), you can use your credit card to make the purchase this year, take the deduction this year, and pay your credit card bill next year. When you pay with a credit card, the IRS considers the expense deductible in the year that the charge is incurred, not necessarily when you pay for it.

• **Prepay your state and/or local taxes.** If you believe that your tax bracket next year will be no higher than this year and you won't be bothered by any alternative minimum tax issues, consider making your state and/or local tax payments before the end of this year. After all, you're going to owe the money anyway, right? So why not make those payments before December 31 and take the federal tax deduction this year?

• **Catch up on your 401(k) contributions.** As you know, there are maximum limits to 401(k) contributions each year. Generally, your 401(k) contributions must be made throughout the year, but did you know that some 401(k) plans allow for "catch-up" contributions in December if your contribution level is less than the maximum allowed? Using your December bonus to fund the balance of your 401(k), when allowed, might be a good way to dodge some current taxes. If your employer matches some of your catch-up contributions, you're in even better shape.

• **Get rid of worthless stock.** How about those stocks you own that have completely fallen off the radar screen? Perhaps the company is in bankruptcy . . . or delisted . . . or worse! You might have some worthless stock on your hands that might generate you a capital loss. But the term "worthless" is a technical one from a tax standpoint. It means more than just the bottom dropping out of the price of the stock or a suspension of trading of that stock. There are some tricks that you might be able to use to sell these shares before the end of the year, so you don't have to fight over the term "worthless" with Uncle Sam. But make sure that you understand the rules.

TAKE ADVANTAGE OF CREDITS

As wonderful as deductions are, credits are even more wonderful, because they're much more powerful. As an example, let's say that you get a $1,000 deduction for something and you're in a 28 percent tax bracket. If so, your deduction will save you $280 (0.28 times $1,000 equals $280). But if you qualify for a $1,000 *credit*, you'll likely save a full $1,000. In this case the credit is nearly four times as valuable as the deduction. Credits offset your tax bill dollar for dollar.

There are many credits that you should be aware of, and it should come as no surprise that we haven't the space to go into them in detail here. Still, below you'll find a handy list of some (of many) available credits. Place a check mark by the one(s) you think you might qualify for and then seek more information on them either with a tax pro or by doing some research online. Might we suggest a visit to www.Fool.com/taxes?

_____ The Child Tax Credit: If you qualify, this credit can offset your tax liability by up to $600 or more per child. (Learn more in IRS Form 8812.)

_____ The Adoption Expense Credit: This credit can be worth as much as $10,000 per adopted child to you (and in some cases more), if you've shelled out at least that much in qualified adoption-related expenses. (Learn more in IRS Publication 968.)

_____ The Hope Scholarship Credit: This offers up to $1,500 (at the time of this writing) toward educational expenses for the first two years of an undergraduate program, if you and your expenses qualify.

_____ The Lifetime Learning Credit: This offers up to $1,000 (at the time of this writing) toward educational expenses that help a student acquire or improve job skills. This credit can be claimed over many years, even for expenses incurred at some vocational schools. Of course, as with all of these credits, there are various requirements for qualification.

_____ The Earned Income Credit: This is designed to aid low-income taxpayers. (It's confusing, but you can try to figure it out with IRS Publication 596.)

_____ The Child/Dependent Care Credit: This credit can be used to offset those dependent/child care costs that enable *both* spouses to work. To qualify, the dependent must be under the age of thirteen or disabled. (Learn more in IRS Form 2441 and IRS Publication 503.)

_____ The General Business Credit: This encompasses a number of credits designed to encourage certain business activities. It includes the Investment Tax Credit (composed of the Rehabilitation Credit, the Energy Credit, and the Reforestation Credit), the Work Opportunity Credit, the Alcohol Fuels Credit, the Research Credit, the Low-Income Housing Credit, the Enhanced Oil Recovery Credit, the Disabled Access Credit, the Renewable Electricity Production Credit, the Empowerment Zone Employment Credit, the Indian Employment Credit, the Employer Social Security Credit, the Orphan Drug Credit, the Trans-Alaska Pipeline Liability Fund Credit, the Community Development Credit, and the Welfare-to-Work Credit.

_____ Credit for the Elderly or Disabled: If you're sixty-five or older and have a modest income or are permanently and totally disabled. (Learn more in IRS Publications 524 and 554.)

_____ The Electric Vehicle Credit: If you purchase a qualified electric car. (Learn more in IRS Publication 535.)

_____ The Disabled Access Credit: For eligible small businesses that incur expenses to provide access to persons with disabilities. (Learn more in IRS Form 8826.)

_____ The Foreign Tax Credit: If you've paid foreign taxes, whether abroad or through investments. (Learn more in IRS Publication 514.)

CALCULATING CAPITAL GAINS

One of the most important tax concepts for investors to understand is that of capital gains, which occur when you sell a qualifying asset and the proceeds exceed your cost basis. (In other words, you have a profit, or gain—which is taxable.) Related to this are capital losses, which can be used to offset your gains and thereby reduce your tax.

Which capital gains tax rate applies to you depends on:

- The type of asset you sold
- Your cost basis
- The length of time you held the asset before selling it
- Your income level

Qualifying for the lowest rates are stocks, bonds, mutual funds, and many other capital assets. Taxed at a slightly higher rate are business or rental real estate, collectibles, depreciation, and certain other things. We'll just focus on securities here, though, such as stocks.

Your cost basis is important to understand and calculate correctly. If you buy one hundred shares of a stock at $30, the value of that bundle of equity is $3,000. But that's not the number that should figure into your taxes. For that, you need to calculate your cost basis, incorporating any expenses incurred in carrying out the transaction. If you paid a $25 commission to your broker when you bought the shares, that means your cost basis is now $3,025. If you sell the hundred shares when they hit $45, your proceeds for the sale will be $4,500, less the commission. If it was also $25, your net proceeds would be $4,475.

Is calculating your cost basis a pain? Yes. But it's worthwhile. Look at what it has done to your gain. Instead of reporting a $1,500 gain ($4,500 less $3,000), you'll report a gain of $1,450 ($4,475 less $3,025). If you would have paid 20 percent tax on the $50 difference, you've just saved ten bucks. This might not seem like much, but it adds up. For those Fools who haven't yet switched to a discount broker and who pay commissions in the neighborhood of $100 and up per pop, this makes a big difference.

Try the math out yourself, in the following example.

---

1. You bought 200 shares of Octopus Garden Supplies, Inc. (ticker: ARMSS) at $25 each.
2. You sold them all later, for $48 each.
3. You paid a $12 commission on the purchase and again on the sale.

WHAT'S YOUR CAPITAL GAIN?

Cost basis:

200 × $25 =   _____
Add the $12 commission and you get: _____

Proceeds from sale:

200 × $48 =   _____
Subtract the $12 commission and you get: _____

Capital gain (or loss):   _____

Subtract the cost basis from the proceeds and you get: _____

[The answer is $4,576 ($9,588 − $5,012 = $4,576.)]

Now that you know what your gain is, what's your tax on it? Well, that depends mainly on how long you held the asset and your income level. There are two holding periods. Assets held for a year or less are considered short term. Those held for more than one year are considered long term. Here's the upshot:

If you're in the 10 percent or 15 percent tax bracket:

Assets held for a year or less: Taxed at the ordinary income tax rate

Assets held for more than a year: 10 percent tax

If your tax bracket is greater than 15 percent:

Assets held for a year or less: Taxed at the ordinary income tax rate

Assets held for more than a year: 20 percent tax

Even lower rates may apply to assets held more than five years. You can learn more about them in our online Tax Strategies area (at www.Fool.com/taxes).

Tax bracket	Tax on: $4,576
1. 28%	_____
2. 31%	_____
3. 36%	_____
4. 40%	_____
5. 20%	$915.20

(Remember that these are just sample tax brackets.)

[Answers: (1) $1,281.28; (2) $1,418.56; (3) $1,647.36; (4) $1,830.40.]

Also, understand that these tax rates are correct as of press time but may be changed from year to year.

But back to you and the shares of Octopus Garden Supplies that you sold, netting you a gain of $4,576. What's your tax bill on that? Well, it depends on how long you held the stock. If you held it longer than a year, you'll most likely be taxed at the long-term rate of 20 percent, costing you $915.20. If you held the stock for a year or less, it's a short-term gain and will be taxed at your income tax rate. Below are some possible tax brackets. Calculate the tax on each for a gain of $4,576:

Do you notice anything? There are a few lessons to glean here. For starters, if possible, it's usually better to have a long-term gain than a short-term one, as you'll likely pay more for the short-term gain. This is truer the higher your bracket. You can't always control when it's best to sell a stock, but if you're about to sell one after eleven months, think about whether it might make sense to hang on for another few weeks.

A final thing to understand about capital gains is that you can offset them with capital losses, if you follow the rules. You must first offset all of your short-term losses against your short-term gains. Then you must offset all of your long-term losses against your long-term gains. Finally, offset (or net out) these two results. If you have large short-term losses and small short-term gains, some of those "excess" short-term losses may then be forced against your long-term gains. This may not be ideal, as you may want to wait for a future tax year when you anticipate some large short-term gains that can eat up those short-term losses.

If your capital losses exceed your capital gains, you can still get some mileage out of the excess losses. Go ahead and offset every dollar of capital gains with your capital losses. With what's left, you can deduct up to $3,000 from your income via Schedule D. (Note: For married people filing separately, the limit is $1,500 each.)

Any excess loss beyond $3,000 (or $1,500 each for married folks filing separately) can be carried forward and applied against capital gains in the following year. And anything remaining beyond your gains can be applied against income—up to (again) $3,000.

For more information on offsetting gains and losses, and to see how it's done, check out Schedule D.

DECIDING WHICH SHARES OF STOCK TO SELL

If you want to make things easy on yourself, whenever you sell shares of stock you own, sell *all* the shares of stock that you own in that company.

That's not always the best course of action, though, investment-wise. Sometimes you need to sell just *some* shares. In that case, it can sometimes make a big difference *which* shares you choose to sell. For example, if you've been adding to a pile of shares over the years and you then sell some, have you sold ones you bought long ago or the last ones you bought? The difference matters because the tax rate varies according to the holding period, and your choice can save you much moolah. In addition, you might have paid much less for the earliest shares, so your gains would be bigger if you were to sell them.

Let's consider your options. Note that in this section, we're dealing only with individual securities and not mutual funds (they have their own rules, which we'll discuss later). With individual securities such as stocks, you have only two options when determining the basis (or cost, for tax purposes) of shares. They are:

- Specific Identification Method
- First-In, First-Out (FIFO) Method

First, the Specific Identification Method. Let's say that you made the following purchases of stock in the Florida Ballot Co. (ticker: CHADZ):

June 1, 2001: 100 shares @ $10 each
June 5, 2001: 200 shares @ $11 each
June 10, 2001: 300 shares @ $13 each

The stock is now trading at $15 a share. You decide to sell 300 shares. You also know that you want to sell the shares you bought on June 10, 2001, be-cause you paid more for them and therefore your gain on the sale will be lower than if you sell the first shares you bought. You very emphatically tell your broker that you want to sell the June 10 shares, not the 100 shares bought on June 1 or the 200 bought on June 5.

Understand the tax implications. Crunch a few numbers to see what your capital gain would be in two different scenarios presented on page 156.

It should be clear that you could reap a significant tax saving just by making a simple decision and specifically identifying the shares that you want to sell. A 20 percent tax on the $700 difference between the two scenarios above amounts to $140, which isn't small change.

You'll always need to do a bit of thinking, though. For example, if you expect that you'll soon be in a higher tax bracket (due to a higher salary, perhaps), you might want to sell the earliest shares and take the bigger tax hit now. On the other hand, if the last shares you bought have not yet been held long enough to qualify for the lowest capital gains tax rate, it might be worth it to sell the ones you've held longer. Look at your options from many different angles and see which one saves you the most money—both now and in the long run.

If you choose the specifying share option, note that you'll have to get confirmation from your broker, *in writing,* of which shares you specified. If this seems like too much of a hassle (it doesn't have to be but can sometimes become one), you might opt to use the FIFO method of determining which shares you're selling.

With the FIFO method, you specify that the first securities you bought are the first ones sold. The basis of the stock for capital gains purposes is the cost of the first securities you purchased.

ACCOUNTING FOR MUTUAL FUNDS

The rules and procedures we've presented for securities such as stocks and bonds also apply to mutual funds. Fear not—while mutual funds buy and sell shares of stock each day, you don't have

SCENARIO A: SELL FOR $15 ALL OF THE FOLLOWING SHARES

Cost basis (excluding commissions):

100 shares bought on June 1, 2001, for $10 each $ _____

200 shares bought on June 5, 2001, for $11 each $ _____

Cost basis: $ _____

Proceeds from sale of the shares: $ _____

Capital gain (proceeds minus cost basis): $ _____

SCENARIO B: SELL FOR $15 EACH THE FOLLOWING SHARES

Cost basis (excluding commissions):

300 shares bought on June 10, 2001, for $13 each $ _____

Proceeds from sale of the shares: $ _____

Capital gain (proceeds minus cost basis): $ _____

[Answers: *Scenario A:* The cost bases are $1,000 and $2,200, for a total of $3,200. The proceeds are $4,500. The capital gain is $1,300. *Scenario B:* The cost basis is $3,900 and the proceeds are $4,500, yielding a capital gain of $600. Remember that this is a simplified example, not accounting for commissions.]

to account for each transaction. But you *do* have to account for any shares of a mutual fund that you sell during the year. And if you're like many people, regularly buying shares of various funds each month, perhaps even having your dividends reinvested in additional shares, the accounting can quickly begin to seem insurmountably complicated. It isn't, though—as long as you've kept good records of when and how you bought each share.

The first thing to calculate for the shares sold is their cost basis. This will depend on how you got them. If you purchased them, your cost basis is the purchase price plus any commission costs. If you got the shares as part of a dividend reinvestment plan, the cost basis is their price at the time of purchase. If you inherited the shares, the cost basis is usually their fair market value (the "net asset value") on the day you inherited them. (Things get more complicated if the shares were given to you as a gift.)

Once you have the initial cost basis of the shares, you'll need to continue to add the cost of additional shares purchased to your basis. If you received a dividend that was reinvested back into additional shares in the fund, you should increase your basis by the amount of the dividend, thereby incorporating the value of the dividend into your basis. This can be a hassle, but if you update your records regularly (perhaps quarterly), you'll be very happy you did when you sell some shares. Remember, though—you can avoid all this headache by just selling *all* the shares of a given fund at one time. That way you'll minimize the record keeping involved.

Let's assume that you really need only to sell some shares. Unlike with securities such as individual stocks, you have three options with mutual funds:

THE SPECIFIC IDENTIFICATION METHOD

With this you keep records of when you acquired each share of a mutual fund and you clearly specify which ones you're selling when placing the order, just as with stock.

THE FIRST-IN, FIRST-OUT (FIFO) METHOD

With this you specify that the shares sold were the first ones you owned. So if you accumulate 550 shares over many years and then sell 75 shares, you'll be subtracting the adjusted cost basis for the first 75 shares you owned from the sale price in order to determine your gain or loss. The downside is that this method can maximize your gain, as your earliest shares are likely to have the lowest cost basis. The upside is that since you've held them the longest, these shares are most likely to qualify for the lower long-term tax rate.

THE SINGLE-CATEGORY AND MULTIPLE-CATEGORY METHODS

Here you average the cost of all your shares, which can be done in two ways. Let's look at these more closely.

With the single-category method, you add up the purchase prices of all the shares you have and then divide by the total number of shares. For example, let's say that you started out with 100 shares of the Ominously Overdiversified Mutual Fund (ticker: OOMFX), purchased for $50 each. Later, you bought 100 more shares at $60 each. In the meantime, your dividends have been reinvested and you get a notice that you have received 5 shares, purchased at $52 each. Let's use the single-category method to average them:

COST BASIS (EXCLUDING COMMISSIONS)

100 shares @ $50 = $ _____

100 shares @ $60 = $ _____

5 shares @ $52 = $ _____

205 shares, totaling $ _____

Dividing the total cost basis of $ _____ by 205 shares yields an average cost basis of $ _____ per share.

[Answers: The shares bought for $50 have a cost basis of $5,000. The shares bought for $60 have a cost basis of $6,000. The shares bought for $52 have a cost basis of $260. The total cost basis is $11,260, which when divided by 205 shares yields a cost basis per share of $54.93.]

So if at some point you sell 50 shares for $65 each, you calculate your gain using a cost basis of $54.93. (Note: To simplify, we haven't incorporated commission costs here.) You record your gains or losses on Schedule D, where you must also explain the method you used to calculate any average bases. The basis you calculated stays in effect until you acquire more shares. Then you'll have to recalculate. Note also that you still have to pay attention to holding periods. Whenever you sell any share, you'll have to figure out its holding period and its appropriate tax rate. But no matter what the holding period and tax rate, with the single-category method, the cost basis is the same.

Most mutual fund companies will provide cost basis information for you when you sell your shares, averaged according to the single-category method.

Next up, the multiple-category method. This is pretty much the same as the single-category method, but you average the shares in subsets, ac-cording to holding period. It becomes further complicated when you sell off shares over time. You'll have to recalculate, incorporating new shares acquired in the interim and recategorizing all the shares as their holding periods change.

The multiple-category method is a little more work, but it often decreases the taxes you pay. To use this method, you should make all the calculations whenever you sell any shares. Complete the following exercise to see how this method works.

With this method, when selling shares, you simply use the cost basis that corresponds to the holding period of the shares you're selling. So if you were selling shares you'd held for fourteen months, your cost basis would be $28 per share.

COST BASIS

SHORT-TERM SHARES (HELD FOR A YEAR OR LESS)

Cost Basis (excluding commissions)

200 shares @ $40 = $ _____ (bought this April)

100 shares @ $30 = $ _____ (bought this May)

5 shares @ $32 = $ _____ (bought this June)

Total $ _____

Dividing the total cost basis of $ _____ by 305 shares yields an average cost basis of
$ _____ per share.

LONG-TERM SHARES (HELD FOR MORE THAN A YEAR)

Cost Basis (excluding commissions)

200 shares @ $28 = $ _____ (bought last April)

Dividing the total cost basis of $ _____ by 200 shares yields an average cost basis of
$ _____ per share.

[Answers: In the short-term section, the cost basis is $8,000 for the shares bought for $40 each, $3,000 for the shares bought for $30 each, and $160 for the shares bought at $32 each. The total short-term basis is $11,160, or $36.59 per share. In the long-term section, the cost basis for the shares bought at $28 is $5,600, or $28 per share.]

As time marches on, shares in your short-term category will eventually become long-term holdings as long as they remain in your portfolio.

You should choose the method that serves you best, but realize that, with the single- and multiple-category methods, you'll have to stick with them for as long as you hold shares in that particular fund.

You can read much more about mutual fund taxation issues in IRS Publications 564 and 550, which you can get directly from the IRS (contacts listed below). Many of the issues can be a bit complicated and difficult to understand, but you should become familiar with them if you decide to invest in mutual funds.

You'll find a lot of tax relief through your computer and at the other end of your telephone. To wit:

KEY WEB SITES AND PHONE NUMBERS

- Internal Revenue Service: www.irs.gov (where you can download and print any IRS form or publication)
- The IRS main phone number: (800) 829-1040
- For IRS tax forms: (800) TAX-FORM [(800) 829-3676]

GENERAL TAX INFORMATION WEB SITES

- 1040.com: www.1040.com
- Essential Links to Taxes: www.el.com/elinks/taxes
- Fairmark Press Tax Guide for Investors: www.fairmark.com
- Federation of Tax Administrators' state tax resource list: www.taxadmin.org/fta
- H&R Block: www.hrblock.com
- Quicken.com: www.quicken.com/taxes
- Roth IRA information: www.rothira.com
- Tax and Accounting Sites Directory: www.taxsites.com
- Tax Foundation (featuring many tax facts): www.taxfoundation.org

- Tax History Project: www.taxhistory.org
- taxworld.org: www.taxworld.org
- The Motley Fool Tax Strategies area: www.Fool.com/taxes

TAX PREPARATION SOFTWARE

- TaxCut: www.taxcut.com
- TurboTax: www.turbotax.com
- EDCO tax planning software: www.edcosoft.com

TEN TAX TIPS

Here are ten Foolish tax tips to keep in mind before you sign your tax return and mail it to Uncle Sam.

1. **File if you should.** You, your children, or even your elderly parents might not technically be required to file a tax return, but if you or they worked for wages and/or had federal taxes withheld, the only way you can recover any federal taxes you or they paid is to file a return and claim a refund. For more information, see IRS Publication 4 (Student's Tax Guide) and IRS Publication 554 (Older Americans' Tax Guide).

2. **When appropriate, use the head-of-household filing status even if your ex-spouse claims your child as a deduction.** You might have negotiated the tax deductions available to your ex-spouse during the divorce (usually allowed when the ex makes timely child support payments). Nevertheless, you can still use the head-of-household filing status if the children actually reside with you and you have physical custody of them.

3. **Don't report too much wage income.** If you participate in a deferred-compensation plan at your place of employment—401(k), 403(b), etc.—remember to report as wages only the amount reported to you in Box 1 of your W-2 form. Don't report the salary you actually earned.

4. **Don't report interest earned on Series E, EE, or Treasury bonds/bills/notes on your state tax return.** Remember that while this interest is taxable for federal purposes, it is not taxable for state purposes. Remember to make the appropriate adjustment on your state tax return.

5. **Add your brokerage commissions and other fees to the cost of your stock.** When you buy stocks, you'll pay broker commissions. You might also pay transfer fees. These expenses are added to the purchase price of the stock and remain with the stock until sold. When you sell the shares, make sure to reduce your gross sales price by the amount of these expenses. And don't forget to reconcile your sales to the Form 1099B that was provided to you by your broker.

6. **Make an adjustment for student loan interest.** Did you pay interest on a student loan this year? If so, you might be able to reduce your income by the amount of the interest that you paid, to a maximum adjustment of $1,500. The interest must be paid in the first sixty months of the loan, and the loan must have been used for qualified educational expenses. The beauty of this is that you *do not* have to itemize your deduction on Schedule A to claim the adjustment for student loan interest paid. For more information, read the instructions for line 24 of Form 1040.

7. **Take the property tax deduction for additional home and/or investment property.** Many people are under the impression that property tax deductions are available only for your primary residence. Nothing could be further from the truth. Property taxes are deductible for all applicable real property—second, third, and fourth homes, vacant lots, raw land, and so on. But—and this is a very big but—if you have rental properties, different rules apply.

8. **Deduct refinancing points.** Did you refinance your primary or secondary residence? If so, you might have paid loan points. You might be able to amortize those points over the life of the loan and generate an additional interest deduction. For additional information, check out the instructions for Schedule A in your Form 1040 Forms and Instructions booklet.

9. **Take education credits.** Did you know that you can claim a credit for qualified education expenses paid for yourself, your spouse, and your dependents? It's true. You can even claim credits for your child's college education. The Hope and Lifetime Learning Credits can be valuable tax busters for you. The rules can get a bit complex, and there are certainly restrictions. But if you or anybody in your family attends a higher education facility, it's something that you should take a closer look at. Review the instructions for line 44 on Form 1040 and also review IRS Publication 970 for more information.

10. **Take the child credit.** If your dependent is under age seventeen at the end of the calendar year, you might qualify for a $500 credit when you file your tax return for the year. Why? Just for putting up with the kid. Really. There are no special qualifications other than the age of the dependent and your total income (high-income taxpayers don't benefit from this credit). If you qualify, don't forget to reduce your taxes by the full $500 for each qualifying dependent. Check out IRS Publication 972 for more information and qualification worksheets. This credit is in addition to any child *care* credit that you are able to claim, so don't confuse the two since they are completely different issues.

YOUR BIT-BY-BIT BUDGET ENTRY

We're keeping this Bit-by-Bit Budget assignment simple since we did just make you read an entire chapter on taxes.

Designate a folder (or envelope or desk drawer or warehouse) for all the receipts and statements you'll need to fill out your next tax return. Every time you get a brokerage statement in the mail or buy something that you are going to deduct, stick it in this file. That's it! Just remember where you put the file so there's no panicking come tax time.

On your Bit-by-Bit Budget you'll see two lines under "Taxes": "Income taxes (federal and state)" and "Social Security and Medicare taxes." Those are numbers that you can find simply by looking at your last pay stub. In fact, you probably already dwelled on those expenses in Chapter 2 as you were trying to find out where the heck all your money goes. If you get paid twice a month or once a week, add up a month's worth of your outpourings to The Man and plug them into the part of your Bit-by-Bit Budget that looks like this.

BIT-BY-BIT BUDGET

	AMOUNT FROM MONEY TRACKER WORKSHEET	BUDGETED AMOUNT	MONTH 1	MONTH 2	MONTH 3	MONTH 4	MONTH 5	MONTH 6
Taxes:								
Income taxes (federal and state)								
Social Security and Medicare taxes								

CHAPTER 9

WHEN LIFE HAPPENS

SIXTY-SECOND GUIDE
TO PREPARING FOR LIFE EVENTS

Live your life.

Get married. Have kids. Switch jobs. If you must, get divorced. But no matter what, be prepared for all the financial changes that accompany these life events.

0:60 Gather ye papers.

We know that your honey and your mother can read your mind. But your insurers and the lawyers who are going to handle your estate can't. Fill out the key documents (we'll tell you which ones) to specify your innermost intentions in lawyerspeak.

0:48 File ye papers.

We know that you keep all the warranties for every electronic item you've ever owned in that gray file in the middle desk drawer. So of course your Really Important Papers are assembled in the same painstaking manner. Right? We'll give you a few extra seconds to get this done.

0:37 Tell someone where to find the aforementioned papers.

If you give your daughter durable power of attorney, make sure she knows that she can find the document in the safety deposit box at your bank. And make sure she knows which branch office and on what days they serve free coffee and croissants.

0:21 When life happens, revisit your Really Important Papers.

Whether it's adding a significant other to your family or a driver to your insurance policy, make sure you're covered in the eyes of Uncle Sam, Uncle Lenny's Insurance Emporium, and Crazy Uncle Al.

0:10 Know what to do, and how to do it cheaply.

Every life event is a financial event—but each life event has its own financial consequences. We provide a list of how to anticipate and manage many of Fate's fancies, and maybe save some money along the way.

. . .

Though we Fools believe there's more to life than money, we do recognize that big life events are often big money events. When those events arise, there are steps you can take to stay on a firm financial footing even though your life is in flux. That's what this chapter is all about.

To be prepared for life's milestones—both cheery and dreary—there are things you can do now and things you can do when the time is right. Not coincidentally, we have organized this chapter accordingly into:

- **Paperwork you should complete and legal documents you should execute now** so your affairs will be in order when you become incapacitated, whether temporarily (e.g., you are in a coma) or permanently (i.e., you are in a coffin).

- **What to do, and how to save money, before and after major life events.** The milestones we cover are:

  - Marriage
  - Children
  - Divorce
  - Changing job
  - Being laid off
  - Disability
  - Retirement
  - Death of a loved one

Here's our *strong* recommendation: Definitely complete Part I. Visit Part II when Fate so dictates.

GETTING YOUR AFFAIRS IN ORDER

OK, we really didn't want to bring it up, but the statisticians just told us there is a 100 percent chance you're going to die. We're sure of it.

Barring Armageddon or the total collapse of society (we're willing to concede that these require no financial plan), life will go on after you. And some sad soul—likely one of your favorite people—will be stuck wrapping up your affairs. To make it worse, along the road to this certain end point,

there's a good chance you'll be at least temporarily incapable of managing your financial affairs. (We're relentless, aren't we?)

Wait! There is good news.

It doesn't take much to put a few safeguards into place so you don't have to worry about this stuff and you can get on with skipping through life with that smile we love so much.

Here's all you have to do:

1. Complete four important documents.
2. Pick your heirs and write their names in the appropriate blanks.
3. Let important people know where your stuff is.

Here are the four most important documents:

YOUR WILL (LAST WILL AND TESTAMENT)

What it is: Your will details exactly what happens to your property (and potentially your minor dependents) when you die.

Where to get it: We recommend you see an attorney. It won't cost you much, and you'll get it done quickly and correctly. If you opt for preprinted, fill-in-the-blanks forms and software, be sure they are up to date and conform to the laws of your state.

LIVING WILL (ADVANCE MEDICAL DIRECTIVE)

What it is: This says you want the right to die a natural death, free of all costly, extraordinary efforts to keep you alive when your life can be sustained only by artificial means.

Where to get it: This document is available free at virtually every hospital in the nation.

DURABLE POWER OF ATTORNEY *AND* MEDICAL POWER OF ATTORNEY (HEALTH CARE PROXY)

What they are: These documents allow the person that you select to make decisions on your behalf—financial and legal in the first case, medical in the second case—when you are incapacitated.

Where to get them: We suggest you see an attorney for these, too.

AIN'T THIS FUN?

So maybe contemplating these issues isn't as much fun as envisioning your ideal retirement, but you know what they say: When life gives you lemons, lawyers will find a way to get 40 percent of all lemonade proceeds. Anyway, here's more information on these sunny topics.

Health and Medical Care

Your loved ones should know your wishes for health and medical care. Discuss the use of life support systems when there is no reasonable expectation of recovery and your wishes for organ donation. Remember, before age fifty it's far more likely that you will be mentally or physically incapacitated than that you will die. Obtaining the legal documents we've listed will permit your loved ones to act on your behalf without a court order, saving thousands of dollars in attorney expenses, court fees, and a lot of time—far more than the small cost of drafting these documents now. Use an attorney to draft your powers of attorney and use your state's approved format for the living will/advance medical directive, which is available at most hospitals.

Funeral Arrangements

Your loved ones should also know your funeral arrangement desires. Knowing your wishes in advance will ensure that they are not pressured into high-cost services because they're making decisions during a time of grief or through a misguided sense of respect for the deceased. If you have made advance funeral arrangements, make sure your loved ones know with whom and where the pertinent documents may be found.

Last Will and Testament and/or Living or Testamentary Trusts

Review these documents to make sure they clearly express your wishes and intent. If you have personal property not included in these documents, specify through an addendum or codicil (a fancy word meaning "postscript") how these personal effects are to be distributed. If these documents have not been developed yet or if a lawyer hasn't reviewed them in more than five years, get thee to an attorney! It's worth the price to get peace of mind to know that your wishes are accurately communicated in the necessary legal Swahili. If you have minor children, specify who their guardian should be in the event both parents are deceased.

Be aware that a failure to execute this document prior to your death will almost certainly cause your family needless expense, grief, and time as they struggle through the probate process of your estate. In addition, the state will almost certainly dictate a distribution of your assets that does not fit with your desires. So please don't put this off.

You can get a living will and a health care power of attorney by visiting your local hospital or downloading the forms from the Partnership for Caring (www.partnershipforcaring.org) or the Northwest Justice Project (www.nwjustice.org).

Not everything will pass to your loved ones via a will. Some assets (such as real estate, residences, taxable investment accounts, and checking accounts) may be owned as joint tenancy property. If that's the case, when you die they will pass outside of your will to the joint owner. Additionally, things such as retirement accounts and life insurance policies require a designated beneficiary or two. Those proceeds will go to the designated persons on the owner's death, which means your will won't govern the distribution of these assets.

The moral here is that in addition to completing your will, you should consider two things:

1. **Ownership of your home, bank accounts, taxable brokerage accounts, and so on:** Are they titled/owned jointly or individually?
2. **Beneficiaries of all retirement accounts [including 401(k), 403(b), pension, profit sharing, and IRAs] and insurance policies.** Keep 'em up to date!

Update all of your property title and IRA/retirement plan/insurance policy beneficiary information. Don't forget any life insurance or retirement plan beneficiary designations you have made regarding employer-provided benefits in your current job. Review this information whenever a major life event (marriage, divorce, birth, death) occurs. If changes are needed, you can get the necessary forms for changing your beneficiaries from your human resources department (for job-provided insurance and retirement plans) or from the insurance company, brokerage, mutual fund, or IRA provider (for personal insurance policies and investment/retirement accounts).

WHERE'S WILL-DO?

If something were to happen to you, would your loved ones knew where to find all of your accounts? Does your partner know where to find the safe deposit box key? And what about your will? Your lawyer's phone number? The dog's heartworm pills?

It doesn't do any good to have your affairs in order, all of your important papers filed, and your beneficiaries up to date if no one knows where to find your records.

Well, today's your lucky day, because we just happen to provide in this book—at no additional cost to you—a handy-dandy Really Important Stuff Worksheet (see page 166). It provides you with a list of important documents and a place to write down where your loved ones can find your stuff in a pinch. It's mind-numbingly comprehensive, so take it one bite at a time. But it's important, so

spend a few minutes a week filling it out until you're done.

And remember to tell your family where you keep the list! Make a few copies and give them to trusted friends and relatives. There's only one thing worse than filling out a dead guy's tax forms, and that's doing it without access to his financial records. Believe me, your posse will thank you posthumously.

1. Before you fill anything in, make a few blank copies. Give one to any adult who lives with you. Heck, make a bunch of copies and pass them out to friends and family. People love this stuff.

2. Next, work your way through the big table. Expect this to be dull and endless. Chip away at it slowly but surely.

3. Pay close attention to these two columns in the table:

- "How Owned?" for property titles and bank/brokerage accounts
- "Beneficiary" for retirement plans and life insurance policies

Get these two right, and the processing of your estate will go smoothly. Mess 'em up, and you risk subjecting your loved ones to years of haggling over your stuff.

4. Develop a complete list of all documents, information, and records that may be needed by your loved ones, and specify their location. We've provided space in our celebrated Really Important Stuff Worksheet for you to do this. Besides the items mentioned above, your list may include:

- Marriage certificates or divorce decrees
- Pre- or postnuptial agreements
- Birth certificate
- Previous years' income tax returns (local, state, and federal)

- Social Security number
- Auto, life, health, and disability insurance policies (include premium amounts and due dates)
- Employee benefit plan information (health, disability, retirement)
- Investment, checking, and savings accounts
- Location, deeds, and mortgage information for all real estate
- Debts owed or due to you (personal loans, auto loans, credit cards, charge accounts, notes payable, notes receivable from others)
- Business agreements relating to corpora-

tions, partnerships, or sole proprietorships (location, names, buy/sell arrangements)
- Names and phone numbers of persons to be notified in the event of your incapacity or death

5. When you're done, make a copy of the ultra-fabulous Really Important Stuff sheet and leave the copies in two safe places. The person to whom you assign durable power of attorney should know exactly where to find a copy. Note: If this person is not a signatory on your safe deposit box, she won't be able to get into the box.

WORKSHEET: REALLY IMPORTANT STUFF

PERSONAL INFORMATION

FULL LEGAL NAME	DATE OF BIRTH	SOCIAL SECURITY NUMBER

IMPORTANT LEGAL DOCUMENTS

DOCUMENT	PERSON YOU'VE AUTHORIZED IN DOCUMENT (EXECUTOR FOR LAST WILL AND TESTAMENT)	PHONE NUMBER	LOCATION (DESK DRAWER, SAFETY DEPOSIT BOX, FILE CABINET, ETC.)
Durable power of attorney			
Medical power of attorney			
Last will and testament			

MEDICAL-RELATED PAPERS	IMPORTANT INFORMATION	NOTES	LOCATION
Organ donor card	Are you an organ donor? ____ Yes ____ No		
Living will	Have you signed a living will? ____ Yes ____ No		

OTHER PAPERS	LOCATION
Birth certificate	
Marriage certificate	
Military papers	
Divorce/separation papers	
Copies of tax returns	
Mortgage documents	
Business agreements	

PROPERTY TITLES

(BE SURE TO NOTE WHETHER PROPERTY IS OWNED JOINTLY OR ONLY BY YOU)

PROPERTY	ADDRESS/DESCRIPTION	HOW OWNED?	LOCATION
Home			
Other real estate			
Automobiles			
Other			

(continued)

WORKSHEET: REALLY IMPORTANT STUFF, continued

BANKS AND BROKERAGES

(LOCATION CODE REFERS TO WHERE THE ACCOUNT DOCUMENTATION IS)

ACCOUNT	ACCOUNT NUMBER	OWNERSHIP	PHONE NUMBER	LOCATION

CHECKING/SAVINGS (INCLUDE ALL OF THEM, PLEASE, ESPECIALLY THE OFFSHORE TAX DODGE)

CREDIT AND CHARGE CARDS

CDS, MONEY MARKET ACCOUNTS

BROKERAGE ACCOUNTS (DO NOT INCLUDE IRAS HERE)

RETIREMENT ACCOUNTS

ACCOUNT	ACCOUNT NUMBER	CONTACT	PHONE NUMBER	BENEFICIARY	LOCATION
IRAS [INCLUDE 401(K) AND OTHER EMPLOYER PLANS THAT YOU ROLLED INTO A SELF-DIRECTED IRA]					
EMPLOYER-PROVIDED RETIREMENT PLANS [SUCH AS 401(K), 403(B), PENSION, PROFIT-SHARING AND DEFERRED-COMPENSATION PLANS]					
OTHER					

INSURANCE POLICIES

(BE SURE TO LIST BENEFICIARIES WHERE APPLICABLE)

POLICY	ACCOUNT NUMBER	CONTACT	PHONE NUMBER	PAYMENT DUE	LOCATION
Health					
Disability					
Homeowner's					
Auto					
Life	**Beneficiary:**				
Other					

(continued)

WORKSHEET: REALLY IMPORTANT STUFF, continued

DEBTS

DEBT	ACCOUNT NUMBER	CONTACT	PHONE NUMBER	DUE WHEN?

FUNERAL ARRANGEMENTS

(LIST ANY WISHES IN REGARD TO YOUR FUNERAL AND BURIAL. IF YOU HAVE ALREADY BOUGHT A BURIAL PLOT OR MADE OTHER ARRANGEMENTS, PROVIDE CONTACTS.) _____

CONTACT	PHONE NUMBER	FOR WHAT

PERSONAL ADVISERS

TITLE	NAME	ADDRESS	PHONE NUMBER	E-MAIL
Emergency contact				
Attorney				
Accountant				
Primary physician				
Guardian for children				
Minister/priest/rabbi/yogi				
Other				

TOP SIX WAYS TO MAKE YOUR LOVED ONES MISERABLE

1. Execute a durable power of attorney, naming your daughter to speak for you when you can't, but forget to make her signatory on the safe deposit box where you store the document.

2. Take out a long-term disability policy but neglect to tell your spouse. Then go into a coma for six months so that snookums has to take out a second mortgage to pay the bills.

3. Play a good joke on the poor soul who will complete your final tax form and leave your important papers under mountains of less important papers scattered all over the house.

4. Get divorced and forget to change the beneficiary on your life insurance policy. That way your first husband—the lunatic who ran off with the Krishnas—gets the entire lump-sum death benefit, while your second husband and family of fifty years get zip.

5. Forget to tell your wife about that great new financial planner you're working with—the one who mysteriously boards a flight for the Cayman Islands the day of your unexpected demise.

6. Repeatedly leave the toilet seat up (or down) and just two squares of tissue on the roll.

PART II: TIPS FOR LIFE EVENTS

Congratulations! Your newborn baby is adorable (she looks just like your spouse . . . fortunately). But do you know how reproducing affects your taxes?

Oh, you say you're changing jobs. What are you going to do with the investments in your 401(k)? And how will you maintain health insurance for your family?

Don't worry. We have tips for how to navigate the intersections, turnoffs, and pileups along the road of life.

MARRIAGE

Working your way through this list may feel as tedious as the weeks you spent listening to tapes of wedding bands playing "Celebration" and macarena medleys. But nothing says "I love you" like saying "Honey, I just named you as my beneficiary."

- **Review the allowances you claim on your W-4.** Getting married will change your tax situation, and you want to make sure that you aren't having too much—or too little—taken out of your paycheck. Due to the "marriage penalty," many couples—especially those with two relatively equal incomes—are unexpectedly hit with a tax hike when they file their first return as a married couple. (Incidentally, you will pay taxes as a married couple for the entire year, regardless of how long you were actually married during the year.) While you really shouldn't postpone or avoid marriage just for tax reasons—though if you do, we'd love to hear how you explain it to your beloved ("See, honey, line 47 on the 1040 says . . .")—you ought to be prepared for any changes. To get an idea of how many allowances you should claim, ask your employer for a W-4 calculation sheet or visit the IRS Web site to download the form or use its Deductions and Adjustments Worksheet.

- **Change your beneficiaries/emergency contacts.** Remember when you filled out forms ages ago for your 401(k) plan or insurance? Your beneficiary is the person you named to be the recipient of those monies when you die. Bummer stuff, we know. Thankfully, the paperwork is pretty easy. Just ask your human resources manager at work for a "life event kit" (she or he may refer you directly to the companies providing these services). You'll also need to change any accounts that are not work-related. Here's a checklist of work-related and non-work-related forms:

- 401(k), pensions, profit-sharing accounts
- Any miscellaneous programs your company may offer
- Insurance: life, car, home, or health insurance (make sure to change contact information)
- IRAs and other investment accounts

- **Think about insurance changes.** Your life has changed: you got a better half, maybe a new pet, and a precious George Foreman grill. Your insurance should change, too.

- **Life insurance:** Life insurance is meant to help with expenses if one spouse dies and the surviving spouse's income is insufficient to cover household expenses.
- **Disability insurance:** The average twenty-year-old is twice as likely to become disabled than to die before retirement. In other words, it's important to have disability insurance.
- **Homeowner's/renter's insurance:** Even if you already have homeowner's or renter's insurance, you may want to update it to include your engagement ring and any particularly valuable wedding gifts.
- **Health insurance:** Coordinate your health and dental insurance if you are both covered by your respective employers. Eliminate any duplicate coverage and maximize your benefits if one of you has a more generous employer.
- **Car insurance:** Car insurers in particular want you to be married (almost as much as your parents and smug married friends do) and will discount your insurance when you get married (especially for young men). Combining your auto policies (as well as any other insurance policies—renter's, homeowner's, and so on) should get you a discount since you will become a bigger (and better) customer to them.

- **Put the wedding-gift money to good use.** Sure, a large flat-screen TV might make a fabulous one-month anniversary present. But the best use for your wedding money is to pay down any debts you incurred throwing the wedding or to set up an emergency fund (a good rule of thumb is to have three to six months' worth of income on hand). How nice to start your life together with the honeymoon paid off!

- **Alert the authorities if you change your name.** While it may be emotionally important to you to change your last name, it is not financially important. If you have to choose between spending an annoying afternoon opening an IRA account or an annoying afternoon filling out forms to change your name, the IRA is the better financial step. But for those who are changing their names, here's what you need to do:

- **Contact the Social Security Administration at (800) 772-1213:** The phone system will walk you through the process of getting a new blue card with your new name. You can also download the form at www.ssa.gov/replace_sscard.html.
- **Visit the Department of Motor Vehicles:** Bring a bunch of forms of identification (it tends to be fussy) and your original marriage certificate with the pretty seal.
- **Contact lots of people once you have your Social Security card and your driver's license:** Banks, credit card companies, the phone company, anyone who sends you bills or mail that you want to have the correct name on. For a while you may get twice the junk mail. Promptly shred it, then use it for kindling.

- **Write a will and set up a power of attorney.** Alas, we are back to the death theme. When you write a will, you should visit an attorney (maybe you have one in the family who would do this as a wedding present). It will cost $100 to $300. Avoid using a preprinted fill-in-the-blank form or off-the-shelf software. They are often out of date and may not comply with your state's laws. Also have your lawyer set up a durable power of attorney that names your spouse or someone else you trust to make financial, investment, and health care decisions on your behalf if you can't act for yourself.

- **Decide how to handle premarital debt.** Perhaps you'll be lucky enough to marry someone who is debt free, but among student loans, credit card debt, car loans, and mortgages it's highly unlikely. If you do find that debt-free Prince/Princess Charming, score! On the other hand, perhaps *you're* not debt free. In either case, you and your spouse will have to figure out how to deal with debts that one or both of you incurred prior to getting married. To begin with, it's important to get this out onto the table as soon as possible. You may be surprised to find out what you don't know about a person's finances, even if you've been dating him or her for years. Once you've established where the two of you stand, important questions naturally follow: How much of your income or savings would you be willing to direct toward paying off your spouse's debts? And vice versa? If you decide that the person who incurred the debts should pay them off with just his or her own income, how will this affect his or her ability to contribute to joint savings and expenses? Refer back to the chapter on debt for help paying off debts.

- **Figure out your banking.** For many couples, the fact that you'll be sharing most of your lives together means you ought to pool your money as well. However, the decision may not be so simple. There are advantages and disadvantages to both joint and separate checking accounts. Certainly, a joint checking account will be easier from an organizational standpoint, and you'll probably pay less in banking fees. In addition, handling mutual expenses for children or your household will be easier with a joint account, rather than having to figure out "who pays for what." Finally, joint accounts should encourage plenty of communication, as you'll certainly have to check with each other before making any significant purchases.

On the other hand, there are plenty of advantages to separate accounts. You're less likely to make errors since both of you won't be using the same account. Separate accounts will also enable some independence within your marriage and help you to avoid disputes over every last dime of hobby-related or frivolous spending.

- **Go through this workbook together.** Decide on your goals, create a budget, plan for retirement, and so forth. Grab a leftover bottle of champagne, order some Chinese food, and find your bank statements to see what the two of you bring to the marriage (a modern dowry). See if you can cut down on some redundancies.

CHILDREN

Babies are adorable, drooly, fun, smelly, and . . . expensive. The U.S. government estimates that it will cost $160,000 to raise a kid born in 1999 to adulthood, and that doesn't include the opportunity cost of that money not being invested. But babies *are* an investment, one that pays immense dividends, and no matter how expensive it gets to raise a child, most of us decide it's one of the most worthwhile ways to spend our hard-earned money.

- **Review the allowances you claim on your W-4.** The number of allowances you claim determines how much in taxes is taken out of your paycheck. The more allowances you claim, the fewer taxes are withheld. You might be able to claim a tax credit for having kids. That's right—a tax credit for no reason other than your child is living with you. If your modified adjusted gross income (AGI) is $110,000 or less (for married people filing jointly), $75,000 (for single or head-of-household filers), or $55,000 (for married people filing separately), you will be able to claim a credit for any child living with you. The amount of the credit will increase to $1,000 per child over the next few years. Here are the credit amounts that you can look forward to:

- 2002 through 2004: $600 per child
- 2005 through 2008: $700 per child

- 2009: $800 per child
- 2010 and thereafter: $1,000 per child

To get an idea of how many allowances you should claim, ask your employer for a W-4 calculation sheet or visit the IRS Web site to download the form or use its Deductions and Adjustments Worksheet. You may find that this credit generates a very large federal tax refund. While this might make you happy for a short period of time, it's not a good practice. Think about it: it's never a good idea to have Uncle Sam hold on to your money all year long. Sam doesn't pay you any interest on tax refunds. If you will receive a hefty refund, consider revising your federal withholding form for the remainder of the year *now*. If you anticipate a large refund come tax time next year due to the child tax credit, change your W-4 form *now* and get that extra cash in your pocket right away.

- **Think about insurance changes.** You now have one more person (or two or three more) relying on you and your income. You should definitely make sure you have enough life insurance and disability insurance coverage. Also, you may have to update your health insurance so that you have family coverage. If you are married and both spouses work, evaluate which employer provides the best family policy.

- **Buy Baby Bargains**, by Denise and Alan Fields. It's chock full of ways to save money on kid accoutrements and also has some handy reviews and consumer information.

- **Visit the Parents and Expecting Parents discussion board at Fool.com.** Discuss money-saving and child-rearing tips with other moms and dads.

- **Start thinking about college**. We know—why think about Junior's B.A. when he can't even control his B.M.s? But a degree ain't cheap, so the sooner you start saving, the better off you'll be. Right now, the best deal going is the 529 savings plan (see Chapter 7).

DIVORCE

Sorry to interrupt the happy vibes that come with talk of marriage and kids. But it's time to interject a downer topic. We'll try to make this quick.

The laws that govern divorces vary from state to state, so the best advice we can give you is to learn the rules for your state. But we do have a few considerations that transcend state boundaries.

- **Review the allowances you claim on your W-4.** Once you are divorced, your filing status will change—probably married filing jointly to filing singly. Also, depending on your divorce decree and who gets to claim the kids as exemptions, to deduct the mortgage interest, and so forth, the amount of taxes you owe Uncle Sam will most likely change. You don't want to end up having too much—or too little—withheld throughout the year. To get an idea of how many allowances you should claim, ask your employer for a W-4 calculation sheet or visit the IRS Web site to download the form or use its Deductions and Adjustments Worksheet.

- **Change the beneficiaries on all your accounts.** Chances are, if you're no longer married to someone, you probably don't want that person to inherit your retirement accounts or receive your life insurance payout.

- **Consider alternatives to court.** If the divorce is mutual and amicable and the two parties make comparable salaries and brought comparable assets to the marriage, consider professional mediation instead of high-priced lawyers. You can learn about this much less expensive option at www.divorceonline.com

- **Know the tax implications of alimony and child support.** Child support payments are not taxable to the person receiving the payments and are likewise not deductible by the person making the payments. Alimony payments, on the other hand, are completely different. If a payment qualifies as alimony, that payment is taxable to the person receiving the payment and deductible by the person making the payment. For a payment to qualify as either alimony or child support, it must be stated as such in the "divorce or separation instrument"—generally the divorce decree. A sloppy or unclear drafting of the divorce agreement can subject you to additional unexpected (and certainly unwanted) taxes. If you would like to read more about the tax implications of separation and divorce, check out IRS Publication 504 (available at www.irs.gov).

- **Decide whether to file joint or separate tax returns.** It depends, but if you're divorced or legally separated by December 31, the government considers you single for the entire year. If you're not divorced or legally separated by December 31, you are considered still married, and you must file a joint return, a married and filing separately return, or perhaps a head-of-household return, if you're eligible. Though the tax laws don't favor married and filing separately, you may want to make that choice or file as head of household, because if you file a joint return, you will be liable for any unpaid taxes due to your soon-to-be ex-spouse's mistakes or fraud.

- **Be aware that there are many other tax implications.** Divvying up retirement accounts, investments, stock options, real estate, and other assets could potentially have serious tax consequences. And your attorney or mediator probably won't know all of them. This is a time when consulting a tax pro may well be worth the money.

CHANGING JOBS

Whether your job change is by choice or not, keep the following tips in mind. If you have been laid off, take a look at this list and the next, "Being Laid Off."

- **Make sure you have continuous medical coverage.** The government has given you some breathing room by mandating your right to remain insured under your former employer's policy for a period of time. Called COBRA (no, not the snake, but shorthand for Consolidated Omnibus Budget Reconciliation Act of 1985), the law provides for continued coverage when you leave your job for reasons other than gross misconduct. COBRA says you are guaranteed the right to continue your former employer's group plan for individual or family health care coverage for up to eighteen months, at your own expense. In certain instances, spouses and dependents may continue coverage for up to thirty-six months. You have sixty days from the time you are laid off or from the day your current coverage ends (whichever is later) to choose to stay with your employer's plan. You must pay the employer's cost for such coverage, and the employer may, and probably will, charge you an extra 2 percent for administrative expenses. Be aware that the cost of this coverage can be hundreds of dollars a month for both families and single persons. However, it is usually cheaper than getting a policy on your own. Check your company's policy prior to leaving that job.

Generally, COBRA is available from companies with twenty or more employers. If COBRA is not available to you or your benefits have expired, check out HIPAA (which stands for Health Insurance Portability and Accountability Act of 1996). If you're like us, you're DTOA (darn tired of acronyms).

- **Roll over your defined-contribution retirement savings.** We're talking about the assets in your 401(k), 403(b), 457, SARSEP, or SIMPLE plan. Unless you know exactly what you are doing, you do *not* want to have temporary possession of any money in employer-sponsored retirement accounts. If you move these funds, it's usually best to request a direct transfer from your old company plan to a self-directed rollover IRA at the brokerage of your choice. Also, it's safest to establish a "conduit" IRA (in which the funds are not mixed with other IRA funds) so that you can roll the money back into your new employer's retirement plan, if this turns out to be your best option. Holding or cashing a rollover check could result in some nasty tax consequences. Also, if you have a loan out against your account, the loan will be due when you terminate your employment. As for your defined-benefit (i.e., traditional) pension plan, in most cases you will not be able to access that money until you retire.

- **Decide if you want to exercise stock options.** If you were granted stock options at your former job, you can't take them with you. Some employers won't let departing employees exercise their options; others will require the options to be exercised within a certain period of time—such as one to three months—or lose them altogether. If your options are worth anything, find out your company's policy *before* you quit.

BEING LAID OFF

If you've been the victim of a "downsizing," a "restructuring," or a "chainsawing," heed the tips in the "Changing Jobs" list above, but also consider the following items.

- **Look into unemployment benefits.** If you didn't receive any severance pay, or after your severance runs out, you can apply for unemployment benefits at your local Unemployment Insurance Claims Office, Employment Service Office, or Mom and Dad's Generous Check-Writing Office. The benefits will replace only a portion of your former salary, but they're better than nothing. Eligibility rules and the amount of benefits are determined by each state. Keep in mind that this is not welfare; this is insurance that your employer has paid for as part of your benefits. (We should note, however, that benefits are available only to those who have lost their job through no fault of their own.)

- **Use the Web for your job search.** There are numerous online resources for folks looking for a job. We're not just talking about "Help Wanted" listings. Many sites provide tips on assembling a résumé, doing well at an interview, and career advice. Here are a few:

> www.monster.com
> www.hotjobs.com
> www.vault.com
> www.careerbuilder.com
> www.wetfeet.com
> www.corporaterefugees.com
> www.careerjournal.com
> www.helpwanted.com
> www.careermag.com
> www.salary.com
> www.6figurejobs.com (ya gotta dream, baby!)

- **Press for more severance benefits.** If you feel as though you deserve a better deal from your employer, make your case. Maybe you can get an extra week or two of severance pay or an extension of health care benefits. Perhaps your employer will permit you to use some of its resources for your job search. We're talking about things that go above and beyond what your former employer legally owes you. So ask nicely. If you are the victim of a large layoff, then make your case soon; your employer won't be able to accommodate everyone's requests.

DISABILITY

If for some reason you are not able to work, you may think you are disabled. However, your insurance company and the Social Security Administration may not agree. Thus begins the odyssey!

- **Contact your provider of disability insurance.** This will be your first source of funds. Check with your employer's benefits specialist if you have disability insurance through work. Otherwise, contact your insurance provider directly. It will be able to tell you if you meet the necessary definition of "disability" and when you'll be eligible for benefits. Many policies have an "elimination period," which is the amount of time you must be disabled before benefits kick in.

• **Contact the Social Security Administration.** Promptly call the SSA toll free at (800) 772-1213. Be forewarned that Social Security has a narrow definition of disability and that benefits will be distributed only if you are expected to be disabled for a year or more. If you are eligible, your dependents—if you have any—may be eligible for benefits as well.

• **Tap your retirement funds . . . but only as a last resort.** Hopefully, your emergency fund will be enough to sustain you until you can return to work. However, you may be able to withdraw some of your retirement funds without a penalty (though you will have to pay taxes). This, again, depends on whether you meet the proper definition of "disabled" (contact your plan's administration/custodian for more information). But more important, you should use this option only as a last resort. Do all you can to tap other resources—even use credit cards, as long as you get a competitive rate and know you will be able to pay them off—before you shortchange your retirement fund.

• **Keep records of all medical bills.** All unreimbursed medical expenses that exceed 7.5 percent of your adjusted gross income are tax deductible. In general, you're allowed to deduct unreimbursed amounts paid for your own medical care and the care of your spouse and/or dependents. "Paid" is the key word here, since, with very few exceptions, you are allowed the deduction only in the year when you pay the medical expense. The scope of medical care includes the diagnosis, cure, mitigation, treatment, or prevention of disease, procedures affecting a structure or function of the body, related transportation, qualified long-term care services, and medical insurance. But it does not include expenses paid for the benefit of overall general health or well-being.

• **Know whether your benefits will be taxed.** If your employer paid for your insurance—or if you're self-employed and you deducted your premiums as a business expense—any proceeds from a disability policy will be taxed. If, on the other hand, you paid for your policy out of your pocket with after-tax money, the payout will be tax free.

RETIREMENT

You've waited your entire working life for this day. The folks on the shuffleboard court won't know what hit 'em. Use the following tips to increase the shine on your golden years.

• **Move some of your assets to safer investments.** A few years before you retire, you should gradually move some of your assets out of stocks and into bonds, money market funds, and Treasury notes. This should preserve your principal as well as produce income. However, don't get *too* conservative or you'll outlive your money.

• **Contact the Social Security Administration.** The SSA recommends that you contact a representative in the year before the year you plan to retire because, according to the SSA Web site, "the rules are complicated, and it may be to your advantage to start your retirement benefits before you actually stop working." Visit the Social Security Web site (www.ssa.gov) or call (800) 772-1213.

• **Decide how much to withdraw from your retirement accounts.** You'll have to determine how much of your stash you can safely take each year to ensure it will last your lifetime. On top of that, you'll have to heed the different rules that apply to the different types of retirement plans:

• **Defined-benefit plans:** A traditional pension—technically known as a "defined-benefit plan"—provides a specific and *guaranteed* retirement income, typically based on the number of years of employment, an average of the final few years of salary, and a percentage multiplier. This benefit can be received as a lump sum or paid out as a monthly pension for life, with an additional percentage payable to a surviving spouse following the death of the pensioner. It's your choice, and it'll determine how much you receive and when. Also, bear in mind that only one option may be elected, and once it's chosen, that election can't be changed, so make sure you know the ramifications before you make your choice.

- **Defined-contribution plans:** Some defined-contribution plans—for example, 401(k)s and 403(b)s—may permit only a lump-sum payment. Many other plans, though, will allow you to take annual installments paid typically over a period of not less than two or more than fifteen years. A few plans will even allow you to convert your plan proceeds to an annuity payable over your life or the joint lives of you and your spouse.

- **Traditional IRAs:** If you haven't taken all the money out of your traditional IRA by the time you're $70^{1}/_{2}$ years old, you have to begin minimum required distributions (MRDs). The calculations are complicated, so see IRS Publication 590 or ask the custodian of your IRA for more information.

- **Roth IRAs:** As long as the money has been in the account for at least five tax years, just take the money . . . tax free!

- **Reassess your tax withholding.** Just because you stopped working doesn't mean you will stop paying taxes. Just as when you were getting a paycheck, you have to determine how much of your income is withheld and sent to Uncle Sam. And also just as during your working life, if you don't send the government enough in taxes during the year, you could face penalties. You might opt to not have any withholding taken from your retirement payments. In that case, become aware of how estimated taxes work and how to play that game in order to avoid underpayment penalties. Another fly in the ointment: at certain income levels, up to 85 percent of your Social Security benefits will be taxable.

- **Plan your estate.** For most people, this means taking care of all the paperwork we mentioned

in Part I (a will, power of attorney, etc.). However, if you have a large estate—worth $500,000 or more—you should look into more complex estate planning in order to reduce the tax burden to your heirs. For that, see an estate-planning expert.

DEATH OF A LOVED ONE

When a loved one passes away, money is the last thing on your mind. However, if your financial future was in any way dependent on the decedent, there are some important things you should know.

- **Contact the Social Security Administration.** Promptly call the SSA toll free at (800) 772-1213. Depending on your relation to the deceased, you may be eligible for survivor's benefits and/or retirement benefits. Also, you may receive a onetime lump-sum benefit of $255.

- **If you inherit an IRA, know the rules.** Those rules can be complicated, and they're different for spouses than they are for other beneficiaries. So read IRS Publication 590 (available at www.irs.gov) and avoid a 50 percent penalty!

- **Know the cost basis of inherited assets.** If your rich Uncle Louie left you some twenty-five-year-old Wal-Mart stock before he joined that great discounter in the sky, your cost basis for that stock will not be what Uncle Louie paid. Generally, the cost basis of inherited assets is the fair market value of the assets on the date of the benefactor's death.

TEN TIPS ON ORGANIZING YOURSELF FOR LIFE EVENTS

1. We can't stress enough the importance of keeping your beneficiary and emergency contacts

up to date. You don't want your employer to call your ex-boyfriend when you break your arm on the photocopy machine. And in the case of your untimely demise in the aforementioned photocopy machine mishap, you sure as heck don't want your lemonade stand fortunes to go to your ex-husband, leaving your current Schmoopy with only your loving memory and ninety-three nylon bags of lemons in the garage.

2. Getting hitched has its obvious perks. Take advantage of the one insurance companies offer by getting lower rates for being paired up. While you're at it, see if your insurer offers other kinds of policies, such as renter's or homeowner's insurance. Combining your policies can shave dollars off the bottom line.

3. When you add to your family—through marriage, babies, or live-in parents—remember to adjust your life and disability insurance. After all, you want to protect everyone who depends on your income and your annual karaoke concert.

4. Do not buy life insurance for your kids. We said it in the chapter on insurance, and we repeat it here: unless Junior contributes significantly to the family income with his movie career as a midget stand-in, there's no reason for him to be insured. Instead, invest that money you would have spent on a policy in his college fund.

5. When you leave a place of employment, roll over and play Buffett. The assets in your 401(k), 403(b), 457, SARSEP, or SIMPLE plan no longer have to be handled by your company's plan administrator. Reread the chapter on investing and have your dough transferred directly from your old company plan to the brokerage of your choice. Then start making your own investment decisions!

6. It's worth a separate tip to note that in order to avoid hefty taxes on your old employer-sponsored retirement funds, do not cash out your plan or take even temporary possession of the money. Your new brokerage company can take care of all the paperwork for a swift and simple rollover.

7. If you need some cash in a crunch, try to avoid tapping into your retirement funds. Some employers let you borrow against your 401(k) and pay it back on a regular schedule. But should you lose or leave your job, you'll have to repay all the money in one lump sum.

8. There are some life events you can see coming a mile away. If you're nearing retirement, prepare your finances for that banner day by moving some of your assets into investments that will preserve your principal. If you know you're expecting a child (and we hope it's kind of obvious), ready your revised paperwork before rushing to the delivery room.

9. Copy the Really Important Stuff Worksheet for friends and relatives to fill out for their loved ones. (We won't sue.) Let them know that peace of mind is just a few mind-numbing hours away.

10. Better yet, buy them their own copy of this action-packed workbook. It makes a memorable gift and a lovely coffee table stabilizer.

BIT-BY-BIT BUDGET

Lucky you! You deserve a break after working so diligently to fill out every item on your Really Important Stuff Worksheet. Take out your Bit-by-Bit Budget Kit and put it right back into the folder. There's nothing for you to fill out tonight! Go have a glass of chocolate milk. On us.

CHAPTER 10

HIRING A FINANCIAL PROFESSIONAL

SIXTY-SECOND GUIDE TO HIRING A FINANCIAL PROFESSIONAL

You're smart (you bought this workbook, didn't you?), making you a prime candidate to handle most financial matters you might encounter. But occasionally (or even more than occasionally, for some folks) we all could use a hand. Here's the quickie on hiring a financial professional.

0:60 Determine whether or not you need help.

There are times in life when a second opinion is especially welcome: when dealing with estate issues after the death of a parent; handling complicated stock option decisions; making sure that your kids, not Uncle Sam, are the major beneficiaries of your estate. At times like these, a clearheaded pro can be worth her weight in gold.

0:48 Start sleuthing.

Ask trusted friends and family for recommendations. Who have they used? Were they happy with

the service? How did they find the pro? Would they use that person again?

0:36 Do your homework.

Start your reconnaissance with the folks who were recommended to you. Get some information on the phone, then make appointments with those who look promising.

0:24 Gather your papers.

Even before you meet, you'll need to do a bit of the legwork. Arrive prepared with necessary records, papers, and a granola bar, just in case you get hungry during the meeting. It'll save you and the pro time and (lunch) money.

0:19 Grill the professionals.

How often will you meet? What specific services will they provide? What if problems or questions arise? Will you work directly with them, or will your file be handed off to an associate? Have they handled situations like yours before? It's pretty easy to find out the answers to these questions—just ask!

0:03 Follow their advice.

Not blindly, of course. But you've done your homework (and read this workbook), so you'll know if it's solid information. If you trust them, take their recommendations. After all, you paid for them!

• • •

Whew! Since we have a few seconds to spare, let's go over some details of finding and hiring a financial professional.

WORKING WITH A FINANCIAL PROFESSIONAL

We Motley Fools have always maintained that you are the very best person to manage your money. After all, you are the CEO of your personal financial empire (or rural two-by-two-foot plot of swampland, for some of us).

Like any successful executive, though, you must sometimes seek out the best help you can get. We recognize that there's a need for expert, affordable, independent advice on an as-needed basis. When it comes to your money, then, get all the help you need from whatever source works best for you. But remember that ultimately *you* make all the decisions. When you pay for advice, it's the information you're buying, not a scapegoat to blame for any future bumps in the road.

Of course, it's important to know your team members and their allegiances and to weigh all advice accordingly. We encourage you to become an educated consumer. It is in this spirit that we've included this chapter on obtaining paid financial advice.

WHAT KINDS OF FINANCIAL PROFESSIONALS ARE THERE?

There are pros for just about every subject—from stock analysis to assessing the role of zero-coupon bonds in your portfolio. People can earn accreditation in taxes, estate planning, credit counseling, real estate, investment advice, and the classic serve-and-volley game. Though we don't recommend taking financial advice from your tennis pro. (Keep that elbow up, though.)

Some financial pros are like hands-on personal trainers, assessing your financial health and determining what steps you need to take to get the coveted six-pack abs, er, six-figure retirement account. Others would rather you hand the whole kit and caboodle over to them so that they can work their magic in private while you read out-of-date magazines in the waiting room. Most financial pros fall somewhere in between these two extremes.

The one thing all financial pros have in common is that their advice isn't free—at least after an initial consultation that some provide gratis to potential clients.

The one thing that Fools should heed when hiring any kind of financial pro is this: The more you know, the more effectively you can work with the pro. We don't think you should ever relinquish all the thinking to a third party.

Following are some general suggestions to help you decide if you need a pro and to find and evaluate the best one for you. Then we'll offer some specific tips for finding help in the areas of financial planning, taxes, real estate, portfolio management, and dog walking (just kidding).

WHEN TO PAY FOR ADVICE

Would you be better off working with a pro? It depends on the following factors:

- How much money you have
- The complexity of your finances
- Your interest in doing the research
- The value of the time, to you, that could be spent *not* studying money matters
- Your expertise in money matters
- Your level of confidence in your understanding

Let's take a look at the two extremes.

LOW MONEY, LOW COMPLEXITY, LOW INTEREST, LOW CONFIDENCE

Let's say that you don't have a lot of money and your financial life isn't all that complicated. Nonetheless, you're a little uneasy about some debt you've picked up along the way or a decision you just made about your company retirement plan. And frankly, you'd sooner read the instructions for replacing the gook inside your lava lamp than slog through a stack of financial how-to pamphlets.

In this scenario, you might seek an hour or two of a professional's time just to sketch out a basic financial planning framework. In this short time the pro may:

- Answer a few specific questions (about taxes, estate planning, selling your home, or paying off your debts, depending on why you contacted the pro in the first place)
- Quickly organize and orient your overall financial picture
- Ensure that you're maximizing your retirement savings
- Furnish a much-needed wake-up call regarding your debt
- Check to be sure you have all of the basic insurance you need
- Make sure that you're filling out your 1040EZ tax form accurately—and legally

- Congratulate you on your stellar money management so far and send you away grinnin'

If you fall into this low-money/low-complexity category, one thing you probably don't need is a full-blown, detailed financial plan or historical tax audit in exchange for $2,000 of your meager savings. You also don't want a free consultation with a life insurance salesperson. Trust us on that one. You just want to check in and chat with someone who can add a little expert, objective context to your general financial situation.

HIGH MONEY, HIGH COMPLEXITY, HIGH INTEREST, HIGH CONFIDENCE

You may be the type who actually enjoys researching all the angles of every financial decision. Your friends and family all look to you for advice. The tax code is your favorite bedtime reading. In short, you don't need no stinkin' financial planner.

WHERE DO YOU STAND?

Hopefully you'll recognize yourself somewhere in the middle of the two extremes. To help you put it down in black and white, put a check mark by the items that best describe where you fall on this basic range and then fill in the blanks (high or low).

_____ High money	_____ Low money
_____ High complexity	_____ Low complexity
_____ High interest	_____ Low interest
_____ High confidence	_____ Low confidence

_____ money   _____ complexity   _____ interest   _____ confidence

Give some thought to where you stand on this continuum. As usual, Fool, *you* make the call as to whether you need to call in a hired gun.

OTHER TIMES TO HIRE A PRO

Okay, let's say you are one of those people who thrive on the intricacies of tax-loss selling and setting up escrow accounts. (We sure hope you have some outdoor hobbies that improve your cardiovascular health, too.) There are probably a few occasions when even you will need to call in support.

Life has a way of squeezing important, high-dollar decisions into small time frames, just when you happen to be overwhelmed by other responsibilities. In moments like these, a financial pro may earn his fee many times over by helping you through sticky situations such as:

• **The death of a parent:** You may be the executor of the estate, but is now really a good time to bone up on all the complexities involved or to decide how to invest a substantial inheritance? Would you feel better having a trusted, clearheaded pro on your team?

• **Marriage:** You've just tied the knot, and you've decided to blend your finances into one. Sure, your Schmoopy trusts you, but maybe an independent voice will smooth the way and even point out some tax implications.

• **Divorce:** You've just untied the knot. It's hard enough working through all the divorce lawyers and emotional turmoil, but what about the financial implications? Do you still file taxes jointly this year? Can the stay-at-home former spouse still make a contribution to a spousal IRA?

• **Complex financial products:** Term life and automobile insurance are simple enough that almost anybody can effectively research and purchase them online. But what about complex products such as disability and long-term care insurance? And do you need an umbrella liability policy?

• **Buying and selling a house:** The hallmark of these transactions is a sudden string of big-dollar decisions with little time to think them through. Can you really afford this house? What are the cash flow implications? Should you plow all of your savings into the down payment or keep a little for a rainy day?

• **Saving for college:** It's the last day of the tax year, and you have a little money coming back. You want to make a contribution to a tax-sheltered college savings account for your kids. What are the pros and cons of all the options?

• **Estate planning:** It's *not* just about avoiding taxes. Have you thought about who will manage the kids' inheritance should you die unexpectedly? Do you really want them controlling what's left of the life insurance payout at age eighteen? Should you set up a trust?

• **Retirement:** Your employer has hit the skids and you're being offered an early-retirement package. Should you take it? Do you have enough money to retire? Perhaps four different brokers have shown you four different plans; two say you can afford to retire, two say you can't. Could you use an objective review of all four plans?

• **Employee stock options:** Should you exercise your employee stock options this year or next year? What are the tax implications?

There are many reasons to seek the services of a paid financial adviser, ranging all the way from a helping hand in getting off to a solid start early in your life, to, later in life, calling in support to help with a complex mess at a critical moment.

WORKSHEET: GATHER YE PAPERS

Regardless of the type of financial pro you're going to hire, you'll need to cough up a few key financial documents. We offer the following list of items for you to gather ahead of your meeting. The breadth of the financial inventory listed here is geared more toward preparing for a tête-à-tête with a financial planner. But even if you're meeting someone to discuss taxes or buying a home, having a handle on all of these items will give you and the pro a rough overview of your financial health.

There's a lot here, but the more detail you have on hand, the better advice you'll get. So get started early. After you've located—or developed—each item, stash it in a file.

1. A rough outline of your **monthly budget.** Use the one you've developed in this workbook. If you need to hire a pro before you're finished with the Bit-by-Bit Budget, just estimate your regular monthly payments: utilities, rent/mortgage payment, car payment, other loan payments, phone, cable, and so on.

Where to locate:
Added to folder: (Checkmark when completed)

2. A recent **pay stub** from work that shows income, payroll deductions, and taxes paid. If you are self-employed, or if a significant chunk of your income is derived from commissions, bonuses, recording contracts, game show appearances, and so forth, try to put together a rough timeline of this less predictable income over the last year or so.

Where to locate:
Added to folder:

3. A copy of your most recent **tax return.**

Where to locate:
Added to folder:

4. Recent **account statements for all retirement plans** (pension, 401(k), 403(b), profit sharing, IRAs, etc.) showing current balances and how they are invested (stocks, bonds, funds, etc.).

Where to locate:
Added to folder:

5. Your most recent annual **statement from the Social Security Administration.** If you can't find it, you can order a replacement online at www.ssa.gov (it will arrive by mail in two to four weeks).

Where to locate:
Added to folder:

6. The most recent **bank and brokerage statements** for all accounts, including savings, checking, money market, college savings, and brokerage accounts.

Where to locate:
Added to folder:

7. A **list of your major assets** and their estimated market value: home, car, savings bonds, stock options, Beanie Baby collection, and so on.

Where to locate:
Added to folder:

8. A recent statement showing the outstanding balance and next payment amount for **all debts,** including mortgages, student loan, auto loans, home equity loans, payday loans, and so on.

Where to locate:
Added to folder:

9. The most recent statement from all open **credit card accounts** and other revolving credit accounts showing their total outstanding balances and rates of interest.

Where to locate:
Added to folder:

10. A copy of the latest declarations page from your **auto, homeowner's/renter's, life, and disability insurance.** This is the page that tells you exactly what coverages you have and what you are paying for each. If you get disability and life insurance through work, try to hunt down a brochure from your company that explains the plan.

Where to locate:
Added to folder:

11. **Records for any other account, trust fund, legal judgment, and so on** that have a major impact (or potential impact) on your finances.

Where to locate:
Added to folder:

12. **The folder in which you're stashing all this stuff.**

Where to locate:

HOW TO HIRE A FINANCIAL PLANNER

Now to the nitty-gritty of hiring a financial pro. We'll start with financial advisers—the generalists in the field of money management. A financial adviser (also referred to as a "financial planner" or "CFP") assesses your overall financial picture with an eye on your retirement investments, savings, debts, insurance, and other big areas of your money life. Some are equipped to offer estate-planning advice or input on your tax situation.

When it comes to hiring a financial planner, it pays to screen them carefully. Thankfully, you can do so for free since many financial planners will give you an hour of their time for free, upfront, to explore your needs and explain how they operate. A big chunk of this initial meeting will be devoted to establishing—in the planner's mind—a rough overview of your overall financial health.

But you also want to leave plenty of time to evaluate a candidate and get a solid understanding of how the relationship will work: how often you'll meet, what the planner will and will not do, how well the planner answers tough questions, and **how the planner is paid.**

HOW ARE FINANCIAL PLANNERS PAID?

How is a planner paid? That's an important point—so we wrote it in boldfaced type and included this section detailing the point.

It's important to understand exactly how planners are paid so that you can make an informed decision. But remember, not many worthwhile pros work for peanuts. Don't get so ruthless about cost that you end up with worthless advice.

Financial planners are paid in four basic ways. Many mix these options.

1. Commissions

There are essentially three types of commission payments:

- Onetime sales rewards, such as mutual fund "loads" or the upfront payments that come from selling annuities and cash value life insurance policies
- Ongoing, annual service payments, such as annual commissions paid to insurance agents upon policy renewal
- Commissions paid for transactions, such as buying and selling shares of stock

2. Fee Based on Percentage of Assets

Some planners charge a straight percentage of your total assets on an annual basis—either all assets (from your personal balance sheet) or just the assets they are helping you manage. This is the most common arrangement for paying an independent financial planner and is increasing in popularity.

3. Fee Based on an Hourly Rate

Under this arrangement, you do the bulk of the work and pay the planner for information and advice on an as-needed basis—like the typical arrangement with a personal lawyer.

4. Flat Fee for a Onetime Financial Plan

You pay a hefty upfront fee, often in the many thousands of dollars, for a glossy write-up of your total financial empire, complete with recommendations for action.

These four ways to make a living aren't mutually exclusive. In fact, the majority of financial planners are compensated by a combination of fees *and* commissions. It's important to know a bit about where a planner derives her paycheck. Here are a few tips to help you weed through the gobbledygook:

- Don't be misled by labels. Ask planner candidates exactly how they will be paid. "Fee only" should mean that the planner accepts no sales or trading commissions. Ask directly to be sure.

- "Fee based" and "fee offset" are *not* the same as "fee only." The fundamental basis of these relationships is a fee, but subsequent commissions are also part of the package—either charged on top of fees ("fee based") or subtracted from fees ("fee offset").

- Find somebody with whom you can develop a long-term relationship, even if you will rarely seek advice. You don't want to have to start over again every time, especially if a tight timeline is at the root of your next money problem.

- In the best case, even a well-intentioned commission-based planner might overlook the best option for you if he's not trained and paid for selling it. In the absolute worst case, commission-only planners are thinly disguised salesmen with no interest at all in your finances—beyond selling you the one product for which they are most highly compensated.

- Unless you know exactly what you're after, stay away from the "complete financial plan for a few thousand dollars" option. The resulting plans are often long on glossy charts but short on specific advice to solve your unique problems. Moreover, there may be no ongoing advice to service your constantly evolving needs.

- The more money you have, the easier it will be to find a fee-based financial planner, particularly one that charges a "percentage of assets" fee. Having a lot of money doesn't necessarily mean that your finances are more complex, but it does make it more likely that a planner can save (or make) you enough to more than offset the ongoing fee.

- Folks with a net worth below $100,000 will have a tougher time finding a fee-based planner. Moreover, if they are just looking for occasional advice, an annual, asset-based fee is usually an expensive proposition relative to the payback. An hourly charge usually makes more sense. If this is you, expect to take a little more time and effort to find a good planner. It's unlikely that one will knock on your door.

If you are looking for some independent, salesperson-free advice, we do offer a fee-only service called TMF Money Advisor that, for a fraction of what you would pay a financial planner, helps you work up your own plan with the help of an online interactive planning tool and exclusive phone access to ask any financial question you have. Visit http://TMFMA.Fool.com for more information.

CONDUCTING THE FINANCIAL PLANNER INTERVIEW

Just because they work at big-name firms with slick TV commercials doesn't mean that financial advisers—or the firms they work for—are automatically up to snuff. By the same token, EZ Lenny's House o' Money Matters may seem dinky and dingy, but Len may give extraordinary financial guidance to his clients. It's up to you, Fool, to run your own background check.

Grab a pad of paper, don your rumpled Columbo raincoat, and stretch out for the interview. We help with this sleuthing by providing an interview worksheet. Most of the questions you'll pose to a financial planner fall under four categories that you can remember with our favorite Foolish acronym: FACE. It stands for:

F is for Fees: How much will the expert charge? How is he or she paid? Know this in advance so that there are no surprises.

A is for ADV form (or the state securities agency equivalent): This is a document filed with the Securities and Exchange Commission that discloses educational and business background, compensation, and investment methodology. It's best to get your hands on this before you meet with the planner.

C is for Credentials: The sad fact is that anyone can call him- or herself a financial planner in most states. There is no licensing requirement and very lit-

WORKSHEET: QUESTIONS TO ASK A PROSPECTIVE FINANCIAL PLANNER

Make copies of the following worksheet to fill out when interviewing prospective financial planners.

Name _____

Address _____

Telephone _____

Date interviewed _____

Action taken, if any _____

How big is your firm?

You want to determine whether you'll be a little frog in a big pond and just how important your business would be to this person.

_____

_____

Who exactly will be doing my work—you or somebody else? If I have problems or questions, can I speak with you personally or will I be shunted off to another person?

Make sure that you're comfortable with the answers here. Ideally, you should be able to speak with the person who will actually be doing your work.

_____

_____

What are your educational background and experience?

People always like to talk about themselves. See if you get the information in a matter-of-fact fashion or if you're treated to a dog-and-pony show. Although educational background is important, the way in which the person articulates himself is even more so. Ask how long the financial professional has been doing business in this location/town/area. The longer, the better. We like five years. Why? It tells us he must be doing something right because no one has run him out of town on a rail yet.

_____

_____

_____

What professional credentials do you have?

Look for the diplomas on the wall and the initials after the name. You want to see something like Certified Financial Planner (CFP), Chartered Financial Consultant (ChFC), or Certified Public Accountant (CPA) with a specialty designation as a Personal Financial Specialist (PFS). These designations don't ensure that the person does good work, but they do say the person has had extensive training and experience.

_____

_____

_____

Have you done similar work in the past to what I'm asking of you?

If yes, ask for a sample of that work and get the names of three clients you can call for references. The good pros will comply. Review the sample and call the people. As to the latter, we all know the person is going to give you only the names of folks who think highly of him or her. Call anyway and ask one question: What don't you like about the services you receive(d)? People are basically honest, and they'll tell you.

Names/numbers of references

_____

_____

_____

Feedback

_____

_____

_____

(continued)

WORKSHEET: QUESTIONS TO ASK A PROSPECTIVE FINANCIAL PLANNER, continued

How do you operate? What will you expect me to provide you, and what will you provide in return? How often are we likely to interact?

Here you want to get an idea of what your relationship will be like. Will you just mail in all needed papers once a year and get a prepared assessment back a few weeks later? Will the pro want to meet with you face to face for any reason (perhaps a planning or strategy session)? Will you receive tips or updates from the pro throughout the year?

_____

_____

_____

_____

_____

Speaking of fees, how do you set them? Can I get an estimate of what my fees would be? What are your billing policies?

With this you'll come in prepared. You've read up earlier in this chapter about how financial planners set their fees (right?). We also suggest that you ask the planner's office to send you a copy of their Form ADV. Any person who provides financial planning services and manages investment assets of $25 million or more has to file Form ADV with the Securities and Exchange Commission. (Those who manage less than $25 million in assets must disclose similar information with their own state's securities agency.) Check out the information about commissions and then verify that information with Schedule F. What if the individual provider or the firm principal is not registered with the SEC or the state securities agency? Leave. Get out of the office. Don't do business with that person or firm under any circumstances.

Along the same lines, any professional who sells securities will have a Central Registration Depository (CRD) file. You may obtain CRD information through your state securities agency. The CRD will give you a ten-year history of the provider, including any disciplinary actions taken against that person.

_____

_____

_____

tle regulation, but the charlatans don't have and can't use these designations, so the credentials become your seal of quality. (For more on this, see the box on common credentials below.)

E is for Experience: How long has the financial professional been doing business, and has she done similar work in the past?

Will you find the perfect planner overnight? Not necessarily, unless you have a *really* productive evening. But so what? This isn't something that you want to hurry. When you need expert advice, you want to be certain you've found the right person.

Draw a Turkey

Got a few minutes to kill waiting for your interviewee to call you into her office? Use a blank page to outline your hand and draw a turkey. (Hint: The head goes where your thumb is.) Extra credit goes to those who show their artwork to the potential financial adviser and get a laugh. And not one of those polite "I'm laughing because it might help me win you over as a client" laughs, either.

COMMON CREDENTIALS—FROM CFA TO XYZPDQ

What's that alphabet soup trailing the name of so many financial pros? Those letters usually stand for academic degrees, professional designations, and licenses used in the world of personal finance and investing. To help you decipher those fancy acronyms embossed on letterheads, we spell out the most common—and not-so-common—credentials here:

CFA: Chartered Financial Analyst
CFP: Certified Financial Planner
ChFC: Chartered Financial Consultant
CPA: Certified Public Accountant
MBA: Master of Business Administration
RIA: Registered Investment Adviser
RR: Registered Representative

Others that you may come across are:

AAMS: Accredited Asset Management Specialist
CFM: Certified Financial Manager
CIC: Chartered Investment Counselor
CIMA: Certified Investment Management Analyst
CLU: Chartered Life Underwriter
CMA: Certified Management Accountant
CMC: Certified Management Consultant
CMFC: Chartered Mutual Fund Counselor
CMT: Chartered Market Technician
CPCU: Chartered Property Casualty Underwriter
PFS: Personal Financial Specialist
REBC: Registered Employee Benefits Consultant
RHU: Registered Health Underwriter

XYZPDQ: Examine Your Zipper Pretty Darn Quick

Of course, credentials don't tell the whole story of how much skill an investment professional possesses. Some credentials can be easily attained in a number of days with minimal experience, while others are extremely difficult to receive and take years of study. One of the most important credentials is often overlooked: experience. Be sure to ask a professional what sort of work experience gives him the skills needed to effectively provide his service.

The bottom line is that if you're using and paying for the services of a financial professional, make sure that those you are trusting with your money are qualified to do the job correctly.

HOW TO HIRE A TAX ADVISER

Finding a good tax pro is similar to finding a good financial adviser. In fact, many of the questions you'll ask are identical.

Make sure that the answers you receive are reasonable to you. Remember that although most taxpayers might not need a pro, spending a few hundred dollars to have a return professionally prepared might save you much more money than that. Another consideration, if your income and

WORKSHEET: QUESTIONS TO ASK A PROSPECTIVE TAX ADVISER

Make copies of the following worksheet to fill out when interviewing tax professionals.

Name _____

Address _____

Telephone _____

Date interviewed _____

Action taken, if any _____

How big is your firm?

You want to determine whether you'll be a little frog in a big pond and just how important your business would be to this person.

_____

_____

Who exactly will be doing my work—you or somebody else? If I have problems or questions, can I speak with you personally or will I be shunted off to another person?

Make sure that you're comfortable with the answers here. Ideally, you should be able to speak with the person who will actually be doing your work.

_____

_____

What are your educational background and experience?

People always like to talk about themselves. See if you get the information in a matter-of-fact fashion or if you're treated to a dog-and-pony show.

_____

_____

_____

_____

How many continuing professional education (CPE) hours are you required to take, and how many do you normally take on an annual basis?

If you're not comfortable with the answer, ask to see his/her written CPE report, which is required to be filed with his/her professional organization. You don't have to be rude about it. You can just say, "I'm just curious about your areas of CPE interest. Would you mind showing me your written CPE report?"

_____

_____

_____

What research materials do you use or subscribe to? Commerce Clearing House (CCH)? Research Institute of America? Bureau of National Affairs (BNA)?

If you find that the only research material is a copy of the *Federal Tax Handbook,* run—don't walk—to the nearest exit. Taxes evolve from regulations and court cases. Sometimes complicated problems arise that require deep research. You don't want your tax geek to give it his or her "best shot." Being correct is always best when dealing with the IRS.

_____

_____

_____

If my return is audited, will you represent me before the IRS in examination on my behalf? Not with me, but instead of me? And what will the fee for any audit work be?

If the accountant sources out the audit work, think twice. If you're asked to be present at an audit, think a third time. The worst situation in the world can be when both the accountant and client are present at audit time. Then the IRS will be able to ask just about any question it wants and expect an answer. If you're not there, when asked some questions, the accountant may be able to say that he'll have to ask you and submit an answer later—perhaps by mail. When you're present, experienced auditors may be able to get a lot of extra information out of you. They might in a friendly manner, for example, strike up a conversation about cars and car repairs or about nice vacation spots—hoping that you'll mention a

(continued)

WORKSHEET: QUESTIONS TO ASK A PROSPECTIVE TAX ADVISER, continued

Mercedes or fancy vacation in Bali that you don't seem able to afford. Don't let yourself be put into the hot seat in an audit!

_____

_____

_____

How do you operate? What will you expect me to provide you, and what will you provide in return? How often will we likely interact?

Here you want to get an idea of what your relationship will be like. Will you just mail in all needed papers once a year and get a prepared tax return back a few weeks later? Will the pro want to meet with you face to face for any reason (perhaps a planning or strategizing session)? Will you receive tax tips or tax law change updates from the pro throughout the year?

_____

_____

_____

_____

_____

_____

Speaking of fees, how do you set them? Can I get an estimate of what my fees would be? What are your billing policies?

_____

_____

_____

tax life are fairly stable, is that you might use the pro just once, for one year, and then use that professionally prepared return for reference in future returns.

Again, as with any professional financial service, make sure you understand the fee structure and that it is spelled out for you in black and white.

HOW TO HIRE A REAL ESTATE AGENT

A home is probably the biggest purchase any of us ever make (unless you're into piloting your own fleet of jets or collecting live panda bears). This is an area where it's important to make sure all the *T*s are crossed and *I*s written legibly so that they don't look like *T*s.

Many people use a real estate agent when shopping for and ultimately purchasing a home. When a person gets a real estate license, he's called a licensed real estate professional or an agent. He's not, strictly speaking, a broker, though you'll hear the person who shows you houses loosely called your "broker." Brokers actually have advanced training and a different license; they generally need to have been licensed for three years before becoming a broker. This doesn't mean that you're getting second-class service if you get an "agent" instead of a "broker." The only benefit of being a broker is that a broker can start his own company; some brokers choose simply to manage the office rather than going out and showing houses. (Here, as is commonly done, we'll use the terms interchangeably.)

Some people like the extra attention that a hands-on real estate agent can provide. Others just want to be left alone as much as possible so they can look at houses and peer into the under-sink cabinets undisturbed. If you've read our chapter on big purchases, you've begun educating yourself about the entire home-buying process so that you won't need as much hand-holding as some people.

At the Fool, when it comes to stocks, we encourage individuals to use discount brokers since we have little confidence in the services provided by full-service brokers. The same argument can't necessarily be made against full-service real estate pros.

Buying a home is a serious endeavor. There are a lot of legal and financial hoops to jump through, and an agent can help you wend your way through the process. They can inform you about all of your rights and responsibilities. Real estate agents can offer a one-stop shop for all the homes available to you. What's more, real estate agents can help you find and evaluate financing and steer you toward a good home inspector and settlement attorney.

If you want to go it alone, you can. But be realistic about your time frame for buying a house and about the amount of time you'll be able to devote to the process.

HOW IS A REAL ESTATE BROKER PAID?

A real estate broker is essentially a middleman who is paid for a service, based on commission. The broker generally takes about 6 percent of the sales price as a commission. On a $250,000 house, $15,000 in fees ends up going to the broker.

Fools would do well to wonder why real estate brokers aren't paid a fixed amount rather than a commission, which would very likely result in substantially lower fees. (And—surprise!—this idea would not be very popular with the real estate brokerage community.)

How valuable is the service that brokers are providing? As we said before, the process of buying a home is complicated business. Real estate agents can provide invaluable services, such as introducing you to neighborhoods you might not have known about and shepherding you through the settlement process.

But there are many reasons why folks prefer to go the process alone. Supposing there were no agent in the picture, would the price of that $250,000 home be $15,000 less (taking out the realtor's fees)? You and the seller could save that money and split it. Any time you can leave out a middleman, you're going to save money.

However, this is not always practical. It's the same reason why most of us go to retail stores and not wholesalers—we'd rather buy a pen at Wal-Mart than go to BIC's manufacturing plant and ask if we can buy it direct. The retailer is providing a service (chiefly convenience) and for that we are prepared to pay the markup.

CHOOSING A REAL ESTATE AGENT

This list will look familiar to those of you who have read the pages before this one.

Ask for Referrals

If you're staying in an area you know, ask friends and family if they can recommend someone to you. If you're moving to a new area, ask the Better Business Bureau or the Chamber of Commerce for the names of brokers in your new town that are members of their organizations. Call at least five of them and actually meet at least three.

Interview Agents

Remember that this person is going to have a huge effect on your life for at least several months. Make sure that you trust the agent, above all else. On page 197 we provide an interview worksheet you can use when talking to real estate pros.

Ask the Broker to Show You One House

Take a tour of the house with your broker wannabe. Has she listened to your requests? Did you want to see a single-family detached home on two acres of land and are being shown condos instead? A good real estate agent will let you know if your desires are out of whack with reality but should also try hard to find you what you want. Is she showing you what you like—or what she likes?

If You Don't Hit It Off

Interview another agent. These people are professionals and are used to having prospective buyers shop around for their services. Thank her for her time and say that you have decided to use another agent. Don't waste her time (and yours!) if you'd rather work with someone else.

What if an agent does a bad job? You can call the local real estate board if you feel you are being treated unfairly. Agents are held to certain standards by a state regulatory board, and if they violate any of the rules or regulations, they can lose their license.

FSBO: FOR SALE BY OWNER

If you are able to find a house that is for sale by owner, one that you like and that you feel is priced at or below market price, by all means go for it. It may be that someone you know has decided to sell or that you've found the place simply by driving through a neighborhood and seeing a sign out front. You may have found the place through the classifieds in your local paper. You'll need an attorney to step you through the legalities and the paperwork, but you could end up saving a pile of money.

Similarly, if you can find a seller-financed home, where the seller may even be amenable to a rent-to-own situation (wherein the rent you pay goes toward buying the house if you should decide to buy at a later time), again, go for it. The opportunities do exist.

Note that it's much more difficult to *find* a house without an agent, since the overwhelming majority of houses are listed with agents. If, however, you can do so, more power to you.

CHOOSING A BUYER BROKER

Over the years there have been a lot of changes aimed at protecting the house-hunting consumer.

One of the biggest has been the establishment of the "buyer broker."

Traditionally, the real estate agent has always represented the *seller* of the house. So whenever you walk into an agent's office and say something like "I'm ready to offer $150K but would go as high as $160K if I had to," that agent is duty bound to tell the seller about your conversation.

Even though a traditional agent may spend hours and hours with you, her allegiance isn't to you at all. It's to the *seller,* and in this regard her main motivation is to get as much money out of you as possible. There are two reasons for this. One, it makes the seller happy to get a lot of money. Two, as we've seen, the agent's commission is based on a percentage of the selling price. The more you pay, the more she makes.

There are many agents who take exception to looking at their business so coldly. And there are many fine and ethical agents in the world (some of the parents and spouses of Fools are in the biz. Hi, Mom!). But the bottom line is that sellers' agents are salespeople who make their living off commissions. Never forget that, no matter how nice they are.

So how can a good Fool make sure that the guy who is helping him is *really* helping him? Enter the "buyer broker."

A buyer broker works for you. The two of you will negotiate a fee based on several criteria, according to the state in which you're looking. Most of the time the fee comes out of the seller's proceeds, but sometimes buyer brokers are paid up front with a flat fee.

Usually, however, the broker is compensated by commission based on the *sale price* of the house. So in spite of what we're about to tell you, know that the payment structure still favors a higher sales price—and that does not benefit you (unless you negotiate a commission with the buyer broker, as described later).

Practically speaking, the amount the buyer broker will make in commissions if you get the house for, say, $247,000 versus $249,000 (3 percent of the difference, or $60) isn't enough for her to jeopardize her relationship with you. After all, the deal may fall through, and she wants you to have no qualms about using her as your agent until you find the house that you eventually end up buying.

Negotiating the Buyer Broker Fee

You can negotiate a flat fee with your buyer broker. Start with what you expect to pay for your house. Then take 3 percent of that amount (or half the standard commission rate in your state). For

WORKSHEET: QUESTIONS TO ASK A PROSPECTIVE REAL ESTATE AGENT OR BUYER BROKER

Make copies of the following worksheet to fill out when interviewing potential real estate agents and buyer brokers.

Name _____

Address _____

Telephone _____

Date interviewed _____

Action taken, if any _____

(continued)

WORKSHEET: QUESTIONS TO ASK A PROSPECTIVE REAL ESTATE AGENT OR BUYER BROKER, continued

What are your training and experience?

People always like to talk about themselves. See if you get the information in a matter-of-fact fashion or if you're treated to a dog-and-pony show. Ask how long the agent has been doing business in this location/town/area. The longer, the better. We like five years. Why? It tells us she must be doing something right because no one has run her out of town on a rail yet. An agent who knows the town well will most likely serve you better than a newcomer.

_____

_____

_____

What can you tell me about the area of town in which I'm interested?

Does the agent seem knowledgeable? You want a strong agent. That is, you want someone who knows the market well enough to advise you on any given house.

_____

_____

_____

What do you know about the type of house I'm looking for?

Be sure to first describe some of your housing desires. Does she ask *you* questions about what it is that you want?

_____

_____

What have you found is the most challenging part about negotiating with sellers? Do you have a lot of experience doing that?

You want someone who's had experience in negotiating with sellers, and with closing.

_____

_____

_____

If I need a settlement attorney or a building inspector, can you provide me with a list of ones you like?

You want someone who can steer you toward at least three excellent settlement attorneys or building inspectors if you so desire.

_____

_____

_____

Who exactly will be assisting me—you or somebody else? If I have problems or questions, can I speak with you personally or will I be shunted off to another person?

Make sure that you're comfortable with the answers here. Ideally, you should be able to speak with the person who will actually be doing your work.

_____

_____

Can you give me a few referrals?

Get the names of three clients you can call for references. The good pros will comply. As to the latter, we all know the person is going to give you the names only of folks who think highly of him or her. Call anyway and ask one question: What don't you like about the services you receive(d)? People are basically honest, and they'll tell you.

Names/numbers of references:

_____

_____

_____

(continued)

WORKSHEET: QUESTIONS TO ASK A PROSPECTIVE REAL ESTATE AGENT OR BUYER BROKER, continued

Feedback:

_____

_____

_____

How do you operate? What will you expect me to provide you, and what will you provide in return? How often are we likely to interact?

Here you want to get an idea of what your relationship will be like.

_____

_____

_____

_____

_____

_____

Speaking of fees, how do you set them? Can I get an estimate of what my fees would be? What are your billing policies?

Let any prospective real estate agent know what you expect from her.

_____

_____

_____

example, if you're looking for a condo that costs $100,000, tell your buyer broker that you'll pay her a flat $2,500 commission and then another $100 for every $1,000 that she saves you under $100,000. This means that she will make money no matter what. Plus she has an incentive to make it as cheap as possible for you.

But remember, you are going to be signing a contract. Make sure that the services and method of compensation you expect are spelled out in the agreement. Will you still have to pay the fee if she hasn't found a house that meets your criteria in three months? Probably not, but get it down on paper.

Now it's time to start interviewing agents!

HOW TO HIRE A STOCKBROKER

Thinking about hiring a broker to buy and sell stocks for you? Circle the appropriate answer:

No.

If you haven't gathered this already, we Fools believe that if you don't want to research individual stocks, you should just buy a broad-market, passively managed index fund for the stock portion of your portfolio. But, as always, Fool, *you* make the final call.

WHAT'S WRONG WITH FULL-SERVICE BROKERS?

Here at The Motley Fool, we have a pretty set opinion as to whether you should use a full-service broker or a discount broker. We favor discount brokers, who execute trades for about one twentieth the amount that full-service brokers often charge.

Yup, that's right . . . *one twentieth* the amount that full-service brokers charge. Whereas discount brokers typically charge between $5 and $20 for an individual online trade, you'll probably pay around $150 for the average trade done through the typical full-service (really, full-price) broker. Further, full-service firms often charge annual "maintenance" fees through which they grant themselves a generous slice of your assets, say about $150 a year or more. Alternatively, full-service brokerages might grant "unlimited free trades" in an account but will charge you around 1 to 1.5 percent of your total assets—per year! In other words, full-service brokerages provide help at a high cost. Very high.

So do you get twenty times the value by using one of those expensively dressed souls who work for Merrill Lynch, Salomon Smith Barney, Morgan Stanley, and other companies?

We don't think so. Most brokers who give advice are just salesmen, shopping around their brokerage house's stock picks or pricey mutual funds. Brokers are paid a percentage (commission) for every sale they make. While there are some knowledgeable brokers who do a knockout job for their clients, many aren't actually very good investors and lack impressive or even average performance histories.

Another problem is that full-service brokers usually receive commissions on each trade, so their compensation is closely tied with *how often* their clients' accounts are traded. In other words, part of the commission *you* pay to the firm may wind up directly in your broker's pocket. *So your full-service broker may be paid not for how well your investments perform (which is in your best interest, obviously), but rather on account activity (often the opposite of your best interest).* Highly distressing.

HOW TO FIND A FULL-SERVICE BROKER

If you *are* looking for a broker, for whatever reason, we have gleaned some excellent, candid advice from a practicing broker who posts on our discussion boards at Fool.com. He gave us some guidelines to sizing up practitioners of his trade:

- **Pick out a broker to meet.** Some say that you should look only for people with designations, CFP being the most common one referred to. This is a decent starting point, but the only ones who believe it should be carved in stone are the designation holders. A better place to start is by asking family and friends who have worked with a broker. From this list—gather three to five names—see if there is a common thread. If a broker is mentioned more than once, you might want to start with him or her. A little-known advantage to coming in as a referral is that you carry a little more weight, especially if the person who referred you is a good client.

- **Set up appointments.** Remember that you are interviewing the person to be hired as *your* money manager. You have the right to ask anything you want, but also remember that he or she has the right not to answer a question. Some brokers will not divulge the size of their practice, nor will they acknowledge having anyone as a client, unless they are the one who referred you.

- **Be prepared.** This is a job interview. Be honest with the broker. You should have an idea of what

WORKSHEET: QUESTIONS TO ASK A PROSPECTIVE STOCKBROKER

Make copies of the following worksheet to fill out when interviewing potential stockbrokers.

Name _____

Address _____

Telephone _____

Date interviewed _____

Action taken, if any _____

What licenses do you hold? And what are your training and experience?

People always like to talk about themselves. See if you get the information in a matter-of-fact fashion or if you're treated to a dog-and-pony show. If the broker does not have a Series 7 license, he may not sell individual stocks and bonds. If he does not have an insurance license, he may not sell an annuity. It is amazing how many brokers with just a Series 6 (Investment Company/Variable Contract Representative) think that individual issues are not worthwhile—when, oddly enough, they can't sell them.

_____

_____

_____

_____

What is your general philosophy on the markets?

Everybody has favorite investments, and that is where they tend to put money. For instance, if your broker doesn't like bond funds and you are interested in bond funds, the relationship probably isn't a good fit. Also ask what mutual funds he uses. There are literally hundreds of fund families, but people usually use only from one to ten families. Check out the fund families and their fees when you get home.

_____

_____

_____

How big is your firm?

You want to determine whether you'll be a little frog in a big pond and just how important your business would be to this person.

_____

_____

Who is your broker dealer?

Some of the best brokers have broker dealers whom you never heard of but are well respected in the business. This is especially true of independent broker dealers. The only independent firm most people have heard of is the second largest of them, and that is because a football stadium is named after it (Raymond James). You can check out whatever broker dealer the candidate uses at www.nasdr.com.

_____

_____

_____

What is your disciplinary record?

If the broker will not respond to this question, thank him for his time and leave. This is one question where a nonanswer is unacceptable. You can see if there have been any actions against the broker by logging on to www.nasdr.com.

_____

(continued)

WORKSHEET: QUESTIONS TO ASK A PROSPECTIVE STOCKBROKER, continued

_____

_____

Who exactly will be doing my work—you or somebody else? If I have problems or questions, can I speak with you personally or will I be shunted off to another person?

Make sure that you're comfortable with the answers here. Ideally, you should be able to speak with the person who will actually be doing your work.

_____

_____

Have you done similar work in the past to what I'm asking of you?

If yes, ask for a sample of that work and get the names of three clients you can call for references. Beware: the broker may have to call and get permission from his clients before revealing their names and contact information. Review the sample and call the people. As to the latter, we all know the broker is going to give you only the names of folks who think highly of him or her. Call anyway and ask one question: What don't you like about the services you receive(d)? People are basically honest, and they'll tell you.

Names/numbers of references:

_____

_____

_____

Feedback:

_____

_____

_____

How do you operate? What will you expect me to provide you, and what will you provide in return? How often are we likely to interact?

Here you want to get an idea of what your relationship will be like. Will the broker want to meet with you face to face for any reason? Will you receive information or updates from the broker throughout the year?

_____

_____

_____

_____

_____

Speaking of fees, how do you set them? Can I get an estimate of what my fees would be? What are your billing policies?

_____

_____

_____

you like and don't like about past investing experiences. You should have a general idea of the time frame in which your money will remain invested. Is it for retirement, college savings, or a down payment on a bigger house? These all have different time frames and should be invested for differently. If you lie about the amount of money you have to invest or your risk tolerance, you will get advice based on false information and it will not be worth anything to you.

• **Don't sign anything at the first meeting.** Go home, do your checks, and think about whether you want this person handling your money. Think hard.

In the end, as with all hiring decisions, you need to trust your gut. If you don't like the broker, don't do business with him. Never mind that Uncle Charlie has used his services for years. You don't have to.

Finally, always remember, it's *your* money. *You* are the one ultimately responsible for it. If you're not honest with the broker about your risk tolerance and expectations, you won't get good advice. If you don't get the level of service you want, start looking elsewhere. If your questions are not answered to your satisfaction, don't agree to the investment.

Don't be railroaded into anything. It's not necessary to "act now or lose out!" for any good long-term investment. In the words of the candid broker who gave us these guidelines: "Yes, there are opportunities that you will miss if you sit on the sidelines and think about it, but there are also a lot of opportunities to lose money by acting without thinking. Unless you are looking to trade rather than invest, chances are the security will still be worth investing in tomorrow. Even if it isn't, something else will be."

TEN TIPS ON WORKING WITH A FINANCIAL PROFESSIONAL

Here are ten general rules of thumb that will help you form a happy, healthy, and warm-and-fuzzy relationship with your financial professional:

1. **Know exactly why you are hiring a pro.** You should know precisely what questions you want answered—and what you're paying for—before you write the first check. If you only want the pro to help you make sense of your 401(k) options, then say so or you may end up discussing life insurance for fifty of your sixty minutes together.

2. **If you are hiring a tax pro, find one who is familiar with your business or industry.** Avoid those who try to convey that they know everything about everything. Everyone has areas of expertise; make sure the pro meets your needs. For example, if you have issues such as employer stock options, make sure the pro has expertise in those issues.

3. **Don't sign anything that you don't understand.** And don't write out checks directly to a financial planner for financial products and investments. Most important; don't sign a "discretionary authority" unless you know *exactly* what you are doing. This enables a planner to buy and sell investments without consulting you ahead of time. The same goes for other types of financial pros.

Make sure you understand all documents before you commit your John Hancock to the dotted line.

4. **Interview all potential candidates as if they were job applicants.** Ask for an interview. In most cases, he or she will be glad to give you an hour of advice at no charge to discuss your situation and assess your specific needs and desires. It should be a two-way effort, with both of you probing for a good fit. In particular, be wary of somebody who either desperately wants your business or can't "lower himself" to your level. And beware of "Just trust me" kinds of responses.

5. **See if the professional has any questions for you.** If she's established and successful, she doesn't have to take any old Fool who walks in the door. The more questions she asks, the better. At least it shows some interest.

6. **When you ask questions, do you understand the answers?** When you ask for clarification, does the subsequent explanation make more sense? Are you comfortable admitting that you don't understand something?

7. **Make sure you take the advice you paid good money for.** If your adviser's guidance makes sense, make sure you follow it. As Berkeley professor Matthew Rabin has argued, procrastination plays a big role in economics. So if your adviser says you need to open a Roth IRA and you agree, do it. Not doing so is a waste of your money.

8. **Unless you are specifically looking for stock picks from a broker, be wary of any pro who is preoccupied with these.** This is especially true if he generates commission income by getting you to trade actively. A good financial adviser always puts the basics—such as insurance and cash flow—before investment advice. All specific investment recommendations should be fit into a larger framework built around your financial goals. And if your

tennis pro starts offering stock tips, run for the baseline!

9. Any discussion of investments should involve the level of risk. If any type of financial adviser promotes any investment—be it in a stock, insurance, real estate, or collectible Cabbage Patch dolls—as a risk-free "sure thing" or offers you "exclusive access," find another pro, *especially* if the promised reward is very attractive.

10. Try to find financial pros on your own, rather than waiting for salespeople to descend upon you. Ask for referrals from friends and family with good instincts and financial sense. If possible, talk to people with financial concerns similar to yours or ones who have just dealt with one of those pressing issues that called for a quick decision.

In the end, it's most important to select someone you're comfortable with. You want someone skilled, but if you're uneasy with his or her style, you may hesitate to call for further information and might not provide the information that he or she needs in order to do a good job for you. Once you've verified the person's technical competence to the best of your ability, evaluate the comfort factor.

As always, Fool, the money decisions you make—regardless of the advice you paid for—are yours and yours alone.

CHAPTER 11

DOING A FINANCIAL CHECKUP

SIXTY-SECOND GUIDE TO DOING A FINANCIAL CHECKUP

As you've worked through this book, you've assessed various aspects of your finances, then charted a course so you can meet your goals. To make sure you and your finances stay on track, open wide. It's time for a financial checkup.

0:60 Decide on a place, time, and ambiance.

Set an appointment with your checkup. Write it in your calendar, personal digital assistant, or date book or on your forehead. And do all you can to make it an enjoyable task.

0:55 Update your records.

Gather your most recent account statements for all bank, credit card, mutual fund, and brokerage accounts. If you are maintaining a Bit-by-Bit Budget, make sure the information is up to date.

0:43 Ready . . . set . . . review!

Take some time to peruse your statements, balances, and goals.

0:30 Go through the checklist.

Your personal finances have many facets. To help you keep them all straight, we provide a checklist of topics to review and discuss.

0:15 Make resolutions.

You've perused, you've discussed, you've reviewed. Now it's time to take action.

0:08 Give yourself a pat on the back or a slap on the knee.

Find a way to reward yourself for keeping up with the program. We know that improving your financial situation and potentially increasing your net worth by thousands of dollars are not always enough to get you to sit down with your bank statements.

0:03 For couples.

If you have a partner, we have special considerations for how to manage your money with your co-CEO.

• • •

So far in this book, we've covered most of the limbs and organs that make for a healthy, robust financial life. It'll take a bit of work to get everything into shape, but once you've set up your program, it should be as easy as a jog in the park.

But every once in a while, you should get a checkup. You know, take the pulse of your spending, check the weight of your retirement accounts, bend over and try to touch your taxes.

Most important, this is the time to evaluate whether you're on track to meet your goals. You'll take a look at your account statements and decide whether you're saving enough. Or you'll review your credit card statements and see if you're paying off your debt quickly enough. How are your investments doing? Where is your money going? You'll answer all these questions during your checkup.

HOW OFTEN SHOULD YOU TAKE YOUR FINANCIAL PULSE?

If your finances are complicated, or if you're in a situation where every penny must be counted, review your finances every month or every three months. If you are actively trying to pay down debt, a monthly tally will help you chart your progress and spur you on. And, hey! You might even start looking forward to it!

For others, every six months might be fine. However often you choose to review your situation, make it an actual event—set a couple of hours aside in your calendar, let the answering machine take the calls, put the kids to bed early . . . or maybe even get a babysitter.

If you're married or in a relationship where you share finances or belong to a hippie commune where ownership is meaningless but someone still has to pay the electric bills, you should probably meet quarterly. With two people (or more) handling the finances, communication is important. Later in this chapter, we'll have some pointers for discussing money with your honey.

INJECTING CHEER INTO YOUR CHECKUP

We know that talking about insurance and taxes is about as invigorating as a walk in an industrial park. So come up with ways to make the event more bearable. Here are ways to bring some levity to the task and maybe—just maybe—make it enjoyable:

- Go to your favorite coffee shop or restaurant.
- Accompany the checkup with your favorite dessert.
- Do the checkup in the bathtub.
- Take a blanket and your dog (or a friend's dog) to the beach. Play some Frisbee and look over your financial papers during breaks.
- Discuss your retirement under a furniture fort, among many pillows.
- Play Christmas music and drink hot cocoa.
- Just get it over with and reward yourself with a movie.

WHY BOTHER?

If you've completed this book, you've already done a lot of reviewing and evaluating. Why do you have to do it again every few months? Here's why:

• **You'll be able to chart your progress.** Give yourself the satisfaction of seeing your debts decrease and your investments increase.

• **You'll get to where you want to go.** You'll be much more likely to achieve your goals if you know you're on track and can make adjustments along the way.

• **You'll have more control.** If you completed the money-tracking exercise in Chapter 2, you probably saw money going to places that weren't so important to you. We know you want to have more control of your money and you want your money to do more for you. Otherwise, you wouldn't be reading this book.

• **You'll build a better life for your family.** Making sure that you are properly insured, that you have enough savings, and that you're getting the most bang for your buck all put your family onto a firmer financial foundation.

• **You'll keep up with your and your family's evolving lives.** Your priorities may change; the size of your family may change; your job and income may change; your hair will definitely change. Your personal finances should change accordingly.

Convinced? We hope so. We'll make it even easier for you by breaking down the checkup into five steps, complete with a handy checklist.

THE FIVE STEPS

1. MAKE IT A DATE

This isn't one of those "I'll get to it when I can" tasks. Decide on a definite time to perform your checkup (e.g., the first Thursday evening of every month). Or after each checkup, set the next date. We suggest you try performing a checkup once a month as you start out, then maybe go to once a quarter (i.e., every three months) when you feel your finances are on course.

2. PREPARE

Gather the following accoutrements:

• Your Bit-by-Bit Budget, if you're maintaining one

• Your most recent bank, brokerage, IRA, retirement, and credit card statements . . . and any other pertinent financial paperwork
• A calculator
• Your budget
• A whoopee cushion

3. ASSESS YOUR ASSETS . . . AND YOUR DEBTS

Relax, get comfortable, and get ready to review your entire net worth. Really, this won't hurt a bit.

Generally, what you're looking for is your debts to be decreasing and your assets to be increasing. If, in general, your debts are going down and your savings are going up, congratulations! Stay the course. If, however, your debt is getting bigger and your savings are going nowhere, there can be only one cause: you're spending all of what you make—or even more—on a regular basis. Unless you can come up with a way to markedly improve your income, you're going to have to cut some spending. Go back over your budget. Resolve to focus on reducing spending as your top financial priority.

To address specific aspects of your finances, use the following worksheet. If it works for you, great. However, you may want to create your own worksheet to address your specific situation. You probably don't need to answer all of these questions each time you review your finances, but each question should be addressed at least once a year.

OTHER ISSUES TO DISCUSS

This Financial Checkup Worksheet should be used as a guideline. Being the unique and quirky individual that you are, you'll have your own list of concerns that'll need regular—or irregular—review. Here are some other issues you might consider:

• Paying off low-interest debt (e.g., mortgage, student loans) or investing more for retirement

WORKSHEET: FINANCIAL CHECKUP

Directions: Review this checklist as part of your financial checkup. Noted in each category is the chapter you can consult for more information.

	DATE OF CHECKUP:	DATE OF CHECKUP:	DATE OF CHECKUP:	DATE OF CHECKUP:
Spending and saving (Chapter 2):				
Do you have the pulse of your pennies? Knowing where your money is going is the first step to taking control.				
Have you stayed within your budget? Make sure your money is going to your priorities, not frivolities.				
Are you living below your means? Look for ways to shave $100 off your monthly budget . . . or even more.				
Others:				
Debt (Chapter 3):				
Has your credit card debt increased or decreased? Credit card debt is a leading cause of financial downfall.				
Is there a way you can get a better interest rate on your credit cards? Companies want your business, so call around for the best rate.				
Have you checked your credit history recently? Errors occur, or you may have forgotten about a loan. Keep your record clean.				
Others:				
Insurance (Chapter 4):				
Do you have adequate coverage?				

(continued)

WORKSHEET: FINANCIAL CHECKUP, continued

	DATE OF CHECKUP:	DATE OF CHECKUP:	DATE OF CHECKUP:	DATE OF CHECKUP:
Could your dependents survive if you were to die? Become disabled? Total your car?				
Has there been a change in your life that would affect your coverage? Job change, birth, marriage, and death should trigger a coverage reevaluation.				
Have you checked around for lower premiums recently? Check with other companies to compare rates or with your existing provider for possible discounts.				
Others:				
Investments (Chapter 5):				
Do you have an emergency fund? Setting aside 3 to 6 months' worth of expenses could save you from debt—or worse.				
Are you getting the best return on your investments? Is your stock portfolio beating the market? Are you getting the best rate on your short-term savings?				
Is your brokerage providing good service at a reasonable price? The brokerage and mutual fund industries are very competitive. Get the best for your money.				
Others:				
Retirement (Chapter 6):				
Are you on track to retire when you want to? Monitor your progress using the process in Chapter 6 or an online calculator.				
How have your retirement investments been performing?				

	DATE OF CHECKUP:	DATE OF CHECKUP:	DATE OF CHECKUP:	DATE OF CHECKUP:
Make sure that your investments keep up with their respective indexes.				
Are you taking advantage of the best available savings vehicles? Make sure you understand the benefits of traditional IRAs, Roth IRAs, and work-sponsored plans.				
Others:				
Taxes (Chapter 8):				
Have you done your taxes for the year? Why wait until April . . . unless you owe a lot of money?				
Have you reviewed what deductions and/or credits you're entitled to? The tax laws are always changing, so check out the IRS Web site each year.				
Are you taking advantage of all possible tax-friendly retirement accounts? Contributing to a 401(k) or IRA saves on taxes and increases your nest egg.				
Others:				

- Paying for recent minor catastrophes (e.g., belching furnace, disintegrating automobile)
- Triplets (!)
- Saving for upcoming projects that will take a chunk of money (e.g., landscaping, building a swing set, remodeling the kitchen)
- Financing your plan for world domination or a new couch
- Paying for the kids' college education
- Reviewing potential investments
- Determining how much to spend on this year's vacation

4. ARRIVE AT A PROGNOSIS

Now that you've reviewed your financial health, do you need to take action? Conclude your checkup by writing down and resolving to perform the tasks that should be done by the next checkup. These actions should be:

- **Specific:** Try "Get three quotes on car insurance to see if there are cheaper options" as opposed to "Find ways to save on insurance."

- **Realistic:** Don't come up with a list of chores that you'll never accomplish. Choose the few that are the most important and will make the biggest financial impact.

- **Optimistic:** We know that "to do" lists are never fun, but do your best to look at your resolutions not as burdens but as steps to bringing you closer to early retirement, a vacation home, a new car, or whatever other goals you have.

- **Hedonistic:** Not really, but we needed another word that ended in "ic"—and it sounds more fun than the previous three.

5. REWARD YOURSELF

Congratulations! If you've completed a financial checkup, you deserve a reward. Ideally, have a re-

ward in mind before you do the checkup as extra motivation to actually get it done.

The reward is up to you. It shouldn't involve an exorbitant expense, of course; that would defeat the purpose of the checkup. But spending a little something on life's little luxuries isn't uncalled for. If you're doing a swell job of righting your finances, there's no reason you shouldn't reap some of the benefit along the way.

From here on, this chapter addresses how to perform a checkup with more than one person. If you're single, you're done! If you're a double, or even a triple or quadruple, read on.

RELATIONSHIP REPAIR KIT

Prepare for financial checkup fallout: make an Emergency Relationship Repair Kit. Take a toolbox (or any old box) and place items inside that will help you get over a spat with your co-CEO. You may want to include coupons for eating out, a pair of movie tickets, some old love letters, a poem, or a joke book. Plan on not every money talk going smoothly. Then plan to make up.

A BUDGET BUILT FOR TWO

We all know that money is one of the biggest causes of marital strife. However, it doesn't have to be that way. Managing money as a couple can be an opportunity to grow even closer, to build a prosperous life together, and to fight over the price of two-ply toilet paper. But before we get into the nitty-gritty, let's have a little fun.

THE FOOLY-WED GAME

Remember *The Newlywed Game*? We've created the fun, financial version for you and your partner. The only things missing are the cardboard signs (we discourage smashing objects over loved ones' heads). Take a few minutes to answer the following questions. Read the question aloud; then each partner should record his or her answers on his or her own sheet of paper. Don't peek at each other's answers. The fun part of this exercise is comparing your responses at the end.

---

1. What would your partner say is the annual income your family would need to be happy?

$ _____

2. Place the following items in order of importance (1 = top financial priority; 5 = lowest financial priority):

_____ Furniture   _____ Retirement   _____ Car   _____ Clothes   _____ Vacation

3. When was the last time you made financial whoopee—or at least talked about your finances?

4. How much would your bank account have to sink to before you panicked? $ _____

5. How much is too much to spend without consulting your partner? $ _____

6. If your main squeeze were a superhero, which superhero would he or she be?   _____

7. What are the three best purchases you've made as a couple? The three worst?

Best:

_____

_____

_____

Worst:

_____

_____

_____

(continued)

continued

8. You get $1,000 back as a tax refund. What would you spend it on? What would your partner spend it on?

I would spend it on: _____

My partner would spend it on: _____

9. You view money as (circle one):

    A. A necessary evil

    B. The path to happiness

    C. Nice to have, but I won't sweat over it

    D. Where's my wallet?

10. Which of the two of you is more likely to:

    _____ Know how much is in the checking account

    _____ Buy an expensive gift

    _____ Look for the best deal

    _____ Know how the stock market fared

    _____ Do the taxes

TEN TIPS ON PERFORMING A FINANCIAL CHECKUP

So did you learn anything? Did you find more areas of agreement or more areas of disagreement? Are you still in the same room? C'mon . . . it's time for a group hug.

We're not marriage counselors. (Lord knows, Tom can't even make a commitment for dinner twenty minutes in advance.) But we have heard from some knowledgeable sources—mostly our happily married friends—that anticipating problems and heading them off at the pass are the first steps to healthy comingling. Therefore, keep the following ground rules in mind and you'll be on your way to a lifetime of productive financial conversations.

1. **Agree to try.** You may be skeptical about doing things differently or even of opening financial conversations.

DIVVY UP THE DUTIES

A lot of tasks are required to keep a family's financial engines running smoothly. To make sure all the jobs are covered, it might be helpful to decide who will be in charge of what. Here's a list of potential duties that could be assigned:

_____ Checkbook balancer	_____ Budget monitor
_____ Investment manager	_____ Grocery shopper
_____ Coupon clipper	_____ Bill payer
_____ Tax preparer	_____ Car/house maintenance monitor
_____ Asset/debt tracker	_____ Paperwork manager
_____ Chief gratification delayer	_____ Researcher/assessor/fact finder

2. **Accept equal responsibility for changing your lives.** Creating a better financial future falls to the lot of both members of the couple. That means you share the angst, the jobs (balancing the checkbook, filling out spreadsheets, cutting coupons, etc.), and the rewards (taking that great European vacation! sending your kids to college!).

3. **Don't play the blame game.** No fair bringing up outside issues and attacking your partner's views. You can play the blame game with your tone of voice and posture, too, so watch out for these silent accusations as well as the louder ones.

4. **Be honest.** It won't do any good if you hide expenditures when you're trying to make a joint budget and assess your spending habits. If you feel the urge to lie, ask yourself what's going on—what are you afraid of? If you know this is a problem in your relationship, deal with it constructively and creatively—such as keeping some money separate in a small account earmarked for you.

5. **Be realistic.** You don't want to say you'll have a two-hour conversation about money every Sunday if the two of you never have even fifteen minutes to sit down. Find some small ways to keep each other updated, such as Post-it notes on the refrigerator with your weekly bank balance written on them. Combine your money conversation with another activity you need to do. For example, you might rake leaves together while deciding how much you can spend on your family vacation.

6. **Take a break if your conversation gets heated and unproductive.** Cool down, review your list of ground rules, and make sure you set a follow-up date to talk again. But don't use this rule as an excuse to avoid tough subjects!

7. **Play fair.** If one of you takes on the lion's share of the financial upkeep or picks up the other person's slack, make sure there's a reward for the extra work. Unload the dishwasher for once. Or buy your number-crunching spouse a pair of massaging slippers.

8. **Keep current.** Your summit will go much more smoothly if you update your Bit-by-Bit Budget regularly. If you've slacked off in recent months, do yourself a favor and catch up as best you can. At the very least, whenever you get retirement statements and bills, put them into a file so that you're not searching the entire manse looking for your last MasterCard bill.

9. **Keep it fun.** Remember, you're working toward common goals. Whether it's paying off debt or saving for a pair of vintage Vespas, the financial checkup is all about achieving your dreams.

10. **Stay the course.** If you notice your numbers starting to slip, don't panic! (Well, go ahead and take three minutes and eighteen seconds to let out a primal scream; then it's back to work.) Every business has down cycles. As the CEO (or co-CEO) of your empire, it's up to you to keep your troops on track. If you find that your debts have started creeping back up, resolve to attack them more aggressively in the next fiscal quarter. If you needed to dip into the emergency fund a few months ago, make a mental note to replenish the coffers. Then at the next scheduled financial checkup you can celebrate with a bottle of bubbly juice.

Now, without further ado, it's the moment we've all been waiting for. No, it's not Charo's Reunion Tour. It's time to put it all together. To fill in all the blanks. To blank out as you add it up. It's time to (insert dramatic pause) *finish off your Bit-by-Bit Budget.*

Cue majorettes.

Give the downbeat to the accordion ensemble.

A-one, anna-two, anna-three . . .

CHAPTER 12

THE BIT-BY-BIT BUDGET

SIXTY-SECOND GUIDE TO THE BIT-BY-BIT BUDGET

Yes, ladies and gentlemen, you have reached the conclusion, the culmination, the climax, the *pièce de personal finance*. Just a few more exercises, and you'll be free of our bad jokes—until you read *The Motley Fool Guide to Plumbing, Carpentry, and Romance*.

0:60 Patch the holes.

Your Bit-by-Bit Budget should now be complete—but if it isn't, it's time to fill in the blanks.

0:52 Total up your expenses.

It's time to see how much you have flowing out and compare it to how much is coming in. This is the moment of truth: Are you in the black or the red? If the former, that means you can fund your future with the money left over—congratulations! If the latter—read on!

0:44 Play with the numbers.

If your expenses exceed your income, you'll have to see where you can trim the fat, or even the meat. It may take some sacrifice, but remember: you're giving up not-so-important things in order to pay for your priorities. Make sure you consult the "Money-Saving Tips for Living Below Your Means" appendix to find ways to save money.

0:31 Put the "fun" into "budfungeting."

Now that you have a budget, how are you going to stick to it? Don't worry, living with a budget doesn't have to be a complete bore. Make it just a partial bore by adding spice to your bean counting. There are ways to make it more manageable and enjoyable.

0:17 Wimp out.

We realize that this whole budgeting thing requires a lot of work. And we're the first ones to look for an easy way out. Granted, the more detail you can provide—and the more accurate your numbers—the faster you'll achieve your goals. But if you find yourself in a time crunch and just want to get a basic handle on your finances, use the Baby Budget guidelines we provide on page 221.

0:04 Sing, Fool, sing!

You're now in the top 1 percent of your class. Seriously. We dare you to find anyone who has a better handle on his money than you. Now, don't you feel the urge to belt out a Broadway tune?

• • •

THE END IS NEAR

Do you feel as if you're near the end? Can you tell that a conclusion is upon you? Do you sense that things are winding up? Perhaps you should see a doctor (but not before you get a life insurance policy).

Or it may just be that you have realized that this is the last chapter of this workbook. (Don't be sad—we're planning on a five-year reunion in the Bahamas.) Yes, it's time to finalize your Bit-by-Bit Budget. So here we go.

1. FILL IN THE BLANKS

If you've diligently followed the directions in this book, all the meaningful line items in the budget should be complete. Check over the budget now to make sure you're not omitting an important expense.

2. ADD UP YOUR SOURCES OF INCOME

Those are the top line items in your budget—all the sources of your spending money. Total 'em and enter 'em in the "Total income" line, third from the bottom of the budget.

3. TOTAL YOUR EXPENSES

So how much is your life going to cost you? Add up all your expenses and enter the sum in the "Total outflow" line.

4. SUBTRACT YOUR TOTAL OUTFLOW FROM YOUR TOTAL INCOME.

Here's the moment of truth, people. What's winning the money tug-of-war—your revenues or your disbursements?

5. IF YOU MAKE MORE THAN YOU SPEND

Outstanding! Which of your goals deserves the excess? Decide how to put that extra money to work, adjust your budget accordingly, and—most important—make sure that money goes into the appropriate investment(s).

6. IF YOU SPEND MORE THAN YOU MAKE

Don't worry, you're not alone. And, fortunately, you have many options available to you.

• Consult the "Money-Saving Tips for Living Below Your Means" appendix of this workbook and decide on the best ways to cut back on your costs.

• Perhaps you will have to revise your goals, extending the time horizon (the time at which you want to reach your goals) or reducing their price.

• Really question all the ways in which you spend money. Humans really need only food, clothing, and shelter—and not at retail prices. Despite how we may sometimes feel, cable TV, multiple annual vacations, daily Diet Cokes, and lawn ornaments are not necessities.

LET YOUR COMPUTER DO THE COUNTING

If you are keyboard-inclined, here are some suggestions:

- Develop your budget in a spreadsheet program, such as Excel. It'll take some familiarity with the program to get it to do the math for you, but it's a great way to customize your budget.

- Many money management software products, such as Quicken and Microsoft Money, have budgeting features built in. These programs also make it easy to categorize your expenses and can interface with your bank over the Internet.

- The Budgeting discussion board on Fool.com has many other suggestions for ways to use your computer to count your beans. Drop by and get some help from a whole bunch of Fools.

THE BABY BUDGET

There are several ways of devising a budget. We present the traditional approach: decide how much should go where, and direct your dough accordingly. However, this is just a suggestion; you should design a budget that accounts for your own proclivities, activities, and cavities. For a barebones, no-fancy-stuff budget, follow these steps:

1. RECORD YOUR MONTHLY INCOME

Gather one month's worth of paychecks and indications of other sources of income (dividend income, commissions, paper route). Enter that information into your budget.

2. RECORD MUST-PAY EXPENSES

Start with the basic, unavoidable, pay-or-be-homeless monthly costs. Enter the following expenses into your budget:

- Total housing costs (rent or mortgage payment)
- Grocery costs (assume that you never eat out)

- Utilities (electricity, gas, heating oil, water, phone, etc.)
- Transportation costs (gas, bus fares, etc.)
- Insurance bills
- Loan payments (including credit cards)
- Savings necessary to meet future financial goals

3. SUBTRACT YOUR MUST-PAY MONTHLY EXPENSES FROM YOUR MONTHLY INCOME

The equation should look something like this:

Total monthly income: $ _____

— Total must-pay expenses: $ _____

= Shocking answer accompanied by a quick recalculation that reveals the same number—yes, even the fifth time through: $ _____

This difference represents your "discretionary" money, that is, the money that won't go to your highest priorities. There may be other expenses that you feel should be included in the "must-pay" category, such as clothes or mental health vacations. Fine. After all, it's your budget. The point is, you need to differentiate the expenditures that are very important to you from the expenditures that are nice but not necessary (or even wasteful).

Start apportioning pennies to your various categories, just so you begin evaluating and prioritizing your expenses. Then you can go back to reading novels with Fabio on the cover.

TEN TIPS ON WORKING WITH A BUDGET

Unless you're an accountant, budgeting will never rival a day at Slinky World, but it doesn't have to be torture either. Take a few of our tips and try to create a budgeting system that you might actually follow.

1. **Make it manageable.** An overly detailed, burdensome budget is doomed to fail. You'll give up on it, and the feeling of failure will leave you worse

off than before you started. So be honest: How often will you be able to do this? How often do you need to check on your budget to make sure your finances are solid without driving yourself insane?

Your ideas:

_____

2. Link the process with rewards. Come up with ways to reward yourself for keeping up with your budget. Dinner out? Posters from the National Gallery of Art? A Liberace Beanie Baby? Choose something that will really motivate you (but of course won't break the budget).

Your ideas:

_____

3. Create a fun environment. Watch a video and eat popcorn while you go through receipts; take your balance book to your favorite coffee shop or park; budget in full Renaissance costume.

Your ideas:

_____

4. Share the work. If you have a partner, make sure the tasks—and responsibility—are divvied up. Make sure you both agree on the need for and method of tracking your money. Nothing makes a task more onerous than having to do all the work or fighting the other person every step of the way.

Your ideas:

_____

5. Decide what falls into what category. If you think visits to the pharmacy should fall into "Personal care" instead of "Medical expenses," that's groovy. This budget is up to you. Just make sure you keep track of what goes where. Use the "Notes" section at the end of the budget to keep categories straight.

Your ideas:

_____

6. You decide on the order, too. The Bit-by-Bit Budget is arranged to correspond to this book. Most likely, you'll find that there's a better arrangement—with different categories—that is more effective for you. Once you have completed this workbook, you can create your own budget (on computer or paper) and take it from there.

Your ideas:

_____

7. Once you set up your budget, try to stick to it. One way is the envelope method. Let's say that you have allotted $75 a month for eating out, but you have trouble sticking to it. Here's what you do: Withdraw $75 in cash at the beginning of the month and put the money in an envelope. Go to the envelope for a "withdrawal" each time you visit a restaurant. When the envelope is empty, no more dining out until the following month. If you don't like carrying cash, put poker chips or Monopoly money in the envelope. When you get home from the restaurant, transfer the amount of "money" or chips that corresponds to the amount you spent out of the envelope.

Your ideas:

_____

8. Climb every mountain.

Your ideas:

_____

9. Ford every stream.

Your ideas:

_____

10. Follow every rainbow, till you find your dream.

Your ideas:

_____

BIT-BY-BIT BUDGET

	AMOUNT FROM MONEY TRACKER WORKSHEET	BUDGETED AMOUNT	MONTH 1	MONTH 2	MONTH 3	MONTH 4	MONTH 5	MONTH 6
INCOME:								
Source 1:								
Source 2:								
Source 3:								
Source 4:								
EXPENSES:								
Chapter 1:								
Goal 1:								
Goal 2:								
Goal 3:								
Goal 4:								
Goal 5:								
Chapter 2:								
Room and board:								
Rent/mortgage								
Electricity								
Water								
Oil/gas								
Telephone								
Cell phone								
Trash removal								
House maintenance								
Real estate taxes								
Improvement/furnishings								

(continued)

BIT-BY-BIT BUDGET, continued

	AMOUNT FROM MONEY TRACKER WORKSHEET	BUDGETED AMOUNT	MONTH 1	MONTH 2	MONTH 3	MONTH 4	MONTH 5	MONTH 6
Groceries								
Dining out/take-home food								
Transportation:								
Car loan payment								
Gas								
Maintenance								
Other/commuting costs								
Internal and external care:								
Medical/dental expenses								
Clothing purchases								
Laundry and cleaning								
Personal care								
Recreation:								
Entertainment								
Cable/satellite TV								
Internet access								
Vacations								
Gifts								
Other:								
Business/professional expenses								
Child care expenses and allowances								
Tuition/educational expenses								
Child support and alimony								
Donations to church and charities								

	AMOUNT FROM MONEY TRACKER WORKSHEET	BUDGETED AMOUNT	MONTH 1	MONTH 2	MONTH 3	MONTH 4	MONTH 5	MONTH 6
Chapter 3:								
Debt repayment:								
Credit Card 1								
Credit Card 2								
Credit Card 3								
Credit Card 4								
Loan 1								
Loan 2								
Loan 3								
Chapter 4:								
Insurance:								
Vehicle 1								
Vehicle 2								
Vehicle 3								
Vehicle 4 (you gotta be kidding!)								
Disability insurance								
Renter's or homeowner's insurance								
Liability insurance								
Other insurance (boat, pet, flood, etc.)								
Chapter 5:								
Short- and long-term investments:								
Emergency fund accumulation								
Other:								

(continued)

BIT-BY-BIT BUDGET, continued

	AMOUNT FROM MONEY TRACKER WORKSHEET	BUDGETED AMOUNT	MONTH 1	MONTH 2	MONTH 3	MONTH 4	MONTH 5	MONTH 6
Chapter 6:								
Retirement:								
Employer-provided plan(s)								
IRA(s)								
Other								
Chapter 7:								
Big-ticket purchases:								
Goal 1:								
Goal 2:								
Goal 3:								
Chapter 8:								
Taxes:								
Income taxes (federal and state)								
Social Security and Medicare taxes								
Miscellaneous:								
Total income								
Total outflow								
Windflow/Shortfall								

Notes:

APPENDIX :
MONEY-SAVING TIPS FOR LIVING BELOW YOUR MEANS

WHERE CAN YOU CUT BACK?

What a difference a dollar can make—especially at the soda fountain at 7-Eleven. (Have you seen the size of the Big Gulp these days?) Imagine how much difference a few hundred (or even thousands) of extra dollars could make in your quest to retire early, send the kids to clown school, or put a down payment on a luxury vacation cruise liner.

This entire workbook is filled with strategies to help you save thousands of dollars on major purchases. Here we present some additional tips on shaving money from occasional and everyday events. We asked our community of Fools on the ever-popular Living Below Your Means discussion board at Fool.com for their top money-saving tips. Unfortunately, there aren't enough pages left in this book to list them all. (We begged our publishers for another 1,649 pages, but they wouldn't budge.) So we winnowed the list to the top five or so in each category. Check them out and see which ones you can work into your lifestyle. Then use the following worksheet to add up the savings and start directing your hard-earned dollars to the things that matter most in your life.

HOUSEHOLD MANAGEMENT

1. **Care for your home.** It is your single largest purchase. You can improve its value by keeping it freshly painted, clean, and well landscaped, and you can save a ton of money and get lots of gratification by doing it yourself.

2. **Forgo expensive cleaners.** Use vinegar for glass, alcohol for shower doors and TV screens, and bleach for everything else. Spray dishes with a mix of water and dish soap. A splash of the mix will loosen the grime and use less water than rinsing.

3. **Less is more!** A couple of tablespoons of laundry detergent will get your load clean. A tiny bit of shampoo, dishwashing soap, toothpaste, etc., is also fine.

4. **Install a digital programmable thermostat.** These little wonders make sure you heat and cool your house only when you need it and not so much when you don't (e.g., when you're at work or sleeping). You can buy one at any hardware store, and your local utility may even put it in free of charge (though they're easy to install yourself). Put an insulation blanket on your water heater.

WORKSHEET: MONEY-SAVING PLANS

Category	Money-Saving Strategy	Estimated Savings	Where Will the Savings Go?
Example: Food	Eat cereal at home instead of stopping at the local bagel shop.	$10/week	Retirement fund

5. Close the blinds. During the day it keeps the house cool, and at night it keeps it warmer. Hence, you'll reap major savings on heating and cooling bills.

FOOD

1. Learn to cook. Take the time to learn the hows and whys of cooking techniques. When you know why you should broil instead of bake, you can tweak the recipes you use to meet your own tastes and even make a few spontaneous creations of your own. There's nothing that says "I love you" to your family and friends like a great meal.

2. Cook extra and stock your freezer. Cook twice the amount needed for a meal, then package up the extra and throw it into the freezer. That way, you can pull something out of the freezer rather than go out to dinner. Also, if the grocery store has a great deal on, say, chicken breasts, you can buy more, cook extra, and save it for later.

3. Stretch your meals. Don't waste food. Use leftovers creatively by combining less-than-fresh vegetables, last night's dinner, garlic, lemon juice, carrots and/or broccoli, and cook in a skillet with a couple of tablespoons of vegetable oil. Once you've finished dinner, put the leftovers into meal-size bowls to grab the next morning for your brown-bag lunch.

4. Consider alternatives to cereal. Cold cereal is expensive and a recent American habit. Homemade muffins are easy to make and much cheaper. Leftover rice mixed with brown sugar makes a nice breakfast. Pancakes can be made in a batch, then frozen and reheated in the microwave during the week. If you must buy cereal, bagged cereal is usually cheaper than boxed.

5. Don't go grocery shopping without a list. Plan some meals for the next few days, then go pick up what you need. And don't buy anything that's not on the list!

EATING OUT

1. Schedule times to go out to dinner and stick to them. Don't just stare at each other and say, "Nothing at home sounds good to eat, let's go out to eat."

2. Host a dinner party instead. You could even host a potluck—everybody brings a dish.

3. If your community has entertainment coupon books, purchase one. The cost is usually $30 to $40. They are filled with two-for-one (or 50 percent off, if you dine alone) coupons to local restaurants that are good for one year. If you eat out just twice during the year using the coupons, you've paid for the book.

4. Swear off fast food. That stuff is a lot higher in fat than even Ronald McD. admits.

5. Picnics are a nice alternative to eating out. They're cheaper and more enjoyable. After all, which table in a restaurant is the most coveted? The one with the view!

ENTERTAINMENT

1. Don't subscribe to magazines. Read them at the public library. Give yourself a gift of one afternoon a month at the library to read magazines. Cheap reading and an afternoon of peace and quiet!

2. While you're there, rediscover the splendor of the library. All those books, videos, DVDs, and CDs are just waiting for you to find them and absolutely free! Also, library sales are a great place to find books you want to own.

3. Buy used books, CDs, DVDs, and videos. Check out Web sites such as half.com, ebay.com, and Amazon.com's zShops.

4. When saving for vacations, plan ahead. Trips such as cruises can be booked for a much lower cost if booked well in advance.

5. **Look for bargain airfare to your destinations.** You can often find great prices online. Comparison shop and garner savings by flying at midweek instead of on weekends.

DRIVING

1. **Take care of your car and keep it forever (or as long as you can stand it).** If you're not making car payments to someone else, you can make them to yourself, building up replacement money and earning interest on it!

2. **Don't let your ego get wrapped up in your car.** Proudly drive your old jalopy and think "frugal millionaire."

3. **Know where the cheap gasoline is.** Most cars need only 87-octane gasoline. If your engine doesn't knock, the higher-octane stuff is only a waste of money. Also, save on gas by keeping your tires properly inflated, changing your air filter regularly, and purchasing cars with manual transmissions. If your car pulls to the right or left, get it aligned. It's cheaper than buying new tires.

4. **If you don't do your own car repairs, get to know a mechanic.** If you have someone regular and reliable who will keep records on your vehicle, you will probably get better service—and maybe some tips on whether repairs are worthwhile.

5. **If you don't have to drive, don't.** Walk or ride a bike, or at least carpool (a good way to make friends at work).

CAR INSURANCE

1. **Keep your driving record clean and your car safe.** Insurance companies frequently give discounts to do-gooders who have opted to pay for extras such as air bags, antilock brakes, and antitheft equipment. And something else is obvious but

worth repeating: one accident on an otherwise clean slate can pump up your premiums as much as 50 percent for three years. Besides that, speeding uses more gas. The optimum speed for good gas mileage is about 50 miles per hour. So if you go 70, clearly you're using more gas, you probably don't save all that much time, and you risk being pulled over by Officer Ornery.

2. **Don't file small claims.** If you can afford it, pay for small repairs yourself. Also, since you're going to be paying for those little fender benders anyway, change your deductible to a higher amount. The price difference between a policy with a $100 deductible and a $500 deductible can be as much as 30 percent.

3. **Get smart.** Some insurance companies give discounts to drivers who have taken defensive driving classes. Besides saving money, you might even learn something. This goes double for Junior. Ask about savings if your little pumpkin takes a driver education class. Some companies also reward students who are on the honor roll.

4. **If you drive an older car, carry just liability insurance.** Save on the cost of collision insurance, and use it to pay for repairs or (eventually) a replacement car.

5. **Take the bus.** Make sure that you tell your insurer if you don't use your car to get to work. In fact, don't use your car to get to work. You'll save wear and tear on your car, you won't have to pay for parking, and your insurance premiums will be lower.

BANKING

1. **Know the fees.** Banking regulations state that financial institutions must inform their customers of all the fees that they charge. Look for a staid black-and-white brochure way in the back of the display with all the glitzy sales literature when you

first walk in the door. Be Foolish! If you think the fees are unreasonable, tell the manager. Then walk out the door and go to another bank.

2. **Watch your ATM withdrawals.** Depending on your bank, this is the real budget killer for most customers. In general, use ATMs belonging to your bank, go less often, and take out larger sums of money when you do.

3. **Don't use your debit card for important purchases.** Banks love debit cards—no checks to process! But consumers should beware: some debit cards don't offer the same protection that regular credit cards do. For instance, if you're unhappy with a purchase, there's no middleman to resolve your dispute. When you use a credit card, the credit card company will follow up for you and reverse the charge if necessary.

4. **Ask if your bank encourages direct deposits.** Many banks offer free checking if you have your paycheck deposited directly into your account. Your employer will like you better, too.

5. **Don't sweat the small stuff.** Don't feel as though you need to question every little $2 fee that your bank charges. They're in business to make money. But don't get taken advantage of when your bank goes over the top with a laundry list of $2 fees and takes away your favorite teller to boot.

FIDO AND FIFI

1. **Adopt a pet.** A purebred, pet store puppy can cost anywhere from $500 to several thousand dollars. Why not look into adopting an animal from the Humane Society or a local animal shelter? The costs are minimal, and you get the added bonus of knowing that you may have saved a life. Check out the Web page of the American Society for the Prevention of Cruelty to Animals (ASPCA) (www.aspca.com) for a list of shelters in your area.

2. **Spay or neuter your pet and keep up to date on shots.** OK, so don't tell her beforehand, but your little Fifi LaRue will thank you for it later. Many shelters offer affordable spaying and neutering, as well as inexpensive vaccinations. And think of the money and time that you'll save: you won't have to place "free kitten" ads in the paper or beg your friends to take a puppy. Mark your calendar to get your pets inoculated. Think preventive maintenance. Buying heartworm pills is much cheaper than actually treating heartworm.

3. **Train your puppy.** A puppy kindergarten class can start at as little as $25. The cost of repairing furniture that has been gnawed on, ruined shoes, and your frazzled patience can be much higher.

4. **Be creative with pet toys.** The ones at the pet store look appealing with their glitzy packaging and their glitzy price tag. But sometimes the best toys are free or cost next to nothing. Foil balls, wadded-up facial tissue, and wine corks are great for cats. Experts say that you should rotate pets' toys often so they don't get bored.

5. **Brush your pet's teeth.** We know, "You want me to do what?" But a University of Minnesota study showed that 80 percent of dogs and 70 percent of cats have a gum disease by age three. Vets recommend brushing your pet's pearly whites several times a week.

THE HOLIDAYS

1. **Don't try to be Martha Stewart.** (Secret: She has legions of assistants.) Among making all your gifts, decorating the perfect nine-foot Christmas tree, and cooking a fourteen-course holiday meal, it's enough to make you want to stay in bed until January. Don't get sucked into the "it has to be perfect" mind-set. Remember that holidays are about fun and love and thankfulness—not about how much money you spend or how creamy the fondue turns out.

2. Combine gift giving and charity giving. When you make your gift list, are you faced with some people who truly have everything? Instead of giving them one more thing they don't need, why not give something in their name to someone less fortunate? How about sponsoring a child through, for example, "Save the Children"? You can give the child's picture to your friend with a note that says, "Because of you this little girl will never go to bed hungry this year." Or give to your friend's favorite charity, whether it's a school, the symphony, or the ASPCA.

3. Give your time. Sometimes the last thing a young family needs is one more toy to pick up. Why not offer to play baby-sitter for them a few times instead? Or instead of giving your granddad another sweater, take him to a football game. The time you spend together will often be remembered long after the toy or sweater is forgotten.

4. Make your kids help. If you have children and plan on making gifts or food, get them to help you. Not only will it be a learning experience for them and a bonding experience for you both, but if you screw it up you can blame it on your kids. ("Oh, that's so sweet that little Matthew helped! Look at the purple tree he made" instead of "What? You ran out of green icing?")

5. Use your credit cards wisely. Your credit card companies may try to "help" you with an offer to forgo your January payment to them. Don't do it! Plan now for how much you're going to charge and how you're going to pay it off. The deferral plans offered by some banks usually come with a fee, and you'll still be racking up interest charges.

DATING

1. Make dinner at home. There are three distinct advantages to this ploy. One, it's cheap. Two, it makes you look domestic (if you're a Foolette) and multitalented (if you're a Fool). Three, in case you really hit it off, that couch is just a few feet away. If it's nice outside, go on a picnic. It has the same advantages as making dinner at home: it's cheap, you seem domestic even though you've only made sandwiches, and you'll always look back fondly at "that time we went on the picnic together."

2. Volunteer together. Who says you actually have to spend money? Why not do something good for someone else? Go on a walkathon, clean up a stream, or help with a party for homeless kids. You're guaranteed to come out looking like a star if you do this.

3. Be an early bird. You don't have to wait for the finals of a tennis tournament to see good matches. Go to the qualifying rounds and pay about $3 for a ticket to a professional tournament. Or go to the matinee show of the hot play in town. You'll be able to save about half on admission, and you'll still have time for an early dinner.

4. Take a tour. Take a walking tour of your city's historic district. Many cities offer offbeat tours set around ghost stories or tales of murder and mayhem. Not only will you be entertained, but you'll learn more about your hometown so that you can impress your next date in case this one doesn't work out.

GETTING MARRIED

1. Don't have your wedding on Saturday night. The same goes for having a June wedding. Everybody wants to do it, and you're going to pay a premium for it. Holding the big event at another time is guaranteed to save you money. Heck, getting married in the late morning will save you a bundle. Doing anything nontraditional is going to save you money, whether having a morning wedding or one on a Friday night.

2. Have the reception in a nontraditional place. Check with your county and state recreation departments. Every place has publicly owned properties that are ideal for a ceremony or reception. Forget about the privately owned mansions and country clubs. By going the public route, you can save as much as half on the cost of your site rental and have an equally beautiful location.

3. **In general, don't buy "wedding" things.** Anything that has the word "wedding" attached to it can instantly fetch 25 percent or more. As in:

Take a Word	Add "Wedding," and the Price Instantly Goes Up
Dress	Wedding dress
Shoes	Wedding shoes
Disposable camera	Wedding disposable camera
Bubbles	Wedding bubbles
Super Bowl MVP	Wedding Super Bowl MVP

Wherever possible, try to purchase a "normal" (a.k.a. "nonwedding") equivalent.

4. **Big wedding/small honeymoon or vice versa?** Which is more important to you, the wedding or the honeymoon? Why not be frugal with one and splurge on the other?

5. **Pick the music carefully.** Polls have found that wedding guests remember the music more than any other element of the reception. If you can afford a live band, ask around for recommendations. Bands will usually have videos that they can show you. Don't ever hire a band unless someone you trust has actually seen them in action and really liked them.

GETTING DIVORCED

1. **Make a list of everything.** Chances are that you may not even know what you own together . . . or owe together. And if you weren't involved in mak-

ing the financial decisions, you have a lot of learning to do. But that's OK. First, make a list of everything you own, including such things as real estate, bank accounts, insurance policies, and retirement plans. Then make a list of everything you owe, from the phone bill to school loans. Write down everything about each debt, including addresses and phone numbers of contact people. Now make a list of what your expenses will be *sans* spouse.

2. **Protect your credit.** Make sure that you have credit in your own name. If you have always had a shared account with your spouse, ask your credit card company to issue a new card in your name only. Also, agree with your spouse that neither of you will put any new large purchases on your shared card that you might both be liable for later. If your spouse receives the statements for things such as your brokerage account, ask your broker to send a duplicate statement to your new address.

3. **Protect your future.** Make sure that you understand who will receive the retirement benefits if you have a joint plan with your spouse. Different laws govern this, depending on where you live. Check out the laws in your state.

4. **Protect your alimony and/or child support.** If your spouse is going to be paying alimony or child support, make sure that your divorce agreement stipulates that he or she buy life and disability insurance. This will ensure that these payments will continue should something unexpected happen to him or her.

5. **Protect your investments.** Always split any securities you own straight down the middle. Just because they look equal on paper doesn't mean they will remain that way should they have to be liquidated. Some investments have more capital gains than others, while some are difficult to sell at any price (such as a limited partnership).

6. **Don't forget inflation.** When making plans for the future, it's best to include a provision for in-

flation. That $500 a month in child support won't be worth the same amount in ten years.

7. **Do the best you can, then let go.** Chances are you're afraid you're going to get the short end of the stick in your divorce settlement. Perhaps an inequitable relationship was one of the reasons you're divorcing. Divorce counselors all agree on one thing: make the best deal that you can for all involved and then let go. Try forgiving your spouse and yourself. Then get on with your life. You still have a lot of living to do, and your new life is just about to start!

CHARITY

1. **What causes really float your boat?** How can you choose which ones are worthy? Don't be frozen by indecision. Think about what is most important to you. Did you really love camp when you were a kid? How about sending an underprivileged kid to camp this summer? Does a coworker have AIDS? How about giving money to medical research in his name?

2. **Check out the organization.** Ask the organization to send you more information on what it does. How long has it been in business? What is its main mission? Does it seem to be accomplishing its goal? How does it use its money? How much of its money is going for true charitable work? (In order to pass muster with the charity watchdog group National Charities Information Bureau, groups have to devote at least 60 percent of the money they receive to their mission.)

3. **If you can't give a lot, give what you can.** Does that little box that you have to check ask for more money than you can afford? Don't worry about it. If you can afford only $5 instead of $25, send that. It will be appreciated more than you know. Then vow to yourself to give more when you can afford it.

4. **Keep your receipts for your taxes.** If part of the reason that you're giving to charities is for the tax deductions, don't forget to save the receipts and keep them in a place where you can actually find them come April 14. (Yeah, we know that's when you're going to get around to doing them.)

5. **Itemize.** Are you a Fool who waits until the very last minute and fills out a 1040EZ form? If you want to take advantage of the tax benefits of contributing to a charity, you're going to have to buckle down and fill out a regular 1040 form. Don't worry, it's a breeze. And if you need help, you can always check out Chapter 8. If instead of money you give things such as sweaters or old records, don't forget to get a receipt, especially if you're giving more than $250 worth of goods. If you give more than $500 in noncash charitable contributions, you will also have to fill out IRS form 8283 as well as the 1040. (This is cake . . . don't let it stop you!)

ADDITIONAL RESOURCES AT FOOL.COM

We hope you have enjoyed reading and exercising your way into tip-top financial shape with this workbook. And as we hope it has provided you with valuable and helpful information, we believe there are always opportunities to learn more. Throughout the workbook, you have been pointed toward additional resources and services to help you manage your money. Fool.com offers many of these additional resources at your fingertips. Following is an abbreviated but helpful list of some of the key areas, most of which have appeared in this workbook:

Buying a Car—www.Fool.com/car
- Follow a step-by-step plan for finding the best fit, taking control of the test drive, striking the best possible deal, and actually taking possession.

College Savings Center—www.Fool.com/csc
- Make the most of your or your child's education—develop strategies for saving for college and for ways in which to navigate the financial aid process.

Discount Broker Center—http://broker.Fool.com
- Looking to start investing, to switch from a full-service broker to a discount one, or maybe to select a better discount broker? We can help you compare, choose, and use discount brokers, and even get started investing directly online.

Insurance Center—http://insurance.Fool.com
- We'll help you figure out what types you need, how much of it you should purchase, and how to get coverage at the lowest cost.

Short-Term Savings Center—http://savings.Fool.com
- Everyone needs a cash stash for emergencies. We'll help you determine how much you need and where to keep it.

Motley Fool Stock Advisor—www.Fooladvisor.com
- If you are ready to invest or dig deeper into analyzing stocks, David and Tom offer ideas for you in the *Motley Fool Stock Advisor*. In this monthly newsletter, the Gardners present their outlook on the stock market, individual

stock suggestions, and tips on the best ways to manage your personal finances and investing.

The Fool Community—www.boards.Fool.com
Join other members online to interact, learn, question, and exchange ideas. The Community offers:

- An opportunity to post messages to get your questions answered
- Staff-monitored discussions

To check out what other Fools are saying, take a peek with a 30-day free trial.

TMF Money Advisor—http://TMFMA.Fool.com
TMF Money Advisor provides personalized, objective advice for all aspects of your financial life. With TMF Money Advisor you get:

- Access to an unbiased, unconflicted financial advisor
- An online tool you can use to create a personal financial plan
- A package of ten Motley Fool online seminars

And, as a special bonus for all our book readers, we offer a special discount to our Money Advisor service. To get this special offer, go to http://TMFMA.Fool.com.

The Motley Fool's aim is to help you find solutions to the many and sometimes complex matters of money and investing. Whether you're looking for new investment ideas, home-buying tips, minute-by-minute stock quotes, or just a place to interact with other investors, Fool.com has all of that and more—available twenty-four hours a day.

ABOUT THE AUTHORS

DAVID AND TOM GARDNER cofounded The Motley Fool, an Alexandria, Virginia-based multimedia company, in 1993. They started out publishing a modest investment newsletter for friends and family, started talking stocks online in the early days of AOL, then launched their own investment education Web site, Fool.com, in 1997.

Tom graduated with an honors degree in English and creative writing from Brown University. David graduated as a Morehead Scholar from the University of North Carolina at Chapel Hill. With many ideas and no regrets, he quit his job writing for *Louis Rukeyser's Wall Street* newsletter in order to found The Motley Fool with his brother.

Today, The Motley Fool has grown into an international multimedia company offering financial solutions worldwide to millions of individuals seeking to make better financial decisions and improve their overall quality of life. David and Tom have coauthored four *New York Times* business bestsellers, including *The Motley Fool Investment Guide, You Have More Than You Think, Investment Workbook,* and *Rule Breakers, Rule Makers.* In addition to writing bestselling books, the Gardners oversee a nationally syndicated newspaper column, which is carried by more than 200 newspapers, and they host a weekly radio program on NPR. The Gardners, once voted "Interactive Age's Entrepreneurs of the Year, 1996," recently hosted the award-winning PBS Special "The Motley Fool Money-Making, Life-Changing Special."